HER MOTHER'S DAUGHTER

HER MOTHER'S

A Memoir of the Mother I Never Knew and of My Daughter, Courtney Love

DAUGHTER

LINDA CARROLL

DOUBLEDAY

New York London Toronto Sydney Auckland

PUBLISHED BY BROADWAY BOOKS
a division of Random House, Inc.

A hardcover edition of this book was published in 2005 by Broadway Books.

BROADWAY BOOKS and its logo, a letter B bisected on the diagonal,
are trademarks of Random House, Inc.

www.broadwaybooks.com

Book Design by Chris Welch
Original Jacket Design by Allison Warner
Jacket Photograph courtesy of the author
Author Photograph © Karen Ruckman

Library of Congress has cataloged the hardcover edition as:
Carroll, Linda.
Her mother's daughter : a memoir of the mother I never knew and of my
daughter, Courtney Love.
p. cm.
1. Carroll, Linda. 2. Fox, Paula. 3. Love, Courtney, 1964–
4. Psychotherapists—United States—Biography. 5. Mothers
and daughters—United States—Biography. I. Title.
RC438.6.C37A3 2005
616.89'14'0092—dc22
2005048401

First trade paperback edition published 2008
Hardcover Edition ISBN: 978-0-385-51247-3
Trade Paperback ISBN: 978-0-7679-1788-9

144915995

For my family

and the memory of Judy Carroll

ACKNOWLEDGMENTS

This book is the product of many people's dedication, time, and wisdom.

My agent, Beth Vesel, believed in this book from the beginning, even when I didn't, and never stopped encouraging me to tell my story. My editor at Doubleday, Kristine Puopolo, asked all the hard questions and gave me invaluable guidance, pushing me to make this book the best it could be. Marie France skillfully and patiently helped edit the first few drafts.

Michael Kaye was an encouraging writing coach, who understood the spirit of the story while offering me practical advice.

Five friends were generous enough to read the manuscript in various forms and offer suggestions: Genevieve Arnaut, Ann Ladd, DelNan Morgan, Karen Randall, and Karen Ruckman.

In their commitment to their own writing, Paula Fox and Martin Greenberg have been a source of inspiration since I began this project three years ago.

I have tortured my two sons, Tobias and Daniel Menely, with my comma splices and run-on sentences. They spent months explaining the fundamentals of writing to me, while reading and rereading, editing, challenging, and encouraging me. My daughters, Nicole Carroll and Jaimee King, suffered the most painful parts of this story with me, and their willingness to relive it fills me with gratitude. My adopted son, Joshua, has given support and shared his memories.

Margaret Ronda's gifts as a writer, combined with her patience as an editor, have strengthened this book immeasurably. She has struggled through every part of it with me, and it would not have been what it is without her.

Tim Barraud is my life partner and dearest friend. He has read with care all I've written over three years, and supported me unstintingly through the sometimes agonizing process of capturing an entire life in words.

Each that we lose takes part of us;
A crescent still abides,
Which like the moon, some turbid night,
Is summoned by the tides.

—EMILY DICKINSON, *THE COMPLETE POEMS*

CHAPTER 1

"This is your daughter." Her raspy voice on the telephone turns an ordinary statement into an accusation.

"Hello, Courtney," I say, bracing myself. I can't remember the last phone call that didn't end with screams and tears on her end and stony responses on mine. It has been years since we spoke with ease.

"I thought you'd like to know—I'm three months pregnant."

I hear my own sharp intake of breath and feel the sudden rush of emotions: fear, joy, dread, shock. I search for the next thing to say, *the right thing*; everything I think of seems hollow. It would be absurd if it weren't so painful. For the first time I am going to be a grandmother—yet I cannot even utter a sigh that isn't filtered through the screen of my own caution.

"That's very exciting news, Courtney," I manage.

"Guess what else, Mother? I just married a prince. He's the biggest rock star in the world."

Then I register the shock: she got married, and I hadn't been informed. Now she is going to have a child.

Things didn't start out this way, so guarded, so wary.

Courtney was my first child, born July 9, 1964, in the middle of the afternoon. I heard her cries, soft, then louder, and I reached for her. Nothing prepared me for that moment. Receiving her into my arms, I knew she was a miracle, a mystery entering the world. I couldn't believe this perfect baby had come from my body.

Until that moment, babies had held little interest for me. Yet from the instant I held Courtney, I felt that I was born to be a mother. In those first weeks, I inhaled her scent deeply—she smelled like wildness, wrapped in wind-dried sheets with a hint of Breck baby shampoo in her hair.

Get that baby on a schedule, Dr. Spock advised. But I knew what was right for her; I could feel it in my bones. Instinctively, I matched my timetable to hers, sleeping and waking when she did. She was so smart: she crawled and walked months before the baby charts said she would. At one year, she was using short sentences. People marveled at how articulate she was.

My concern was what happened when she became upset. At times she cried so hard, it was impossible to comfort her.

"Don't worry," the pediatrician said. "It's colic."

Deep down, though, I did worry. Something was hurting her that she wasn't able to express in words. As Courtney grew into a toddler, anticipating her moods became my central preoccupation. If I got to her crib as she awoke, all was well. But if I waited a moment too long, there was no consoling her. She could cry for hours.

Pale in complexion, Courtney had soft, generous features. Most startling were her sea green eyes, which shifted from tears to delight with breathtaking speed. Her radiance and enthusiasm were as extraordinary as her distress. As a two-year-old, she was always ready to climb into our Volkswagen Beetle and go for an adventure. She sat in the backseat as I drove, her pigtails bouncing between the two front seats as she asked her wide-eyed question, "Any news?"

She loved news.

But more than news, she loved music. Whenever the Beatles' hit "Michelle" came on the car radio, she would sing along. Already her voice held the dreamy inflection that would later become part of her fame.

Courtney was my first real love. I believed nothing could come between us.

NOW HERE WE are, twenty-five years later, holding a telephone conversation about a momentous event with such estrangement that I monitor even my sighs.

The life Courtney lives stuns and frightens me. Yet in her latest news, this pregnancy, I sense something hopeful.

"It's wonderful," I say. The words sound empty, concealing the emotions washing over me.

"Yeah, well, I thought you'd want to know," she says. The phone clicks, and she's gone.

I hold the receiver a moment longer before I drop it into its cradle.

I hear my husband, Tim. He is downstairs, pulling a roasted chicken out of the oven. He calls up to me: "Dinner."

We are leaving for Hawaii tomorrow to visit close friends. Our suitcases are packed and waiting by the front door.

"I'll be right there," I call back.

I sit down on the bed. I can't bear to talk to anyone just yet, not even Tim. Our cat, Nelson, sidles over and nudges my arm. I set him on my lap. A current of excitement mixed with dread courses through me. My heart races even faster than my thoughts. Finally, I go downstairs.

I tell Tim the news.

"Why do you call the baby 'she'?" he asks.

"I don't know," I say, preoccupied. "I'm just certain the baby will be a girl."

Something is stirring inside, a feeling on the periphery of my awareness whose arrival I've been expecting for years. It's as though I have stepped into a deep stream and am being carried somewhere new.

TWO DAYS LATER at Puako beach on the big island of Hawaii, I sit on the edge of a lava formation that juts out into the Pacific. I have left a gathering of friends; I feel a need to be alone. Tall palms, with their lush foliage, shade the porous rock around me. I look for that mysterious green flash that sometimes lights up the sky as the sun sinks beneath the horizon.

The water is calm. Below me I see schools of fish—yellow butterfly fish, parrot fish. A pod of spinner dolphins, called the *Nai'a*, play off the shore.

Old ones, young ones, babies. Generations.

Generations.

In my mind's eye, the word flashes. Then, with absolute clarity, I know it is time to find my mother, the woman who gave birth to me.

WHEN I WAS growing up, people asked me how I felt about being adopted, and I always said, "It's not an issue." I believed my own lie. The longing ran too deep to acknowledge: for a family who looked like me, for a genealogy, for the full story of my life. Even deeper lay the fear of what I would discover. Now, with the news of Courtney's pregnancy, the desire to find my birth mother, to unravel the mystery of my own origin, was too strong to ignore.

CHAPTER 2

As a child, I often asked to hear the story of how I became the adopted daughter of Louella and Jack Risi. They never tired of describing the ride home from the hospital when I was just ten days old, in April 1944, laughing at the memory of my bald head. I listened for something else: clues about the unknown woman who had given birth to me before I became "Louella's child."

Before I fell asleep each night, I fantasized about my birth mother. She was a queen, I imagined, searching for her lost five-year-old princess.

Each morning, I sat at the curb outside our house, studying the stream of pedestrians on their way to the streetcar, hoping to see her. The Drunk Lady passed first, as she shuffled toward the corner bar. Though she never glanced my way, I gaped at her ruddy face, with its uneven makeup and bulbous nose, fearing she was The One.

Ginger came later. Glamorous as a movie star, she wore sparkly silver pins on her lapels, and her upswept hairdo ended in a dramatic swirl. She always had a special smile for me as she strode by in her rhinestone-studded shoes. One day she stopped and looked right into my eyes.

"How are you this morning, honey?" she asked.

In my excitement, I could muster only a "fine."

She continued on, but her warmth convinced me she was The One. She would stop again, I imagined, and this time she would say, "Okay, sweetheart, you can come home with me."

I hurried off to share my excitement with my friend Helen. "Ginger is my real mother," I explained, "and soon she'll take me with her." Helen told her mother, who told another mother, and before long, Louella heard the news. When I went in for lunch, I could tell she was angry by the pinch in her meticulously plucked eyebrows. She led me into the living room, where she stood rubbing her hands on a starched white apron.

"Young lady," she said, taking a deep breath to compose herself. "The woman who had you was too irresponsible to care for you. You are a fortunate little girl to have people who wanted you." Tears welled in her eyes.

My face flushed as she left the room. I had never seen her cry before, and I felt ashamed for causing trouble. At once, I grasped what she meant by my good fortune. Not only was Ginger not my real mother, but, just as I had feared, my real mother was someone like the Drunk Lady, or even worse.

After that, I stopped searching the faces of beautiful women for signs that one might be her. I pushed my longing deep inside, and tried to think of Jack and Louella as my "real parents." But it never felt right: I avoided calling them Mom and Dad. Though I referred to them as "my mother" and "my father" to others, they were always Jack and Louella to me.

———

WE LIVED IN a beige two-story stucco house in Ewing Terrace, a quiet cul-de-sac near Lone Mountain in San Francisco. On the mountain's slope lay the ruins of one of the city's first cemeteries, veined with trails leading up toward the summit. In the late 1940s, those paths were the stomping grounds of derelicts and hobos, and my friend Helen warned me that the ghost of a child-murdering gold miner roamed them as well. Helen's story made me curious, and one morning when I was five, I set off for Lone Mountain, zigzagging across lawns to evade the sharp eyes of the neighborhood women who gossiped with Louella. I made it to the mountain and began to climb. In my thin sundress and sandals, I scraped my bare legs against brambles, but kept ascending until my eye caught a flicker of flames through the brush. Intrigued, I clambered off the path. As I drew closer, I saw a bearlike man poking a small fire. The ground around him was cluttered with liquor bottles. Seeing me, he turned and bellowed, "What do you want?"

I froze.

He jumped up and grabbed me. The smell he gave off was foul, like our cat's litter box. He began to grope me roughly, sticking his huge hands under my dress. Terrified, I wet my pants. He released me with disgust.

With more speed than I knew I possessed, I ran home. Only when my badly scuffed shoes touched the sidewalk in front of my house did I stop. I sat in my spot on the curb until my trembling body grew calm.

When I went inside, Louella was waiting. She took one look at my appearance and shut off the vacuum cleaner. "You've ripped your dress," she cried. "Oh, look at you. You just can't keep clean. Go take a bath this instant."

Upstairs, I hid my wet underpants in an old shoebox and drew water for a bath. Louella joined me, adjusted the temperature, and sat down on the toilet seat. "I didn't mean to scare you," she said. Her irritation had ebbed, and she eyed the scrapes on my legs sympatheti-cally. "Those look like they hurt! Have you been climbing trees again?" As she spoke, she lightly scratched my back with her long, red nails. I loved it when she did that. Her hands soothed me. "Whatever did you do to tear your dress?" she asked.

"I fell down," I answered meekly.

"Sometimes I get so angry at what a tomboy you are," she said. "I was never like that, not one day in my life." Then she added, as if to reassure herself, "Everyone says you'll grow out of it."

The bathwater and Louella's calming hands made the ghost miner seem far away. I relaxed even more, sensing that my reputation as a tomboy would spare me further questions about the mess made of my best dress—yellow with red cherries on it—that I wore to Mass on Sunday mornings.

Later that night, I thought about how close I had come to ending up like the child Helen had told me about, stuffed in a jar, my body cut into little pieces like the dill pickles I loved to eat. I studied my picture of Mother Mary, wearing her soft blue and white robes, sur-rounded by golden-haired angels. In a whisper, I promised her I would stay close to home if she would protect me. The next morning, I snuck my soiled underpants into the garbage can and figured my se-cret was safe.

MY SUNDRESS WITH the cherry print was not easily mended.

"You'll have to wear your blue one," Louella told me when Sunday came.

I was glad. I never wanted to see the cherry dress again. I settled into the passenger seat of our white Oldsmobile, and we drove to the Catholic chapel of the Women's College at the top of Lone Mountain. As the car climbed, so did a woman and a little girl about my age. We passed them every week, making their way up the steep sidewalk to the church. This particular morning, a light rain was falling when we noticed them trudging along without an umbrella. Louella stopped the car and rolled down the window.

"Would you like a ride?" she asked.

I was surprised. We had passed them so many times before. Gratefully, they joined us, and we drove on in silence.

After we dropped them off at the front of the church, I offered Louella shy praise: "You're really nice."

"Anyone would help a neighbor," she replied mechanically. A moment later, she added, "Believe me, I know about being poor."

During Mass, I glanced up at Louella several times, seeking a sign to explain her sudden, generous impulse, but found none. So much of what she did was a mystery, even though we spent most of our time together. She was like a familiar stranger whose actions I could never quite understand.

A FEW WEEKS later, there was a knock at our front door. Opening it, I saw a short, fair-haired woman wearing a blue wool suit.

"You must be the little girl I've come for," she said kindly, stepping into the hall. I stared, wondering who she might be. The woman set down her large suitcase.

"Well, you're as pretty as your picture," she said. "We're going to get along fine."

I doubted it. I ran up to my room and shut the door.

Before long, Louella followed. "Linda, what on earth is wrong?" she asked. "Why are you behaving so rudely?"

I saw that the short woman had come upstairs too, and stood outside the bedroom door. Seeing my mother's disapproving expression, I thought I was in trouble again. By then, a neighbor had reported seeing me run down Lone Mountain. "She's too much for us," I heard Louella say with a sigh.

Still, I did not want to have to go off with this stranger. "I don't want her to take me away," I said.

The small woman stepped closer. "Goodness, child," she said gently. "Nobody's going to take you from here. Your mother needs help, and I'm lucky enough to get the job."

"This is Nellie Frances Johansson," Louella announced. "She's come all the way from Minneapolis, Minnesota, to help take care of you. The least you could do is act polite."

I peeked again at Nellie, and she winked at me. I followed her into the spare room and watched her unpack. She took out four gold-framed pictures and put them on her dresser. I asked her who they were. We sat down together on the bed, and she told me about her Swedish immigrant parents and her husband's death in the war. She answered my stream of questions with easy warmth. By the end of the evening, she was tucking me into bed, quietly reciting the Robert Louis Stevenson poem "The Swing" to me as I drifted to sleep.

Not long after she joined our household, Nellie asked to take me to see *Bambi*.

"I love going to the movies, Mrs. Risi. Would it be all right if I took Linda along with me?" The two women were folding sheets, and I was lying on a sofa, watching them.

Louella hesitated. "Well, Nellie, she's such a wiggle worm. Do you think she could sit still for two hours?"

"Oh, please," I pleaded. "Let me go. I'll be good and not wiggle one bit."

Her expression softened. She smiled at us both and said, "Fine. We'll all go together."

The next afternoon Louella drove us to the Coliseum Theater, with its sparkling chandeliers, etched glass, and thick maroon carpet. A bas-relief sculpture of a woman with flowing hair graced the ceiling.

"Oh, she's beautiful," I said to no one in particular, but Nellie heard me and gave me an affectionate pat on the head.

The lights dimmed and the movie began. I was enthralled by the chirping birds and playful animals. When Bambi appeared, I could barely keep from clapping with joy. I tucked my long legs under me to sit higher in my seat, not wanting to miss a thing. I did not squirm a bit.

Midway through the film, the mood shifted. First a whisper of trouble, then hunters and barking dogs, and then Bambi's mother was shot dead. I began to cry.

"Shhh," whispered Louella.

Increasingly upset, I started shaking and sniffling.

Louella kept telling me to hush, but I wasn't able to stifle my whimpers. Exasperated, she stood up and grabbed my hand. With a yank, she pulled me out of my seat and led us out. Nellie followed behind.

Nobody spoke on the ride home. By the time we pulled into our driveway, my tears had dried into quiet shame. Nellie disappeared as Louella marched me into the living room.

"What a waste of money that was," she fumed, drumming the coffee table with her carefully painted fingernails. "My own mother never took me to a movie. Or anywhere else for that matter." She drummed harder. "All you do is spoil a perfectly good time."

Huddled on the couch, I wiped my nose. I had never thought of her having a mother. The idea seemed impossible.

"What was it?" she asked. "What made you act so naughty?"

The death of Bambi's mother frightened me so much I couldn't say the words. "Those mean dogs scared me," I mumbled instead.

She looked startled, and softened for a moment, before a dark cloud passed over her face. "Nothing I do is right for you. Nothing."

I sat still, a small figure hunched on an ornate sofa. Louella began to vacuum the carpet, and I crept upstairs. I lay down on my bed, but misery made me restless. I took down the newest members of my Nancy Ann doll collection from my shelf: Pretty Maid and Doll Bride.

Louella had decided I should collect the fancy dolls, with bisque faces painted like kewpies, and I had acquired nearly a dozen of them. I was not supposed to play with them.

"Dumb Bride, you're stupid and messy," I said. Then I picked up Pretty Maid. "Pretty Maid, you're ugly. It's time for your haircut." I crept down the hall to a cabinet and returned to my room with the forbidden scissors.

"Okay, you stupid dolls. Your real mommy died, and your other mommy left the house because you were bad." I cut Pretty Maid's hair and was preparing to cut Doll Bride's when the doorknob turned. Louella stood in the doorway, her mouth pinched and her face red. Then she screamed, "You are a wicked, ungrateful, wrecker of a child!"

She slapped me on the cheek, stunning us both. We stared at one another. "Now look what you made me do," she cried, and rushed from the room. Grimly, I finished their haircuts, adding a few jabs to the dolls' plastic stomachs. I fell asleep next to Bald Bride and Ugly Maid.

I woke to a gentle hand on my back. Nellie stood over me, a comforting smile on her face. "It's time for dinner," she said. Together we went downstairs. Louella had made hamburgers, my favorite. After dinner, I watched Arthur Godfrey sing on our new television. When I returned to my room, the dolls were gone. Nobody ever mentioned the incident again.

THE FAMILIES IN Ewing Terrace wove bonds tight as a tribe's on a small island. Our days passed on a steady stream of friendship, gossip, and occasional surges of drama. Neighborhood women converged at our house to divulge the latest tales. My favorite pastime was to sit in a corner and listen. I loved gossip, especially tales of drunks and ne'er-do-wells, but was bored by the praise heaped on the neighborhood boy Eric Englehart who survived polio. He lived up the street and spent his days looking out the window from a wheelchair. His frequent visitor was the boy who lived next door, Stevie Kroll, whose birthday was the same as mine.

The women in my kitchen considered Stevie's older sister Roxie "bad trouble," but why remained a mystery. Stevie was seen as the good child. Perhaps this is why he had accumulated such a large stack of comic books. Unlike my meager pile of Little Lulus, his collection included Westerns, war stories, and, most thrilling, Flash Gordon.

Stevie came over to play one day and announced he had a surprise. He led me to Eric's house. The house smelled of cooked cabbage, and in his room, Eric sat wordlessly in his wheelchair. Stevie told me that if I took off my clothes, I could take the comics stacked nearby. With an eye on Flash Gordon, I slipped out of my dress and underwear. The two boys stared at my naked body, giggling. Stevie asked if I would let them touch me, but their grubby hands looked repulsive.

"No, I have to go home now," I said.

As I held out my hand for the comics, I had an idea. Maybe I could uncover the secret life of naughty Roxie Kroll.

"Wait a second," I said to Stevie. "I'll let you touch me if you tell me why your sister is so bad."

The door to Eric's room was ajar, and as I made my offer, his mother, a stern-looking German woman, passed by. She pushed open the door and shrieked.

"Wicked, wicked girl! Come away this instant!" She snatched my clothes and pulled me into the hallway.

As I dressed, she telephoned Louella to vent her anger. "Hasn't he suffered enough?" she shouted into the receiver. "Now you've sent that girl of yours over here to corrupt him." There was a pause as she listened to Louella. Then she said, "I know she's adopted. That's exactly why you need to keep a closer eye on her." Mrs. Englehart turned to me and wagged her finger. "Oh, you'll get what's coming to you."

I stood in the hallway, empty-handed, and braced for the worst. When Louella arrived, she grabbed my hand and we left without her saying a word to Eric's mother. We marched home in silence, her hand tightly clasping mine. "Horrible woman," she muttered as we climbed our front steps. "Kids do this sort of thing," she said, much to my surprise.

Then her mood shifted. "I suggest you find another way to get comics," she said. "And you'd better keep your clothes on, or you'll find out what a spanking is."

THE NEIGHBORHOOD KIDS were never as interesting as Schmoo, our neighbor's handsome German shepherd who followed me everywhere. I was born a dog lover, much to the distress of Louella, who saw animals as germ-ridden beasts.

Jack and Louella's closest friends had a woeful-looking Scottie named Herman. I loved the feel of his wild brindle coat. When we visited, I would snuggle with him in the basement where he was kept.

"Herman is happy to see me," I'd say, causing Jack and Louella to roll their eyes.

"Herman is stubborn and bites other dogs," Louella said. "He's just a dog," she added, as though that would bring me to my senses.

Tangi, our Siamese cat, was the only animal she cared for. Delicate, with blue, crossed eyes, Tangi stared at me with her ears folded back, flicking her tail.

"She hates me," I told Louella.

"Of course she doesn't," she said. She loved that cat more than anything. "My darling, my Tangi," she would croon each day, feeding the cat chopped liver she cooked herself.

I devised ways of showing "sweetheart" who was boss, like an occasional plunge headfirst into the toilet.

Every morning, I took up my position curbside to study the procession of ants. I told them the stories I read in my Little Golden Books. One day, I settled into my usual position, elbows on knees, and chin on hands. The ants were comfortingly predictable as they filed across the pavement. I placed a bread crust in the middle of their path to study their reaction. For some time they climbed over the bread, until one ant broke off a crumb as large as his body and marched away with it. The others followed. Watching the ants haul the bread away, I felt elated. I'd been able to alter their tiny world. Then a thought occurred: perhaps the same thing could happen to me. Perhaps someone larger could change my life with just one tiny gesture: Jesus, Mother Mary, or maybe even someone I did not know about.

When Louella discovered my enchantment with the ants, she laughed warily. It was Nellie who understood.

"Every creature is a work of God," she told me one night, tucking me into bed. "Every one."

CHAPTER 3

"How untidy you are," Louella said, as we stood in the playground on my first day of school. "Your hair is a mess." She smoothed my thick blond mane with her hand.

On this day, her fine, curly brown hair was neatly covered with a black felt hat bearing an alarmingly long ostrich feather. A tailored dress and jacket hugged her petite frame. In contrast, my clothes were in disarray. My beret kept falling off, my new plaid skirt was in a twist, and my blue jacket was already missing a button.

A nun with a gap between her front teeth approached us. "Hello, I'm Mother Sullivan," she said, smiling at me. "And what's your name?"

"This is my adopted daughter, Linda," Louella answered. "I'm afraid she's already gotten her uniform dirty. Perhaps you can teach her to be tidy."

I shifted uncomfortably, as I always did when she introduced me as "adopted," but I couldn't resist the nun's warm smile.

"You'll do just fine here," she said, taking my hand. I turned and waved good-bye to Louella as the nun led me through the playground. Louella waved back, a stiff elegant figure amidst the blur of children playing.

Mother Sullivan and I walked together through the doors of the Convent of the Sacred Heart. She led me to a classroom with little girls playing in tight clusters. I stood by a window at the edge of the room, waiting for someone to call me over. No one did. I looked out at the view of San Francisco Bay, from Alcatraz to the Golden Gate Bridge, longing to be anywhere but where I was. In the days that followed, only sad-eyed Alice Boatwright showed any interest in my arrival. But she had a runny nose and eyelids crusted with sleep, and I knew right away that solitude was better than her friendship.

One day, things changed. Walking into the classroom, I spotted Alice in the back row, absentmindedly picking her nose.

"Look," I whispered to Eileen Anderson. "Look at Alice. She'll rot in her snot."

Eileen giggled, and my words ricocheted around the room.

"She'll rot in her snot. She'll rot in her snot."

The chant grew louder and louder until a tall, stern-faced nun entered the classroom. In one dramatic gesture, she pulled a yardstick from the folds of her habit and smacked it down on a desk. Each of us froze like Lot's wife, pillars of salt in a row.

"I am Mother Mary Muldoon," the nun thundered at us. "I will be your teacher from now on, and I can see that you have much to learn." She eyed me and asked, "Why isn't your blouse tucked in? Are you always such a messy girl?" She bent her face close to mine, and a fleck of spittle appeared at the corner of her mouth.

Mother Muldoon is a baboon, I thought.

I felt panic rising as the rhyme grew louder in my mind. *Please God, I'll be good forever, if you help me not to say those words out loud.* The chant receded, and Mother Muldoon put her yardstick away.

At recess, Eileen offered me some of the jujube candy she kept hidden in her pocket. She and her friends asked me to repeat what I had said about Alice.

"Mother Muldoon is a baboon," I said instead. Giggles all around. Rhymes came easily to me, and I blurted out, "Mother Merrill is a barrel. Mrs. Mahoney smells like bologna." Everyone laughed.

At lunch, Margaret Lester whispered secrets in my ear: "Molly Smith isn't even a Catholic. Annie Palmer's parents are divorced." Eileen asked if I could come over after school.

At home that night, I thought about Alice Boatwright and felt ashamed. The next day, I offered to play with her, but she walked away, her face gloomy as ever.

My mimicking of Mother Muldoon made my new friends laugh and ensured me a place in their circle, if not in heaven. While friendship came easily, schoolwork did not. Directions scrambled the moment they entered my ears.

"Take two steps to the right and cross your feet," one of the nuns might say as we exercised. As everyone moved to the right, I would bump into someone on the left. The nun would continue, "Back two, three, cross over one, two." Inevitably, my feet would cross the wrong way, and I would find myself out of place, my classmates laughing. I learned that if I laughed first and hammed it up, I would be admired as a joker, rather than pitied as a fool.

MOTHER MULDOON HAD beady eyes and a long nose that did resemble a baboon's muzzle. She taught us the Baltimore Catechism and how to make a proper confession, and she prepared us for our first Holy Communion. "We must be very careful how we take the Host into our mouths," she instructed. As she paced the length of the classroom, she eyed each of us suspiciously.

"Now, children," she said, using the voice that made us sit tall and fold our hands on our desk. "Once there was a child who was seven years old, just like you. He didn't listen to his instructions and was not prepared for the Big Day. When the wafer was placed upon his tongue, he bit into it like a breadstick. What do you think happened then?" Mother Muldoon didn't wait for an answer. "Bleeding took place, that's what. First from the Host, and then from the boy himself. It poured out of his ears, nose, mouth, and eyes. Only when the poor lad died did the blood cease to flow."

We sat in stunned silence.

"I am certain none of you will make such a mistake," Mother said with a rare cheerful smile. The unfortunate boy was not mentioned again, but every night, I prayed his fate would not be mine.

AS MY FIRST Communion neared, I bit my nails by day and ground my teeth at night. In the same way I had feared blurting out, "Mother Muldoon is a baboon," I was terrified that I would bite a chunk right out of the Host. The morning arrived, a sun-filled Sunday in April. As we entered the church, which was brimming with vases of calla lilies, I thought of taking the Host into my body. For a moment, I felt electrified. Jesus, I imagined, would melt into me. But as I looked around at the crucifix and all the familiar statues of saints, my fear returned. My mouth grew dry and my palms sweated. I imagined bright blood cascading down the front of my white satin dress.

When the nun signaled, I walked to the altar and knelt. As the priest approached, I held my tongue flat; I did not bite down. Instead, the Host stuck to the roof of my mouth. I could not swallow it. Back at my pew, I put my head down as though in prayer. In desperation, I poked at the wafer with my tongue until it broke apart, and I swallowed each piece, one at a time.

Everyone said I looked angelic in white, a perfect little bride of Christ, but I knew I had not fooled God. I had already concluded that He was often upset by my mean thoughts and messy ways. Now He had something serious to be angry about. Breaking up the sacred Host with my tongue was surely as heinous as chomping on it.

Fortunately, I'd found a source of comfort. Unlike the stern father we called God, Mother Mary was gentle and forgiving. On the first of May, my classmates and I each placed a bouquet of tiny pink roses by her statue. At the May procession, we sang:

O Mary, we crown thee with blossoms today;
Queen of angels, Queen of May;
Oh, thus shall we prove thee
How truly we love thee,
How dark without Mary
Life's journey would be.

The song resounded in my mind: *how dark without Mary/Life's journey would be.* I was not sure what these lines meant, but it felt deep and frightening—like a rocky cliff at the world's edge in a Flash Gordon film. Yet the words also made me think of the woman Jack and Louella called "my real mother." Although they seldom spoke of her, Jack told me her one wish had been that I be placed with a good Catholic family. Speaking to Mary in my prayers, I decided, was a way of speaking to her, to Paula. I knew her name, having overheard Jack tell a friend of his, "Her real mother, Paula, was a fallen woman."

I didn't know exactly what he meant, but I knew it had to do with the seamier side of life, recounted to me through Joe, the taxi driver who drove me and four other girls to school each day. A short, stocky Italian, his hair smelled of Brylcreem, and a cigarette usually dangled from his lips. His father was a drunk who used to wake him at night and beat him with a strap just in case he had misbehaved during the day. His sister had polio and was condemned to live in an iron lung. Whenever he spoke of his late mother, he took his hands off the wheel and made the sign of the cross above his heart. He was a Democrat, and he told us that Adlai Stevenson would save the country.

My adoptive father was as Italian as Joe, but, except for his tan complexion and wavy hair, not the least like Joe in appearance. Jack was trim and always dressed in the latest fashion. He held a filtered Kent until it burned to his fingers, but never spoke with it hanging from his mouth, as Joe did. With his large lips and shadowy eyes, Jack looked like Dean Martin, or so Louella claimed.

One night at dinner, I tried something new. I was different from my parents and it was time they knew it. "I'm for Adlai Stevenson," I announced, reaching for the carrots. "He's the best candidate for 1952."

Jack snickered. "Who put that idea in your head?"

"Nobody," I answered. "I just know he's the only man who can save the country."

Disgusted, he pushed back from the table, causing the milk to slop out of my glass.

"Now look what you've done," Louella snapped at me.

"Better tell us where you're getting this rubbish," Jack snarled. I had rarely seen him so upset with me, and I was quick to admit it was Joe.

A few days later, a taxi came to take me to school, but Joe was not sitting behind the wheel. We had a new driver, Roger Mills, every bit as boring as his name.

"I'm for Ike," he made a point of saying.

CHAPTER 4

At Christmastime, I was allowed to open the holiday cards. One had a cartoon of Little Orphan Annie singing Christmas songs with her dog, Sandy, under a banner that read, HAPPY 1953!

"Please, why can't I?" I asked Jack, showing him the card. "Everyone I know has a dog."

"There isn't anything we wouldn't do for you," he told me. "But not that. Dogs make your mother sick."

"Not my dog. I'd take care of him. She wouldn't even know he was here." At eight, I had been helping Mrs. Smith care for Schmoo for several years.

"That's enough," Jack said. "Dogs belong on a farm, not in a house. The subject is closed."

Not as far as I was concerned. "Look," I said, pointing at the Christmas card. "Annie has a dog, and she's an orphan." I paused for effect before playing my ace. "Just like me."

"You'd break your mother's heart if she heard you. You know you're not an orphan." He sounded flustered, to my satisfaction.

"Well, I used to be, and I'm lonely as one now," I insisted. "If I had a dog, I wouldn't be lonely."

"You don't know how lucky you are to have us," he said. "Not everybody has such good parents. Your grandmother, Louella's mother, was plain no good. Now she's crazy and we have to look after her." He lowered his voice before continuing. "She didn't take care of your mother, I can tell you that."

"What happened?" I whispered.

He looked at me gravely. "One night, when poor Louella was just fifteen years old, her own mother locked her out for good. It was winter in Michigan, and she almost died from the cold. Ging was a cruel woman."

"Ging?" I repeated. "Like Bing? What kind of name is that?"

"I don't know, but it's what her mother goes by," he said. "Now don't you mention this little talk to anyone. And no more nonsense about dogs and orphans."

Later that week, I answered the door, expecting to greet my parents' friends. Instead, I saw a disheveled old woman, struggling to take off her girdle on our stoop. Her lips were brightly painted, and lipstick stained her teeth. The tufts of white hair on her large head made me think of candy floss.

"Where's my baby?" she mumbled. "I want to see my baby."

"Who are you?" I asked, more fascinated than fearful.

"Mind your manners, little girl."

The way she said "little girl" made me think of the wolf in "Little Red Riding Hood," and I slammed the door.

"Who was that?" Louella called out from the kitchen.

"A witch," I answered.

The doorbell rang again.

"Please don't answer it," I begged.

Louella ignored me and hurried over to the door.

When she saw the old woman, she cried out, "Mother, what are you doing here?"

She called to Jack, who helped Ging into the living room. Nellie came quickly and led me off to bed. I felt anxious, Louella's voice saying "MOTHER" still running through my mind. I tried to listen to the murmuring voices below, but the talk was too muffled. The next morning, the old lady was gone and her visit went unmentioned.

A few weeks later, we took a day trip in the car. Jack never drove because he was deaf in one ear, so Louella took her place in the driver's seat while I slid into the back.

Our drive took us to Napa State Hospital, an insane asylum situated on acres of farmland. In one of the brick buildings, we found our way to a room crowded with ancient women in rocking chairs. Many held dolls, and most had the same sugar-bowl haircut and vacant stare. Two orderlies entered with Ging and helped her into a chair.

She turned to me. "Oh," she said, "the little girl who shut the door on an old woman."

Ging lived for another year, but that was the only time she spoke in English to us when we drove out to visit. Instead, she used her native French, which none of us understood. She let us know she liked the treats we brought, though, snatching the candy or cookies out of Louella's hands.

I looked forward to our visits to the asylum. While Louella and Jack sat in the ward, I explored the grounds, fearing nobody except the head nurse. One day I encountered Wanda, who paced up and down an out-of-the-way path and cackled. She held an armless doll in one hand and a cigarette in the other. In the canteen, where I went to buy ice cream, I sought out the enormously fat twin sisters with Down's syndrome, who smiled and hugged everyone they met. All the residents had their own stories, and I yearned to know each one.

"Why does Ging talk in a language we can't understand?" I asked one day as we drove home.

"She lived in France when she was a little girl," Louella said. "That's what she learned."

"Did you live there too?"

"No," she shook her head. "My father was Canadian, and Mother never returned home after she married." She turned to Jack and her voice quivered. "Maybe that's why she was always so unhappy."

Abruptly, she pulled the car over and began to sob. Jack wrapped his arms around her, patting her back and cooing like she was a baby. Then he turned and glared at me, his black eyes smoldering.

"You and your goddamned questions. Look at how you've upset her." His hand thumped her back harder. She shoved him away.

"What the hell are you trying to do to me, Jack?" she asked, starting the car again. "You almost clobbered me to death."

He slumped in the passenger seat and muttered, "You can't win for trying."

Later at home, I asked Louella why we visited Ging when she refused to talk to us.

"She's my mother, that's why," Louella said. "Duty is more important than affection."

I didn't understand what she meant, but I felt a sudden admiration for her, as I had when she offered a ride to church to the woman and her little girl.

CHAPTER 5

Ging died in 1953, but we continued to take Sunday drives into the country. When Jack and Louella argued, I would practice my favorite game: making myself disappear. I did it by dreaming up a story in my head about my "real family." My mother and father might be movie stars, while schoolmates would be siblings. My usual story was that we were marooned on a desert island, and my courage saved us all from cannibals and sharks. I called my make-believe life "Oz."

Sometimes Jack or Louella would turn and ask, "What are you thinking about?"

"The land of Oz."

They thought of the Judy Garland movie, and it tickled them to share my secret life.

I can't remember when I first began to fantasize myself into a different place, but I have a very early memory of Jack coming into my room to tuck me in, smelling like whiskey. He sat on the bed and pulled the blankets up to my neck. "You're my best girl," he whispered. His hands fumbled under my nightgown and I looked away, through the window at the sliver of moon. I had a curious feeling that I was much closer to the moon than my bed.

I was so good at disappearing that I did it whenever I was bored or anxious. During Sunday drives, I listened with one ear to their talk and answered their questions, while all the time my mind was on an island far away.

THE SUNDAY DRIVES stopped when Jack bought us a summer home in Sonoma County. The house looked like a red barn and was built into a gorge. To reach it, we had to cross a creek on a swinging wooden bridge. Oaks, madrones, and eucalyptus lined the water's edge. In summer, deer, foxes, raccoons, and an occasional rattlesnake found their way to the cool water. Two granite rocks rested in the middle of the creek, and I stretched out on them to watch water bugs skim the surface, minnows dart beneath them, and the rare silver glint of a trout. Once I found a scorpion under a cool stone and kept it in a jar overnight, but I remembered what Nellie said about every creature being "a work of God," and let it go the next morning.

We drove out to the house most weekends. As soon as we arrived, Jack fixed drinks: old-fashioneds for himself and Louella and a Shirley Temple for me. We settled on lounge chairs and watched the creek ripple past.

"I wonder what the poor are doing tonight," Jack said, the lines under his melancholy eyes softening as he chuckled at his own joke.

"You've worked hard, Jack," Louella said. "You take good care of us."

"Well," he said, "I'd have nothing without my sweetheart."

I loved it when they were nice to each other. This happened most often, I noticed, when they'd just had a drink.

So I suggested they have a highball one Sunday morning when they were arguing about Jack's not going to church. First they laughed, but then Jack looked annoyed with me. "You don't understand anything about us," he said.

I DID KNOW Jack was raised in a large poor family in Southern California, but Aunt Rosetta was the only sibling I had met. She and her husband were childless, which was, according to Louella, why they were unhappy. How stubborn they were not to adopt a baby, Jack often remarked.

One day I was told that they had finally adopted a child, not a baby, but a seven-year-old girl. I was excited by the prospect of a new cousin, especially one who came from the same mysterious place as me. I wondered if she would look like me. Maybe we all shared some feature that we alone could recognize.

Her name was Patti. She was a tall girl, and the blue dotted swiss dress she wore the day we met was too short for her long legs. In the corner of her bedroom stood two suitcases and a box full of possessions from her past life. I wanted to examine each item, but had been told not to probe.

"As far as we're concerned," Louella informed me, "Patti's life begins here and now."

"But why can't we ask where's she been?" I asked.

"Because her old life was full of trouble," Jack answered. "If you bring it up, you'll just make her unhappy."

"But she knows all about it anyway," I argued.

"Yes, she does, but some things are best forgotten," Louella said, annoyed. "Anyway, it will break Auntie Rosetta's heart if you say anything. Finally she has a child of her own. She doesn't need any reminders about how she got here."

"But where did she come from?" I persisted. "If you tell me, I won't ask her any questions."

"My, you are a nosy girl," Louella said. "What if you found out the girl has bad blood? How would you feel then with your prying questions?"

Bad blood. What did that mean? I knew some families were related by blood, and I had heard that blood runs thicker than water. Our history book at school referred to certain battles as "bloodbaths." But I had never heard of bad blood. Perhaps the badness had something to do with not having a real father and mother. If Patti had bad blood, then maybe I did too. I had to find out more about this blood business. I decided to talk to my cousin. I found an opportunity one night when we shared a room at Aunt Rosetta's.

"Are you asleep?" I asked.

"No," she whispered.

"Do you miss your real mother?"

"Shhh. They get mad if I talk about my family. But, yes," she went on, "I miss my mother, and I miss my sister even more."

A sister—this was even more exciting. "Tell me what happened," I prodded.

"My mother got so sick she couldn't take care of us. I had to live in foster homes."

"Was your real mother mean to you?" I asked, thinking again of the bad blood.

"No. Let's not talk about it anymore. They'll get mad if they hear us." She turned her back on me and pulled her blanket tight.

"I'm adopted too," I said. "I wish I knew what happened, the way you do."

"Don't think about it anymore," Patti said. "My new mother says, 'What's done is done.' "

I WASN'T THE only one with a secret past. No photographs of grandparents, aunts, or uncles hung on the walls of our house. Few stories about family made their way into the dinner conversation.

Jack saw Aunt Rosetta, and Louella had a sister with three daughters we visited, but nobody ever spoke of their early lives. Family lore began the day Jack and Louella brought me home from the hospital: "We wanted a baby more than anything," Louella said, whenever I asked. "I knew you were mine as soon as I saw you."

"You made your mother the happiest woman in the world," Jack agreed, never mentioning his own feelings.

When I was seven, Jack did invite several of his mysterious relatives over for dinner. Louella planned the menu carefully, and set the table with real silver. But nobody showed up that night or called to cancel. While Jack waited for them, he drank himself into a stupor. Louella vowed over the cold roasted chicken, "Mark my words, not one of those people will ever be allowed to set foot in this house."

Two years later, the invitations went out again, with the same result. As we ate solemnly, Jack said, "Well, at least my poor mother isn't alive to see her family so torn apart."

I perked up. "Who was your mother?"

He drained his glass. "She was the definition of the word *saint*," he said. "They don't come better than her."

"She wasn't such a saint, Jack," Louella said. "She dropped your daughter on her head." I hated it when she referred to me that way— *your daughter.*

She turned to me. "When you were two weeks old, we put you in the woman's arms, and she dropped you smack on the floor. She died a week later of a stroke."

"You never stop, do you?" Jack yelled. "Come on," he said to me, "Let's go watch television," and the two of us left the table. In the living room, he let me finish his old-fashioned, as he often did. The prize was the cherry at the bottom, and the rule was that I had to drink what was left to get it. This time there was a lot of alcohol in the glass, and it took me two gulps to get to the cherry. Then I opened the doors of the Motorola television cabinet, just as Rosemary Clooney began to sing.

"It's Linda's bedtime," Louella called out.

"I always watch *Your Hit Parade!*" I said.

Jack turned the television off anyway.

"But it isn't fair," I said. He tickled me and planted sloppy kisses on my face. "At least I have you," he slurred, giggling. "You are my real sweetheart." Suddenly he pushed my face against his crotch. The blue serge fly of his pants smelled rancid. I tried to move away, but he held me tightly. A familiar feeling rose in the pit of my stomach. "I can't breathe," I cried, pushing him as hard as I could.

Louella came into the room. "Not this!" she cried. "No, you don't touch her!"

He released me. She grabbed my hand and silently led me upstairs. Her hand was trembling as she put me into bed.

A short time later, I heard them fighting.

"You're a sitting duck," Louella yelled. "I know you gave that uncle of yours another handout. And look what he gives us in return. This has to stop. I mean it, Jack—and there's another thing." She lowered her voice. "If you touch her like that again, you'll be out of this house." There was a pause. Then I heard his deep voice unleashing an angry tirade. I was frightened when Louella began to cry. I lay in bed hugging myself and chanting my favorite poem by Edgar Allan Poe, "Annabel Lee." Nellie read it to me most nights, so I knew it by heart. Pretty soon I couldn't hear their voices anymore, and I drifted off to sleep.

For days, Jack and Louella only spoke to each other through me. "Please tell your father dinner is ready." "Please tell your mother the neighbor called." I enjoyed a feeling of self-importance, but the situation worried me. What if they never spoke again? Where would we go, and what would happen to me? Would Nellie come with us? It seemed like our lives might fade away, back into the ghost land I had come from.

THEY BEGAN TO talk to each other again when Uncle Harry came for dinner. His real name was Harry Linsky, but I always called him "Uncle." He was a quiet bald man with thick black eyebrows.

Rummaging through a box of photos in a drawer, I came across an old picture of him and Louella at the beach. Both wore black one-piece swimsuits, and they had their arms around each another. I carried the photo to the basement, where Louella was showing Nellie how to shelve the cases of canned fruit she kept "just in case of an emergency." The photograph made her smile. Ever since her brother died, she explained, Harry had taken his place.

"Who was your brother?" I asked.

"George," she answered. "He died in the war. Now stop snooping around." Harry worked as a union electrician, and was a Democrat but never talked politics. In his Mercury station wagon, he carried boxes with the word BROTHERHOOD stamped on them. These intrigued me because he, like the Risis, never spoke of his past. I wondered if the containers held secrets of his family life.

Never married, he lived at the Uptown Hotel "without so much as a hot plate," as I once heard Louella whisper to her friend, Sugar. He often came for dinner, and on Sunday mornings, he brought us pastrami, rye bread, and other treats from the Jewish bakery.

Uncle Harry had served as a Marine in the Korean War, but had been discharged long before the war ended, and he came home with gifts for everyone. Nothing could compare with the present he gave me: a bayonet, which he grandly unsheathed in our living room.

"Come and touch it," he said. Its steel edge felt sharp against my fingertips.

"See that?" He pointed to the blade. "That's not rust. It's the blood of a Korean soldier."

I thanked him, barely getting the words out. I took the bayonet out of its leather sheath every chance I got, imagining it had the same supernatural properties as Aladdin's magic lamp.

IN JUNE, 1953, as we drove out to our summer home, a voice on the radio came on with a special announcement: Julius and Ethel Rosenberg had been executed. Amid the drone of grown-up facts, one detail stood out: the Rosenbergs' children were to be raised by relatives. Thunderstruck, I started asking questions.

"Who were they—the Rosenbergs?"

"Bad people," Jack snapped. "Communists."

"But they had children."

"You're too young to understand," Jack said. "They were guilty of espionage."

The car stopped as we waited for a train to pass. Louella looked back at me sharply. "Now don't you go and make a Sarah Bernhardt drama out of this," she said. "They were spies. They got exactly what they deserved."

The radio's stark words crowded my mind. Spies. Espionage. Communists. Electric chair. I remembered my bayonet, and thought—for the first time—about the Korean man whose blood stained the blade. Perhaps he had children who looked something like my friend Karen Kim and her little brother, Dennis, who always played funny tricks on me.

I started to cry, but stopped when Jack turned and asked, "What's wrong?" I put my head down and pretended I was falling asleep. When we returned home, I took the bayonet down to the basement and hid it on the highest shelf. For a moment I stood there, like I sometimes did in the old cemetery, thinking of the dead. The bloodstain haunted me more than any of those headstones. Then I turned and climbed the stairs. That night I woke up and thought I could see its victims hiding in the corners of my room.

Even more frightening ghosts appeared in my dreams. Usually they came from the large brick building near our house marked by a sign that read ST. ELIZABETH'S. The place resembled a hospital, but there were no ambulances screaming to the curb, no men in white coats bustling in and out, no patients. Shadows would sometimes pass eerily across the curtained windows. Whenever we drove past, tension filled the car.

One time I piped up from the backseat, "What's St. Elizabeth's?"

Louella turned away from the steering wheel long enough to exchange a glance with Sugar. In their profiles I caught a flicker of alarm, but they ignored me.

A few days later, a neighborhood girl answered my question. "That's where bad girls go to give away their babies."

That night, I dreamed of spirits from the building surrounding my bed. "Get out of my room," I cried, but they circled faster and rushed at me. They were trying to take me to the hospital where the bad women and their children lived. I could hear myself crying, "No, No!" Then they faded away, except one. I knew it was her, my real mother.

I woke up screaming. Soon the hall light flicked on and Jack came in. He sat on my bed, stroking my hair to comfort me, but then his hands slid under my nightie. I froze for a moment, then pushed him away, curling up into a ball. He left the room.

After that night, I often had nightmares, but I forced myself not to make a sound.

There were so many ghosts haunting our lives: the phantom of the lost child that Louella mentioned once when she caught me staring at her long abdominal scar. The mysterious woman who had given birth to me. Most haunting of all was the game Jack, Louella, and I played, pretending that we were a family no different from the others who made up our community, where babies were born of their mothers and family members looked like one another.

Late that summer, we moved away from Ewing Terrace and the neighborhood near St. Elizabeth's. I can still remember the last drive past "the home" and the relief I felt to leave it behind.

CHAPTER 6

At the end of the Korean War, the American economy was booming, as was Jack's optometry firm, Ferrari & Risi. Our move from middle-class Ewing Terrace to stately Pacific Heights in 1953, with its view of Marina Bay and the Golden Gate Bridge, bespoke his success. The house sat on the corner of Jackson and Steiner, where at that time the cable car stopped for its return trip. Built of stone and painted pink, our new home had three stories, six bathrooms, and a full staff of help. Nellie came with us, taking one of the four bedrooms for herself. "We have our own apartments now," she joked.

In the quiet enclave of Ewing Terrace, I had feared only the bad spirits that haunted Lone Mountain and St. Elizabeth's. In our new upscale neighborhood, however, stories never ceased about the "riffraff" who endangered life and property. People had to be buzzed through a gate to enter our house, a measure meant to protect us from murderers and thieves.

Every morning at seven, Jack caught the cable car to his office. Dressed in a handsome flannel suit, he wore a hanky in his breast pocket, a silk tie, a trilby hat, and an overcoat. His shoes were shined on Wednesdays, his hair trimmed on Thursdays, and on Fridays he had a manicure, always in the same stall at the St. Frances Hotel. After work, sipping cocktails with Louella, he would sometimes slip into a sentimental reverie, describing the pleasure of walking into his office and hearing each employee say, "Good morning, Mr. Risi." Then he'd look at me and add with a smile, "Not bad for a fourth-grade dropout, eh?"

Our increase in fortune heightened Louella's already acute sense of fashion. One of my favorite places to wander was the closet made for her hats. There, in that hushed space, I would lift down each box, color-coded and stored on its own shelf. Under every lid lay an amazing creation: one gray velvet pillbox with an eye-length veil of black netting, another made of lozenge-shaped felt in pale pink, and hats embellished with rhinestones, birds, beads, and fur. Inside their grosgrain bands were labels like Saucer and Flute.

Louella's attention to appearance extended beyond hats. Tailored suits arrived from Hong Kong sized perfectly for her, and every week she returned to the Beauty Key, where a "girl" named Violet painted a new coat of blood red polish on her fingernails and kept her hair stylish, sensible, and subtly tinted.

Our new wealth increased Louella's desire to entertain, and she developed several social circles. Her frequent gatherings entailed much discussion about who should "mix" with whom. When the company arrived on party nights, Nellie would lead me up to bed. After a few minutes, I would sneak back to the top of the circular staircase to watch what was happening below.

The evenings began stiffly with the women gathering in the dining room, still wearing their fur coats, and the men standing in the living room, discussing Sugar Ray Robinson or the latest Yankees ballgame. Not until the third highball did the atmosphere turn lively, with heated discussions about politics and stocks. One evening the men watched the House Un-American Activities hearings on television, swearing and arguing, tossing out words like "hysteria," "treason," and, with the most contempt, "Commie." The drama enthralled me. Though I didn't understand what was going on, I knew there was poison in the air.

Louella knew how to make friends and how to keep them. She had known Sugar Spinoza for fifteen years. Sugar, true to her name, never visited without bringing a sack of candy for me. She and her husband, Woody, a union representative, sacrificed to send their children to Catholic schools. Sugar was the one friend who dropped by without calling first, and Louella would sit and talk with her for hours. Sugar always paid special attention to me, crinkling her warm gray eyes and calling me "Linda-Lou."

Of Louella's newer friends, I liked Florence Willard least. She was the wife of a famous ophthalmologist, Howard, who did business with Jack and always wore a bow tie. Florence dressed in ugly house-dresses and fretted about her only daughter, whose chin had recently sprouted thick whiskers. I heard Louella say to Sugar: "She'll never get that girl married off." Conversations between Louella and Florence were always vapid: about priests who had come for dinner, or Florence's daughter's triumphs in geography or mathematics. Once Louella slipped in a piece of gossip about a mutual friend, but Florence was uninterested. "Well, as Father Martin always says, if you can't say anything nice, don't say anything at all." Her admonishment brought their feeble conversation to a halt.

Molly Duncan, on the other hand, was glamorous, with pretty honey-colored hair and bright clothes. Her husband was a top eye surgeon, and Molly often arrived at our house slightly breathless, just back from an exotic trip overseas. Louella was noticeably concerned with the impression she made on Molly.

One spring day when she was coming to visit, I found Louella trying to choose between three dresses. I went to her large closet and pointed to the one I liked best. "This one," I pleaded. I could hear the pleasure in my voice as I studied this dream of a dress, yards of gray organza and pearl buttons.

Louella's lip curled. "What would you know?" she said. "Now let me alone so I can decide what to wear."

When Molly arrived, Louella descended the stairs to greet her in beige linen, upright as a uniform. The maid served lunch, and I sat politely at the table, pretending not to listen to their gossip over chicken salad and iced tea. Once during the meal, Louella's glance fell on me. "Big ears," she chuckled and brushed back my hair. She always did seem to appreciate me more when her friends were around.

One hot summer day, Molly and Louella decided to "be naughty" and make themselves gin and tonics long before the cocktail hour. Curled up on two facing couches, they sipped and chatted. I sat nearby, pretending to read my latest Nancy Drew mystery, *The Secret of the Wooden Lady*. The topic that day was husbands.

"Men all want the same thing, don't they," Molly said. "Once you give it to them, they just want more." I peeked up from my book, looking from one woman to the other: Molly's soft face was scowling, and Louella grimaced, like her mouth was stuck at the corners.

I dared not ask what it was men wanted, but it made me think of the monthly poker parties Jack presided over. Occasionally one of the men arrived with a reel of film under his arm. I could tell when the projector began to play on Jack's foldaway screen. The silence gave way quickly to individual murmurs, until they were all hooting and howling.

Sometimes when the parties were over, Jack visited my room. I watched him through half-closed eyes as he stood at the end of my bed. After his silent vigils, he often placed money for me on the dresser. One night, he came to my bed and told me he had left me a silver dollar. Then he asked for a kiss. "No," I said, imitating the sharp tone Louella sometimes used. He walked from the room then,

the hall light shining on his defeated face. I hated myself for hurting him.

DURING HISTORY CLASS the next day, I was playing with the
silver dollar on my desktop when Mother Muldoon demanded to
know why I wasn't paying attention.

"I was just looking at something."

"I ascertained that for myself, Linda Risi!"

She brought the incident up during the school conference sched-
uled with my parents.

"You are a very smart girl," Mother Muldoon said, "but careless,
careless, careless. If you just tried harder and paid attention, you
would be at the top of the class." She turned to my parents. "During
history class," she said, "Linda was playing with a silver dollar instead
of reading." She demanded I show them the coin, and when I put it
on the table, Jack looked away. "Linda's bright, but she can't seem to
sit still long enough to listen."

I didn't understand why school was so hard when it was so easy to
pay attention to conversations, especially those of grown-ups. I loved
hearing Nellie's stories about her family in Minnesota. And I was fascinated to learn how others lived: the food they ate, the photographs
and pictures on their walls, the kinds of books on their shelves, how
they talked to one another. Surrounded by adults, I could drift in and
out without anybody noticing, but in class I could never concentrate.
I spent more time dreaming about life with my secret family than listening to the teacher. By the time third grade ended, I was doing
poorly in every subject except reading. Louella and Jack decided to
transfer me to another school in the fall.

CHAPTER 7

From the grandeur of Sacred Heart, I descended to St. Dominic's, in the Fillmore District, known as "Little Harlem." My parents figured that the Dominicans, with their emphasis on discipline and education, stood a better chance of reforming me.

I entered my new school on a hot September morning. Used to the homogeneity of the Sacred Heart Convent, I was startled by the black, brown, and white faces of the children playing on the sticky tarmac at St. Dominic's. When the bell rang, we hurriedly formed rows under the gaze of the nuns and walked single file into the building.

The moment I came into our classroom, I noticed a girl with a blonde bob and deep dimples. She held court in the back of the room, several kids hanging on her every word. Although it was a warm day, she wore an oversized camel-hair coat with a fake leopard collar. Cracking jokes and gum simultaneously, she chewed and talked faster and louder than anyone I had ever seen. Her roving, mischievous blue eyes caught mine in a flash of acknowledgment. Her name was Judy Carroll.

"You're the tallest person in the class," Judy said to me the first week we met. "Does that feel weird?"

"I hate it," I said. "All my parents' friends say, 'Oh, you should be a model when you grow up,' but it doesn't make me feel better."

For a moment she just looked at me, then she grinned. "Well, I'm always the fattest," she said. I knew by her disclosure I had passed the test for friendship. Soon we found ourselves rolling our eyes in solidarity whenever suck-up Melissa Brown gave one of her virtuous answers in religion class.

Our first assignment together was to make an oral presentation on Saint Catherine of Sienna. Saint Catherine showed us how it was possible to be upright, strong minded, and spunky at the same time. Unfortunately, our esteem for the saint was not apparent in our presentation to the class. While describing Jesus as her divine bridegroom, we erupted in giggles. "Jesus is not happy with you today, Judy Carroll and Linda Risi," scolded the angry nun. "Neither of you has any self-control. You will have detention for a week." We returned to our desks, trying to look both chastised and nonchalant. When school was over, the nun left us to face our punishment alone.

"Why do you always look like you're in outer space?" I asked Judy as we sat in the empty classroom.

"What do you mean?"

"Oh, I don't know. You look far away, like you don't want to be bothered."

"I'm just bored."

"No, that's not it," I persisted.

Judy hesitated for a moment, then leaned toward me. "My family is full of terrible secrets. Sometimes I want to tell everyone what really happens there."

"Mine is too. My parents aren't even my real parents. I'm not allowed to ask about them. I think they might be spies."

"Can I tell you something, and you have to promise never to tell?"

"I swear on a stack of Bibles."

"I think my mom's crazy, at least when she drinks," Judy confessed. "My father's worse. He's drunk most of the time. He smashes furniture and beats her up. But nobody knows it."

"That sounds really scary," I said.

"It is. The worst is that the day after a fight, they both act like nothing happened. It's like they're pretending all the time."

I nodded. "That's just like Louella and Jack. They're so nice to anybody who comes over, but as soon as that person leaves, they start gossiping all over the place!"

"I think we should promise never to lie or talk behind each other's back," Judy said. "That way we'll both have somebody we can trust."

I'd never had a conversation so raw and open. I wanted to be responsible to somebody else—to have someone depend on me.

"Even under torture," I promised, "we'll always tell each other the truth."

SCHOOL SEEMED EASIER with Judy beside me. At the end of each day, I felt a pang when we parted, each to a house on Steiner Street, mine in Pacific Heights and hers in the Fillmore ghetto. We called each other as soon as we got home. And after dinner. And before bed.

"I hate my nickname," she said one night. "Rollo" was the name our classmates had given her. "What a stupid thing to call me," she scoffed. "Well, I'm short and fat. And that's that." She giggled.

"No," I protested. "You're the most beautiful girl I've ever seen. And you're lucky, you know. I hate being so klutzy."

"Well, that's true—you are sort of gawky," she said, "but your eyes are like blue diamonds, only prettier."

This is how we spoke to each other, unless we were fighting. Then it turned nasty fast. Judy could be wildly jealous. "You're worse than my no-good father," she complained whenever I spent the afternoon with another friend. She was masterful at finding the one characteristic that made a person seem repellent or dim-witted. Her aim was deadly.

"The nose on her is enough to knock a person dead," she said about Ann Marie Cortopassi. "Of course she's a snotter," she said about Frannie McKay, who had huge glasses and blew her nose often. "She's the definition of *drip*." Once Judy belittled my friends, I could never see them in a positive light again. They became whatever Judy said they were.

I DIDN'T GET jealous the way Judy did. Instead, I feared she would learn the truth about me and leave me behind. I was not even sure what this "truth" was, except that it had to do with feeling like a fraud, that I wasn't who she thought I was.

Each night, I would lie awake in bed and recall our conversations from the day. *Best friends*. I understood what those words meant. It mattered less that I didn't belong with my family, because I belonged with Judy.

God's universe was a "whirling, pulsating place of light and movement," Sister Madeline told us one day in science class. *Pulsating*: I loved how the word rolled across the tongue. At the desk beside mine, Judy wrote frantically in her notebook. I liked watching her write, her nose wrinkled in concentration, her blue eyes squinting inches from the page. In the universe described by Sister Madeline, frogs croaked and waves broke on the shore, but I had stopped listening, captivated by a word. To pulsate was to talk and write like Judy. Pulsating was the word to describe her laughter.

Many weekends, she joined me in the luxurious backseat of the Olds as we drove to the country house. Relieved that I had settled into school, Jack and Louella were happy to let her come along. Judy and

I shared my double bed, talking into the night about God and lipstick, about boys and brave Saint Agatha who chose to have her breasts hacked off rather than lose her virginity.

Jack and Louella plagued me with questions about my friend. "Where has her mother been all this time? What does her father do for a living? Why don't we ever meet them?" I feigned ignorance, because I had sworn not to tell anyone that Judy shared a bedroom with her mother, and that her father was an unemployed plumber who spent most of his time in jail for public drunkenness.

Although each of us in our home life had her own brand of misery, together in the city we were free. In the mid-1950s, San Francisco's bus system made the city a playground for young girls like us. For lunch, we often visited the Far East Café in Chinatown, where we would devour paper-wrapped chicken and steaming plates of chow mein in a private booth. One day, filled to the gills, we pursued an ancient Asian man through a maze of alleys. We were looking for the notorious tongs, gangsters of the 1920s who operated brothels and opium dens, and who, we were convinced, still thrived in Chinatown. We imagined that we could "bust the case."

Other days, we ran up the stairs of the public library at Civic Center and returned home with armfuls of books. Our choices were fanciful, classics like *Gulliver's Travels,* dimestore paperbacks about adolescent romance and misery, and books with photographs about distant lands we promised to explore together.

In the morning light, we climbed Telegraph Hill to Coit Tower, where we took in the city on the rare days when it was not shrouded in fog. Judy brought me to the music conservatory where she took piano lessons. "This place used to be an orphanage," she told me. "You could have lived here." We invented a woeful tale: my life as a Dickens character.

Once Judy brought a shopping bag to school and pulled out two black Irish wool capes of her mother's. Donning them and carrying stenographer's pads, we boarded the city bus after school to play an elaborate game of detective. Following unsuspecting citizens through their various bus transfers, we took copious notes about their clothes and gestures and invented wild stories. At that time, the city's newspapers were full of stories about a woman named Iva Kroger. Iva had owned a rooming house, and she had disappeared, along with many people who had rented rooms from her. During the police investigation, several bodies were exhumed from her basement. According to rumor, not only had she murdered her boarders; she had eaten various body parts. One day, a woman got on the bus, drunk and crazy-looking, with missing teeth and rubber bands holding up her stockings.

Judy turned to me and whispered, "I bet that's Iva Kroger."

Without missing a beat, I blurted out, "Iva Kroger is my real mother."

We laughed so hard our stomachs hurt. Soon "Iva Kroger" became the code for my lost parent, and always produced the same hysterical result. By then, I had smothered the heart of that five-year-old girl hunched on the curb, desperately wanting to find her real mother.

DURING THE FIRST week of school when we were eleven, Judy got her first period. She called excitedly to tell me the news. The next day, we met at Fisherman's Wharf and I asked her about it as we sat down to share a huge bowl of clam chowder at Alioto's. "That's not the highlight of the day," she said, then reached into her black purse. With great ceremony, she deposited a book titled *The Facts of Life and Love for Teenagers* on the red and white checkered oilcloth.

"My mother gave me this book," Judy said. "I can hardly believe she knew what she was doing, because what's inside is so gross you won't believe it." Somberly we sat side by side, turning pages, until we came to the chapter on sex. We saw the cartoon drawings and gasped.

When we came to the sentence, "The penis becomes erect and is thrust into the vagina," we doubled over laughing.

Our chowder long gone, we left the chilly waterfront and caught a bus downtown. On the bus, Judy murmured in my ear, "Bet you don't have the nerve to say it to that woman."

I glanced across the aisle. The middle-aged woman looked dignified in her pert hat with her matching handbag. She might be a librarian, I thought. I fell silent until we neared our stop, awed by Judy's dare. As we rose from our seats, I leaned toward the woman and blurted out, "The penis becomes erect and is thrust into the vagina." As shock spread across the woman's face, we jumped off the bus, and I covered my tinge of guilt by giggling with Judy.

On the sidewalk, we grew quiet again. "How disgusting," Judy said after we had walked in silence for a while. "We shouldn't have to know stuff like that at our age."

"Let's promise we will always tell each other everything, even if something horrible like that happens," she added.

I promised.

ellie called us the "gold dust twins." Seldom apart, Judy and I reacted to the world in much the same manner. Sometimes this resemblance was comforting, and sometimes it had dire consequences. As sixth grade drew to a close, our class entered the church for a final Mass. Walking through the doors, Judy and I made the mistake of spotting an ancient Italian woman babbling nonstop in front of Mother Mary's Shrine. We turned away from one another, knowing that we were on a slippery slope toward trouble. Although we sat apart, just a shared glance caused us to break into painful spasms of laughter. Trying to suppress it gave me a stomachache, and I began to tremble with fear and pleasure.

Toward the end of Mass, our class filed up to the rail for communion. Kneeling in wait, I watched the long line of people on their knees, each of them sticking out her tongue for the priest to lay the consecrated Host upon. I sensed Judy watching alongside me, witnessing the same ridiculous slithery sight: fat or thin, long or short, pink tongues exposing themselves obscenely. We could barely contain ourselves as we stuck out our own tongues. When Father O'Neill placed the wafers on our tongues, we both lost control. In our explosive laughter, the blessed Host shot from our mouths, landing on the marble floor.

Paralyzed, we waited for the Host to bleed. Father O'Neill glowered down at us, his face turning purple, and we bolted out of the church into the street. The outraged priest followed us, leaving shocked parishioners and our fellow students at the altar. Luckily, Judy knew her way, and we ran faster than Father did. "Follow me," she called over her shoulder. We dashed through the Fillmore neighborhood—past the Mexican woman who sold mysterious red and yellow spices that she kept in huge jars, past the "Lickety-Fingers Fried Chicken" restaurant, down an alley bordered by run-down houses where tenants hung laundry from lines in their windows. By the time we settled into a slow-paced jog, fear had taken over. Yet all we had to do was say the magic word—"tongues"—and our laughter erupted again.

We decided to go to Judy's flat. In nearly two years of friendship, I'd never seen the inside of it. The deteriorated Victorian was divided into three separate living accommodations. Beneath the faded paint, the wood was rotting. Gaps in the banister railing looked like missing teeth, and iron meshing covered the downstairs windows. We collapsed inside the front door and rested for several minutes in the dim foyer, gulping the neighborhood air heavy with the smell of old fried food and stale cigarettes. When we had recovered, Judy led me into the living-dining room. Stacks of newspapers and unopened mail covered the dining table, and someone had nailed plywood over a missing windowpane. Yet the place showed signs of what an older person might have called "culture." Books lay everywhere, and in one corner stood an impressive piano. A tattered print of Van Gogh's *Room at Arles* hung on the wall. Judy showed me the bedroom she shared with her mother, a tiny room crammed with an unmade bed, more books, and a bare-bulb reading lamp.

I wanted to tell Judy how much I liked her house, how it had character, but I feared sounding phony, so I said nothing. She didn't seem aware of the contrast between her house and mine, or else she did not think it notable. That I did made me feel shallow.

All afternoon we stretched out on two ragged pea green sofas, united by our fear of the repercussions of the day's episode and our comfort in each other. We pledged to remain best friends forever, and wrote out a long declaration on a piece of blue-lined paper, which we decided to make official by signing in blood. Judy poked herself with a pin, but I felt too squeamish to do so myself. We called in her older brother, Tommy, who had played hooky from school that day and was sleeping in a back room. He held my hand and eagerly jammed the needle into it. Thus we signed our pact properly, assuring each other our promise extended beyond death.

The sound of high heels on the doorstep broke into our conversation. "It's my mother," Judy announced as a key turned in the lock. Patricia Mae Carroll walked through the door. "She'll either be mean or wonderful," she whispered. "I never know what to expect."

A former debutante, Patricia had married a man with Irish charm and little else. Long demoted to a life of disappointment and hard work, she was still striking: a tall, thin version of Judy, dimples and all. Lipstick enhanced her pale skin, but the kohl around her blue eyes did not mask her weariness.

Patricia scrutinized me with suspicion. "Is this your rich friend?"

"Yes, Ma, but her parents don't like her and won't even pay for music lessons."

Patricia's look softened. "Did Judy tell you how I work every day selling coats so that she can go to a private school, take ballet, and have piano lessons?"

I nodded.

"Look at my poor feet," she lamented, tossing off her black heels. "I have to stand on them all day long."

I mumbled my sympathy, and she grinned at me. She smiled like Judy, full and wide, as if I were the only person in the world. "Why don't your parents like you?" she asked.

"I'm adopted," I said. "I don't look or act like they do, and they say I'm too much for them."

"Well, I'm missing a child. My baby boy died at six months. He was such a wonder. Everyone, even strangers, used to come up to admire him." She gave a woeful sigh and continued. "Get away, I would say. I didn't want them to breathe their filthy germs all over him. But you don't want to hear about my poor dead boy."

She made the sign of the cross, whispered, "Mary of the broken heart," and then looked right into my eyes. "You won't be too much for me. If my Judy loves you, then so do I."

When Patricia wasn't drinking, she treated us like her closest friends, telling us scandalous stories about people she worked with and taking us to dinner on payday. Our favorite restaurant was Green Valley in North Beach, where the customers sat at two long wooden tables. The aroma of garlic floated through the room as we ate sourdough with salads drowned in olive oil and balsamic vinegar. Then our plates would be loaded with piles of spaghetti, and her mother talked to everyone at the table, telling them we were "her girls." She revealed so much about our lives that we would beg her to stop.

Patricia laughed off our altar escapade—"They're just kids"—but other adults were upset. Priests, nuns, and my parents took the matter quite seriously, and decided that Judy and I needed to be separated. Jack and Louella registered me at Saint Rose Academy, where I would start seventh grade the following autumn. Judy would stay at St. Dominic's.

THEY BROKE THE news on a Saturday morning.

"I don't want to go to another school!" I protested.

"You'll get a brand-new start," Jack said.

"That's the story of my life," I said. "I just want to stay with Judy."

I ran upstairs to complain to Nellie, who was packing for her yearly visit to Minnesota. She was usually sympathetic to my troubles.

"My lands," she said. "You know nothing will stop your friendship with Judy. Your new school is just a block away."

I noticed she was cleaning out her entire room.

"You're taking so much stuff," I said. "You'll never fit all that in your suitcases."

"Oh, it's not all for the plane," she replied. "I'm just giving the room a good clean before I go."

"I'll miss you impossibly," I told her, handing her a pile of neatly folded clothes.

"Oh, no," she said, pressing her hand on mine. "Not that much. Why, you're practically all grown up, Linda. You're already twelve years old."

"I'll never be so old I won't need you," I protested.

She hugged me close, and then asked me to help carry her baggage.

On the way to the airport, we sat together, holding hands. I noticed brown patches on her arms and hands.

"Why do you have those marks?" I asked, pointing to her arm.

"Liver spots, honey. You'll have them one day when you're my age," she said, chuckling.

As we approached the terminal, she drew me so close that I smelled her White Shoulders perfume. Then she gave my hand a squeeze and stepped out of the car. I watched her through the window as we sped away. We had not gone far when Jack turned around.

"Nellie won't be coming back," he said with brisk authority. "You're too grown-up to need her now, and she's gotten too old to care for you. Nellie wanted to tell you herself, but we thought it was better this way."

"Better?" I cried. "Better for who? We didn't even get to say good-bye. First Judy, now Nellie. I'll never forgive you!"

Jack hunched down in the front seat as we waited for the light to change.

Now it was Louella who faced me. "This is exactly why we didn't let her tell you herself," she snapped. "We knew you'd make a big scene." I was silent, biting the inside of my cheeks to keep from crying. Back home, I ran to my room and fantasized about a different life.

By now my fantasy family was being replaced by the idea of true love, and I reached for my favorite novel, *Seventeenth Summer*. After falling in love for the first time, Angie says, "It was something I've never felt before." Maybe the same thing would happen to me, I thought as I read it for the fifth time.

James Dean was the only person I could imagine falling in love with. I developed a crush on him after seeing *East of Eden*, just months before he was killed in a car crash. He was my ideal hero: cool, misunderstood, a loner. I kept a poster of him hidden beneath my bed, which I unrolled and stared at longingly. I imagined he hadn't died, making up story after story. We rode down highways on his motorcycle as the sun set. His hair blew back in the wind. I wrapped my arms around his waist and tucked my fingers inside his leather jacket. Nothing would ever come between us. Gradually I stopped feeling so sad.

The next morning, Louella and Jack greeted me cheerfully. "We have decided that you can get a dog," said Louella.

"You've got to be kidding," I said.

"We certainly are not," Jack said. "We'll go to the dog pound to-day." For an instant I felt guilty, as though my happiness were a be-trayal of Nellie, but the joy I felt was too overwhelming. We visited the Humane Society and found Bonnie, a collie with a thick coat of black, gold, and white hair. Her ears stood upright. Uncle Harry fol-lowed us in his beat-up station wagon to carry her home.

In the following days, Bonnie and I spent our time outdoors. She accompanied Judy and me to the Marina Greens, where she dodged cyclists and raced after kite flyers. One day we visited Aquatic Park, a small, sheltered beach next to Fisherman's Wharf where Italian men played bocce for hours and Asian boys fished on craggy piers with homemade rods. I liked to watch the lovers on the beach sharing a blanket and a beer as they listened to the latest technological miracle, the transistor radio. Bonnie was more interested in the cry of pelicans swooping into the waters, and her tail wagged as we ran along the wet sand.

At night, she was allowed into my bedroom with strict instructions to stay on the towel that Louella had placed on the floor to protect against the germs, fleas, and mange she thought all dogs carried. In the middle of the night, I would wake to Bonnie's breath on my face, her big eyes glowing in the dark. She would lumber up into the bed, and we would fall back to sleep, side by side. I finally felt safe when I was asleep, and never had a nightmare when she was next to me.

Louella and Jack took no delight in my pet. Louella recoiled at the sight of her. Jack would give her a perfunctory pat on the head, but plainly did not like her either.

When I started school again in September, I returned home after my first day to find that my dog was not there. "Where's Bonnie?" I asked.

"She's gone to live on a farm," Louella explained. "A nice man came by for her."

"A farm? What are you talking about?"

"We had to think of her well-being, Linda. You don't have the time for her now, and we don't have enough outdoor space for such a big animal."

"But she's mine."

"We shouldn't have gotten such a big dog."

"We need to go and get her right now!"

"I know you liked the dog, but I couldn't stand the dirt."

"You haven't been brushing Bonnie enough. Her long hair was making your mother sick," Jack interjected.

I looked at them. In their expressions, I saw no regret or remorse. I stopped listening to their words. I was watching a silent movie: my adoptive parents pointing fingers with scowling brows. Slowly the words formed in my mind: "I hate them both." My body began to calm as I repeated the words: *hate them, hate them*. With quiet, deadly aim, I spoke. "You are not my real parents. Real parents would never do such a thing to their child."

Without waiting for their reaction, I turned on my heels and ran from the room.

That night, not even my fantasy life could fill the emptiness I felt inside. I went to sleep imagining the look of betrayal in Bonnie's soft, shining eyes when the man took her away.

CHAPTER 9

I settled into my new school, which was on the same block as my old school, more easily than I expected. Although schoolwork remained a challenge, I made new friends, and Judy was right around the corner. In the eighth grade, a girl named Babbs joined our class. She wore pink lipstick called Lilac Pastel and skirts shorter than any I had seen, and had bleached blonde hair with black roots. According to the nuns she was "trouble," and my classmates held her in polite contempt. As usual, I was fascinated with anyone from a world different from mine, and we became friends.

One afternoon, she invited me to her house after school. She introduced me to her mother, a woman who looked just like her, only older, with the same peroxide hair and thick makeup. As we chatted, the doorbell rang. On the stoop stood a lanky boy in faded jeans. His light brown hair was slicked down, and long eyelashes fringed his green eyes. He asked if he could carry the groceries in from the car.

"Sure, Mickey," Babbs's mother said. As she turned toward him I noticed the tightness of her thin red blouse, her soft tone. She was flirting with him, I thought, and he was flirting back with equal candor. Something thrilling simmered here, something I felt but did not understand. I could barely breathe or think. I startled myself with a desire to press my own face against his sweater. In the few minutes he stayed, he told us about his first weeks of high school with a mix of wisecracks and genuine enthusiasm. Before he left, he came right up to me and said, "What a pleasure it is to meet you, Miss Lulabelle."

After he left, I tried to look nonchalant as I asked, "Who was that?"

"Only the cutest boy in the Marina," Babbs answered, eager to tell me all about Michael Patrick Malloy, who lived on Chestnut Street above a bar called Linger Longer.

"It's a tragic thing," Mrs. Barnett broke in, "about that boy's mother. She was quite the French beauty until the father ran off with another woman. Now she's just one more drunk, and his new stepfather's in prison."

"Prison!" I exclaimed. "What did he do?"

"Grand larceny. One of Mickey's brothers is in there too."

"He doesn't look like a hood," I said.

"He's not," Babbs insisted. "He's different from the rest of them. He gets good grades, and works at the Wendell's drugstore every day after school. He's the funniest guy I've ever met." She narrowed her eyes. "Listen, don't get a crush on him. All the other girls are in love with him already. Besides, there's one girl, Kate Bradford, he keeps going back to."

But her warnings were no match for the jittery glow I felt. At home, I found Louella busy in the kitchen making pot roast and sipping her old-fashioned. We chatted about her day. Then I made my announcement, just as I had seen it done in the movies.

"I've met the boy I'm going to marry."

She laughed nervously. "You will need more than teenage fantasies to marry someone. Besides, you know perfectly well that you can't date until you're in high school."

I left her to her cooking, vowing never to tell her anything that mattered again. I went upstairs and called Judy. Now that we went to different schools, Jack and Louella allowed us to be in regular contact again.

When she picked up the phone, I exclaimed, "My life has changed forever." I took a shallow breath. "I mean forever. I didn't know my heart could beat so hard."

"Tell me everything," she shrieked.

I told her every single thing I could remember about him and she sighed.

"I wonder if it will ever happen to me," she said.

But it was a different story the next day. "Where'd you meet him anyway?" Judy asked sullenly, reaching for a record to put on her dusty LP player.

"At Babbs Barnett's house."

"Oh God, not her." Judy rolled her eyes in disgust. "She's the biggest tramp in the Marina! If he's so perfect, why does he hang out with her?"

I shrugged, knowing better than to argue. When the music started, she groaned dramatically, as if overcome by passion, and closed her eyes.

"What's this?" I asked.

"I can't believe you don't know," she answered. "It's Bach, of course. The Brandenburg Concertos."

"Who's Bock?"

"Bach, Bach, Bach—get it right."

I tried to imitate the sound she was making at the back of her throat. "What kind of music is it?" I asked timidly.

"It's classical music. Don't tell me you don't know what that is." Then she caught herself and smiled. "Sorry, that was mean. It's what I study at the conservatory and I think it's the only music that matters."

At dinner I asked Louella and Jack if they knew about Bach, trying once more to enunciate the name the way Judy did.

"Oh goodness, that's for highbrows," Louella replied, putting an end to our conversation.

THAT NIGHT I sat on my bed, looking out at the neighborhood below. I wondered about the lives of the people I saw returning home. I imagined them talking at the dinner table with their families, having happier conversations than my dismal ones with Louella and Jack. I thought about Mickey, and how warm and quivery I had felt around him. Unsettled, I decided to write a letter to Judy, as I always did whenever it was too late to call and I was lonely.

As I sat down at my desk, I spotted the diary I had received at Christmas, which I had yet to pick up. Now I did, writing: *October 7 1957 Dear Diary*. The words came faster than I could write.

Why does Judy's mother pay for her to study at the best conservatory in the city when they are poor, while I take piano lessons from creepy Mr. Miller, who always squeezes my thigh and smells bad, just because he gives us a good deal? The world seems upside down. Judy is the only person I belong with. When I am at home, I feel like I'm with strangers. Maybe it's because they aren't my real parents. My pen had a mind of its own, I discovered.

When Judy's brother, Tom, told us boys will expect us to know how to French-kiss, I almost gagged. The thought of someone's tongue in my mouth is too disgusting. But we practiced anyway, using our fingers in each other's mouths, pretending they were tongues.

Two pages followed about school that day. *In current events we discussed the new laws banning racial segregation. We talked about Emmett Till, the fourteen-year-old from Mississippi. He was murdered because they said he whistled at a white woman and the men who killed him were freed. How can something so bad happen and my parents don't even mention it?*

Then I wrote the most important words of all: *Mickey Malloy. Mrs.*

Mickey Malloy. The boy I am going to marry. I put my pen down and marveled. I had filled four pages. I vowed to write every night.

AFTER SCHOOL THE next day, Judy and I went to Katz's Delicatessen, where Mr. Goldstein gave us free kosher pickles. We walked on to Tom's Drugstore and read articles from *Photoplay* and *True Confessions* until Mr. Martin, with the handlebar mustache, yelled at us and we ran out laughing. Our arms stayed locked until we separated at Steiner Street.

I buzzed the gate and ran up the stairs to find Louella waiting. "Go and sit in the living room, please," she told me. Her eyes were puffy and red. "I'll be with you shortly." I had no idea what was the matter.

The living room was reserved for special occasions. I sat on the white sofa. Louella came in and perched herself stiffly on the Queen Anne velvet chair, as though marshaling her strength.

From her pocket she pulled something out—my red diary. She threw it down. It made a loud whack as it hit the floor.

"How dare you write such things!" she cried.

"How dare you read my private thoughts," I yelled. I ran upstairs to my room and slammed the door.

"After all we have done for you," she shouted after me, "and this is our thanks! Keep up this kind of attitude and you'll end up in reform school!"

At my desk, I took out a notebook and wrote in bold letters: "My real mother would never, ever look at my diary." Before school the next morning, I left the notebook open on my bed.

When I got home that day, Louella was waiting for me at the top of the stairs.

"Where's Judy today?" she inquired, a warm smile on her face.

"Music lessons," I mumbled, not trusting her good humor.

"We're going to the country this weekend. Why don't you invite her to come with us, dear?"

I looked up at her, trying to gauge her mood. She gave me an affectionate smile. For a moment, we stood silently, far apart in the vast hall. Then she came over and put her arms around me awkwardly. I could smell her Arpege perfume.

"You know I love you," she said.

I felt a lump rising in my throat. "I love you too," I managed, moving out of her grasp. I felt ashamed I could not bring myself to call her "Mom."

A FEW WEEKENDS later, I told Louella I was going to a movie with Judy, and instead we went to a party at Babbs's house.

Mickey opened the door, holding a can of beer, a cigarette dangling from his lips.

"Lulu," he said with a smile, "I knew you'd come."

I tripped on the doorstep and stumbled forward. Ignoring my embarrassment, he offered his arm in a courtly gesture and led me inside. Elvis's new hit "Don't Be Cruel" was playing at top volume. The small apartment brimmed with teenagers, girls in short shorts with felt ribbon bows in their hair, boys in T-shirts, jeans, and leather jackets. Everyone stood around expectantly; then a few brave couples started dancing, their bodies pressed close.

Mickey introduced Judy to his best friend, Edward, who shyly offered Judy a Coke. I listened wide-eyed to Mickey's every word. His witty stories about high school made me laugh much too loudly, and he was a storehouse of strange, wonderful facts.

"Did you know," he asked me as we looked out at the marina, "that when the weather's stormy, the Golden Gate Bridge can swing out twenty-one feet in each direction?"

"Oh," I said. After a minute I added: "Really?"

I stared at him, painfully aware of my dumb response.

He invited me to walk to the corner grocery so he could buy another pack of cigarettes. On the way back, he shook out an L & M cigarette. In one motion he lit up, inhaled deeply, and blew a series of smoke rings. Though the night was balmy, a cool ocean breeze came up, and I shivered. He took off his navy blue sweater, slipped it over my bare shoulders, and tucked it around my arms. "My sweater looks good on you," he said. Then he asked, "You have a boyfriend, Lulu?"

"Of course not," I said. "I'm only thirteen." Mortified at how uptight I sounded, I wanted to disappear. But Mickey just laughed.

The hours slipped by and then it was ten, when Judy and I were due home. As I went into Babbs's bedroom for my jacket, Mickey followed me.

"Come here, Lulabelle," he said, imitating the Irish accent of our parish priest, Father Wagoner. "Kneel, please, and close your eyes. I want to give you Holy Communion."

I did as he told me. I would have done anything he asked.

"Open your mouth to receive the holy Host," he whispered. His breath, smelling faintly of cigarette smoke, was warm on my face, and then he was kissing me. My teeth clicked against his and made an awkward sound. Embarrassed, I drew back.

"Relax," he murmured, "it's a sacrament." We tried again, and this time I felt the softness of his lips parting mine.

"Now you're mine forever," he said.

The word hung in the air like a cloud. I believed him.

As Judy and I rode the bus back, we were giddy. Judy begged for details about the kiss. Part of me wanted to keep it a secret, so I told her only that it wasn't as disgusting as we had pictured.

I started visiting Mickey at the drugstore. He seemed totally at ease behind the counter, especially around women. Housewives made most of the purchases, and Mickey was happy to help them choose Burma Shave kits for their husbands and just the right color of Max

Factor lipstick. Joking with these women as they paid for Kotex wrapped in plain brown paper, he was light-years ahead of the boys my age, who responded to the presence of girls by making dumb noises and having burping contests.

He came to the house after school one day and Louella answered the buzzer. "Who is it?" she asked.

"Michael Patrick Malloy. I am here to study science with your lovely daughter, Linda."

She frowned at me and buzzed him in.

"How are you doing, Mrs. Risi?" he asked at the door.

But she turned her back and headed toward the kitchen. I invited him in, wondering why she had ignored him. She was usually so nice to my friends, even the boys who came to visit. Then I realized that she must have seen his name in my diary and knew he was the boy I said I would marry. I walked ahead of Mickey to hide my blush.

We sat in the living room and pretended to look at a book. "I didn't know you lived in a palace," he whispered.

"It's actually a prison."

"Oh God," he intoned. "Can I not save one from the pitiless wave? Is all that we see or seem but a dream within a dream?"

"What are you talking about?" I asked.

"It's from a poem we read in school, 'A Dream Within a Dream,' by Edgar Allan Poe. I love poetry, especially Poe."

Then he said the whole poem again, but this time he crossed his eyes and made faces until I got a side ache from laughing. I could barely believe my good fortune. Not only did I have a boyfriend; I had one who wasn't afraid to say he liked poetry. The fact that I had been forbidden by Louella to date until high school only increased Mickey's appeal.

We met after school and on the weekends. Once we sat through the three-hour movie *Giant* two nights in a row at the Marina Theatre. On the first night we kissed the whole time, to the disgust of the people around us. The second night we sat in the last row. We let our fingers trace one another's skin, the sensation almost too much to bear. The arm he had casually draped around me moved down my shoulder, his fingers slipping inside my sweater. Our bodies were motionless; only his hand moved, cupping my tiny breast. What he was doing was supposed to be a sin, I knew, but it felt too good to tell him to stop.

Afterward, we walked through the city streets. Standing on Marina Boulevard, we gazed north to Sausalito. "I'm going to own that place one day," Mickey boasted. "I'll have the money."

I shook my head, thinking of Louella and Jack. "Money isn't the answer," I said.

"Then what is the answer, Lulabelle?" he asked.

"Love," I said. "True love, like the poets write about."

He snickered. "You're a goner." Then he made a retching sound.

Stung, my eyes filled with tears.

"Just remember that scene in *Giant*," he went on, "where Leslie says, 'Money isn't everything,' and Jett answers, 'Not when you've got it.' "

Then he took my face in both of his hands, his thumbs cupping my chin, and kissed me. My hurt gave way to adoration. I was transfixed.

Mickey filled my waking life and my dream life as well. Even Judy, absorbed by her first boyfriend, Eddie, told me I was a creature possessed. I did not care. In my big hollow house, I desired away the hours.

Whenever he came to see me, Louella looked at him suspiciously, but always let him in. On the night of my birthday, he brought me a vinyl 45 of Marty Robbins's hit, "A White Sports Coat and a Pink Carnation," along with a small bouquet of pink flowers. I vowed to keep them always.

Sometimes Mickey would get in what he called a "dark mood." Then he would be surly and sarcastic, mocking my attempts to find out what was wrong. Usually, though, he was chivalrous and charm-ing.

Then, one day in late spring, everything changed. We were sup-posed to spend the day together, but he called to say he didn't feel like it.

"But why?" I asked.

"Because." His voice was stony. "Why don't you come over here tonight?"

"Okay. I miss you."

He said nothing. I waited a second longer, and then hung up. I knew that when he was in a bad mood, there was nothing I could do. But still, I had to try. I told Louella and Jack I was meeting Judy at the library. Louella raised her eyebrows, but gave me permission.

Mickey answered the door clutching a beer. "My brother got out of jail yesterday," he said.

"I'm sorry," I said. He always told me he hated his brother, but would never talk about the reason.

Mickey took my hand and led me to his mattress on the floor. No-body else was home. We lay down and he lit a cigarette. As I tried to make conversation, I noticed a biology book on the floor. I opened it up to a diagram of an enlarged cell, which looked like a leaf. He leaned over and said, "If you want to learn about biology, Lulu, I'll show you the real thing."

I turned around and looked straight into a huge purple penis.

I froze, not knowing whether to get mad or laugh. Either response seemed wrong.

"Hey, it was just a joke," he said, as I sat immobile. When I didn't respond, he grew cold. "Well, maybe you should go on home," he said, turning away.

I snapped out of it. "No, I'm fine," I said, trying to appease him. But he kept his back turned, and flipped through the biology book, ignoring me. I gathered my things and left.

When I got home, the house was quiet. Louella was in her bathroom, getting ready for a party. I ached to talk to her about my relationship with Mickey. She had always accepted my curiosity about the facts of life. She had laughed good-naturedly when she found Melanie Simmons and me in my bathtub examining one another's breasts. And she explained menstruation and my body's slow development without embarrassment. But this was different: I knew she didn't like Mickey. Still, I wanted her company.

I walked into her bathroom just as she came out of the shower. The line where her breast had been and the jagged scar on her stomach were bright red. I had always wanted to ask her about them, and somehow I had the courage now.

"It's a terrible story," she said. "Are you sure you want to know?"

"Of course I do," I answered.

"At a dance one night, a man hit me in the breast with his elbow. It hurt so much I went to see a doctor. The doctor told me I'd get cancer if I didn't let him cut my breast off," she went on, "and I believed him." She pulled her satin robe tightly around her as she spoke. "Not long afterward, I met a man who said he loved me. We married, and I got pregnant. He brought me to a doctor who was supposed to examine me. Instead, he performed an abortion, right there in his office. I almost died. In the end, I lost all of my female organs, just so I could live."

I stared at her, trying to imagine that pain.

"You have a better chance than I did," she said, her eyes tearing. "I want so much more for you. That's why I'm so worried about that boy you spend time with." She saw my surprise. "He isn't a good boy, I can tell you that." She snapped open her mascara box.

I ignored her words. "How did you meet Jack?" I asked.

"I went with a girlfriend to a dance at the Metronome Ballroom and he came right up to me. I thought he was the kindest man I had ever met," she said. "He said I would be enough for him. He didn't need children." As she looked at me in the mirror, her tone changed. "So what are you up to, young lady? Sneaking out at night, lying about where you've been, and that boy always coming over to do homework. I know his type, charming and witty." Her eyes narrowed. "They are all the same, up to no good. I can tell you that. What kind of family does he have anyway?"

"You wouldn't understand," I said and left the room.

SATURDAY NIGHT, I waited for Mickey at the corner of my street. I'd told Louella I was going to Babbs's house. Mickey pulled up in his brother's car and we parked at the Marina Greens. Tension lingered from our last meeting. He held me tight, kissing my mouth almost angrily. My body tingled. He fumbled with the buttons of my white blouse, unhooked my bra, and moved his face against my little breasts. I squirmed and pushed him away.

"Do you want me to take you home?" he asked, in the cold voice he'd developed since his brother came home.

"No," I said. I couldn't bear the thought of being away from him.

We moved to the backseat. After we had been kissing for a long time, he unzipped his fly.

"What are you doing?" I asked helplessly.

He didn't answer. He found my hands and guided them toward his underpants. I moved them away, he moved them back. I felt excited and frightened, as a voice in my head chanted, "You're just fourteen years old." He moved me on top of him, and I caressed his back as he explored my thighs. I didn't want to run to my dreams to hide from him—I wanted to be in my body, to feel his touch. My insides felt like warm liquid, and I kept reaching to bring him closer to me. Just as his hand moved toward my underwear, a car drove into the parking lot and shone its lights on us. Quickly we moved apart.

HE DIDN'T CALL me all week, so I phoned him.

"Don't call me ever again," he said, and hung up.

For several minutes I sat perfectly still. I could not even cry. I had to see him.

I ran all the way to his apartment, but he wouldn't open the door. I followed him on the street, but he would not stop to talk. I hung around the drugstore where he worked, but he pretended not to recognize me. I had Judy call him. He told her that he hardly knew me, that I made too much of everything.

I was desperate. I didn't understand what I had done to make him go away. Judy grew impatient with me. "You're making me crazy. Stop talking about him."

But I couldn't think of anything else. How could he cut it off with no good-bye or explanation? Having no answer, I pined for him in secret, as I used to yearn for my mother. Over and over, I would recite to myself lines from Edna St. Vincent Millay's "Sonnet Two":

> *Time does not bring relief;*
> *You all have lied*
> *Who told me time would ease me of my pain!*
> *I miss him in the weeping of the rain;*
> *I want him at the shrinking of the tide.*

As I repeated the lines, I began to feel comfortable with my sorrow. The idea of aching for Mickey forever seemed marvelously romantic. I would learn to see him in the rain and the tide.

My parents didn't notice my state of mind because they were dealing with a drama of their own. A few days before my last phone call with Mickey, we had all gone out to dinner, and when we got home, Jack noticed something was amiss.

"Goddammit, Louella," he shouted. "Someone's been into our things."

Louella rushed up the stairs.

"My liquor cabinet has been raided. All the Chivas Regal is gone."

From the other room, Louella shouted back, "So are our cigarettes; the drawer in here is empty."

Frantically, they searched the house. Everything else appeared normal, and after reporting the missing items to the police, we all went to bed. Later Jack told me that the police had found the burglars.

They railed about the burglary for several weeks. I found Jack standing over my bed in the middle of the night more often, just watching me now. One night I heard them fighting in their room. I crept down the hall to hear them better. Louella said, her voice trembling, "You know exactly what you want to do, Jack. You want to take the child to bed, if you haven't done it already!" I turned back to my room. For the first time, I did not want to hear the rest of a conversation.

CHAPTER 10

Louella decided I should go to boarding school in the fall and chose Dominican Convent, across the Golden Gate Bridge in San Anselmo. I didn't think I could bear another change, but Louella's decision was firm.

At assembly, in September 1957, cheerful girls stood in lines, waiting for the speech that would inaugurate the school year. Many wore their hair in a helmet crop, reminiscent of Joan of Arc. I was self-conscious about my unruly pageboy, and I'd developed the habit of blowing on my bangs to keep them out of my eyes.

A nun approached the front of the assembly.

"I am Sister Maxwell," she said. "Welcome to Dominican. And to those of you whose mothers and grandmothers attended before you, I extend a special greeting. For you belong to a long and proud history." Nuns were a species I knew by now, but never had I seen one as self-assured as Sister Maxwell. She spoke with authority, and I imagined that her laserlike eyes could read our minds. She described the distinguished history of the school. "One hundred and eight years of tradition and culture have blossomed here in a place that was once an untamed frontier," she said. After detailing Dominican's goals—harmony, unity, and academic excellence—she peered at us and added, "I am here to help you, so long as you are here to help yourself."

After the speech, I was introduced to a classmate named Beth, who was to show me around. Beth had a perfect blond flip with a tiny bow pinned in it. She rolled her eyes about Sister Maxwell, which reassured me. And the more we talked, the more I liked her: she had a caustic wit and a rollicking, infectious laugh. We discovered we liked the same songs and movies, and she promised to show me her secret stash of *True Story* magazines. When we finished our long, chatty tour of the school grounds, Beth took me to the girls' dorm, St. Thomas Hall. A walkway led to an adjacent building that housed the nuns.

"We are not allowed to go there for any reason," she said. "That's grounds for expulsion." Beth then brought me to a room divided into forty identical alcoves. Each one had a curtain instead of a door. We found, happily, that ours were next to each other. I began to unpack, thinking about the day: the girls with their glistening hair, Beth's friendliness, and the riding and singing clubs I'd been invited to join. Finding myself excited, I remembered the school motto, *Veritas*, Latin for "truth." Judy and I had agreed that there was nothing in the world more important.

I looked over the books for class and picked up my new notebook to record my thoughts. Here at Dominican I could write without the fear of Louella snooping.

In this beautiful place, I wrote, *with groves of oaks, morning Mass, and old nuns that call me "dear," I will change. Here I will come to know God and become an exemplary student. At last, my mind and soul will shine.* I read the lines proudly, then added, *Veritas: Seek Truth in God and His world.*

––––––––––

TROUBLE BEGAN RIGHT away.

I peered out from behind my closed curtain an hour later to find everyone gone. I had lost myself in my dreaming and was late for church. I ran across campus and entered the chapel, panting hard. I was looking for a place at the back of the church when a hawklike nun appeared.

"Where is your veil, child?" she frowned.

"Oh," I stammered. "I'm so sorry, Sister, I forgot." Without another word, she handed me a round cap of lace and disappeared. Change would not be easy, I realized.

THE NUNS AT Dominican often seemed to appear out of thin air. Only the stray wisps of hair that peeked from their headgear reminded us that they had human bodies beneath their habits. I found it difficult to imagine that they slept on beds, used the bathroom, or brushed their teeth. Always polite, they spoke in subdued voices that showed neither preference nor opposition.

"Sister, may I borrow some chalk from your blackboard?"

"Most certainly, Sister, help yourself."

One exception was Sister Maureen, a pretty young nun with frosty blue eyes, rosy cheeks, and a loud, nervous laugh. When she was upset, her pale neck would redden, the color spreading to her face.

Several of the freshmen girls had crushes on her. They would congregate outside her classroom, vying for her attention, which she saved for a cluster of bouncy, athletic girls who lived off campus and brought her stuffed animals and boxes of See's candy. Between classes, Sister Maureen and her admirers formed a huddle in the hallway. When a girl outside this clique approached, Sister would twirl around to look her in the eye. "Yes," she would ask, "may I help you?"

She told us about gold cords, the prize reserved for girls who got the best grades and whose demeanor best exemplified the goals of Dominican. On Wednesdays, each of us received a card grading our behavior. These were presented in front of the entire student body, with commentary from Sister Maxwell. An A card meant a girl was on her way to receiving a golden cord. A B demanded improvement, implying that she would be wise to, for example, stop letting loose hair collect in her hairbrush. A C was a danger sign, issued when one had collected too many demerits for missing homework assignments or yelling in the hallways. The D card was reserved for someone who had been caught smoking or sneaking out of the dorms. Smoking, we were told, was the precursor to far worse behavior. Once down that road, a girl rarely turned back.

Initially, my troubles were linked to schoolwork. Fidget and Squirm were like an angry couple that lived in my body. Their constant warring made it impossible for me to sit still. In history class, I found myself drawing prehistoric animals in my notebook instead of taking notes. Worse yet, Sister Alonzo, our humpbacked teacher, looked enough like a dinosaur that I could hardly face her for fear of laughing. Religion class was absorbing until I learned that speculation and debate were not well regarded. Round-faced Sister Edwina read straight from the textbook, her shaggy gray eyebrows bobbing. Only when she talked about "outside influences" that could cause us to doubt our faith did she come alive. I too found the topic interesting, especially when she talked about the dangers of crushes on boys.

After flunking Latin twice, I was placed in Señorita Hernandez's Spanish class. A native Spaniard, Señorita boasted she could teach her native language to anyone. I found it impossible. Verbs that were regular and irregular? Words with their own gender?

"You do not leesten—ever," said frail Señorita Hernandez, her tiny wrists laden with silver bracelets. "You do not roll your *rrr*'s. I cannot help you!" I flunked the class. No one could believe it. At Dominican, Spanish was akin to basket weaving—impossible to fail. I was sent to Sister Maxwell, who gazed at me sternly.

"Linda, never in the history of Dominican Convent has a student flunked Spanish. What's wrong with you? I have no choice but to give you a C card. This is nothing but laziness on your part."

I felt ashamed to tell her I didn't understand the language; then I noticed her face was alarmingly close to mine. I could hardly believe myself: here I was in terrible trouble, and I was focusing on her bad breath. A nervous smile spread across my face, and Sister Maxwell sighed in disgust.

Demerits for all sorts of minor infractions rained down. There were clothes not folded properly, papers not handed in on time, instructions not followed. B cards were the norm, and more C cards loomed.

Jack and Louella visited on Sundays. Although Louella and I chatted, Jack seemed as uncomfortable with me as I was with him. He paced. He stared at the floor. Though always well dressed, his face looked vacant and spent. His presence distressed me, as did the memories of him standing at the end of my bed. Yet how could I resent him after all he'd done for me?

After one particularly unpleasant visit, I lay on my bed near tears, trapped between guilt and disgust. Maybe Sister Maureen, who had a more direct line to God than I did, could help me sort through my feelings. I knew she didn't like me: she was always correcting my grammar with a frown or telling me to brush my hair again. My stomach tightened at the thought of confiding in her, but she was our dorm nun. She had given her word to be there in times of trouble, and nuns did not lie.

I made an appointment to meet her in the recreation room one evening. All afternoon, I practiced what I would say. That night, we sat down to face each other on a black Naugahyde couch.

"What is it?" she asked, somewhat impatiently.

"I need advice, Sister," I began, my voice weak, and then blurted out, "It's about my father. Whenever he hugs me, I feel like throwing up. I'm scared to be alone with him. I think I hate him."

In the silence that followed, I felt the shock of my own outburst. Sister Maureen's neck turned red, which I took to be a bad sign. For a moment, she sat still. Then she slapped me across the face so hard that I fell back on the couch. Redness spread across her cheeks like a swarm of angry fire ants. "There is no excuse," she said, "for such disrespect." Jaw clenched in fury, she marched from the room.

I sat there for a long time. The betrayal of her promise felt worse than the slap. This would be the last time I spoke of my troubles to any adult, I promised myself. That night I found a holy card on my dresser with a gold-stamped picture of St. Jude, the patron saint of hopeless causes, on the front. On the back was a message: *May God bless you and help you to keep trying.* Sister Mary Maureen O.P.

I took no comfort in her note, but the next morning I found an unexpected source of solace. At six o'clock, the nuns and pious girls went to early Mass, leaving the rest of us to sleep until the first bell rang at seven. That morning, I woke early, feeling uneasy. Too restless to stay in bed, I dressed and went for an early walk. I followed a trail through an oak grove, which brought me to the church, empty now that Mass was over.

I walked into the small chapel and sat in a pew. The spicy aroma of frankincense filled the air, and the early light shone through a stained-glass window. It glowed along with the votive candles that had burned through the night. There were fresh pink roses on the altar. A chandelier hung from a long chain over the center aisle. Its crystal pendants began to sparkle with a light too bright to be natural. The pinkness of the roses intensified to a smoldering red. I was exhilarated by their radiance. For a brief moment, I felt outside myself, drawn into the dazzling color. I was a part of the light itself, pulsating, brimming over. Peacefulness washed over me, then slowly ebbed. Hearing the morning bell, I reluctantly left the chapel.

I returned there often over the next two years, hoping for that moment to recur. And, though I never had the same experience again, being in that place brought me a temporary respite from my worries.

In one bright development, Sister Caroline, Sister Maxwell's assistant, taught our second-year religion class. She was beautiful, strong, and certain, and seemed to feel no need to apologize or win approval. On the first morning of class, she walked straight to the blackboard and wrote the word "REBEL." She asked us to define it with examples.

"A greaser with long hair and a cigarette in his mouth," Molly Perkins said.

"A beatnik," Sandy Maskins offered, "who wears a leather jacket and a beret, and who writes poetry instead of holding a real job."

"Fine examples," Sister commented. "But let me tell you about St. Francis of Assisi." She recounted the story of the wealthy young sensualist who one day stripped naked in the street to renounce the material world, and who spoke to animals and looked after the poor. "Radical" was how she described him: rebellious and defiant. These traits weren't necessarily bad, she told us. They could be a sign of wisdom. Sister Caroline's discussion of St. Francis was as exciting as anything I had heard. She challenged many of the things I had learned by rote, most of which now seemed pointless. Once she asked us what holiness was. Piety, we said. Praying and following the church rules. Compassion, she answered. Developing a sense of humor and accepting the imperfections in people.

One afternoon, I commandeered the sole telephone booth available to students as Beth waited outside. I called Judy and we settled into a spirited conversation. A wizened old nun appeared outside the booth. Quite elderly, Sister O'Brien spent her days dusting and muttering to herself, clutching her dust rag like one of the dolls treasured by the madwomen at Ging's asylum. Sister O'Brien rapped on the glass, wanting me out of the phone booth so she could dust. Ignoring her was no use. Hurriedly, I ended my conversation and left the booth. Beth and I watched as the old nun swirled dust around with her rag. On an impulse that I can't explain, I crouched and waited until she completed her chore. When she tried to exit, I held the door shut.

"Let me out, let me out," she pleaded, rapping on the glass.

I held on to the door.

Beth stopped laughing long enough to plead with me. "C'mon, Linda. We'll be in the worst trouble of our lives."

"Child, let me out!" Sister O'Brien hollered. Panic had rejuvenated her lungs. "You naughty, wicked child."

Suddenly mortified at my meanness, I let go of the knob and Beth and I rushed down the stairs. All afternoon we braced for trouble, but nothing happened. It wasn't until the next day that the incident was mentioned.

"You get it about St. Francis, don't you, Linda?" Sister Caroline said with a smile. "His love of living things makes sense to you, doesn't it?"

"Yes, I admire him," I answered, grateful to be singled out by her.

"Then you understand how important it is to care for all of God's creatures, don't you—even little old nuns?"

Sister Caroline did not threaten me with demerits, shame, or disgrace. She had managed to challenge my behavior without belittling me. I fell in love with her then and began to devise elaborate schemes to cross her path. I invented fantastic stories that all led to the same discovery: Sister Caroline was my real mother.

———————

ONE DAY WE were speaking in the hallway and I saw Sister Maureen watching us both.

She doesn't like either one of us, I realized. Then Sister Caroline turned to look at Sister Maureen. "Can we help you?" she asked. We. She had said *we*. She and I were united against a common enemy.

Because of my bad grades, I was assigned to meet with Sister Caroline once a week in her small office. There, we spoke about all sorts of things.

One day she asked me what I thought was most important in my life.

"My friends," I said without hesitation.

"But that's not you. Who are you when they aren't around?"

I took too long searching for an answer.

"Precisely," she said. "That's the problem—you haven't thought about it. So let me put it another way. What do you spend most of your time thinking about?"

"That's easy, I said. "Judy, and my old boyfriend, and sometimes I imagine how my life will be when I grow up."

"Do you realize not one of those things you are describing has to do with right now? They're all what was or what might be. Think about it—who are you right now, on the inside?"

She let me flounder for a minute.

"Remember what you said about feeling most alive when you were taking early morning walks or sitting in chapel when nobody else was there? You're helping yourself, Linda. That's the clue to finding your way."

She left gifts on my dresser: notes of encouragement, Monterey jack cheese, and, once, a can of Jean Naté talcum powder. I wanted to please her in return, and I made a number of resolutions to do better, work harder, and try to become a true Dominican girl. But my in-domitable curiosity led me astray.

ONE DAY IN late spring, Beth brought us the latest rumors about the nuns' house on the other side of the walkway. When off duty, she explained, the nuns wore regular street clothes, listened to rock and roll, and drank gin. We snickered at the thought.

"*Veritas, Veritas,*" I sang out playfully. "The truth will set us free."

"It's up to you," Beth shot back. "If we're ever going to know what goes on over there, you'll have to find out. You're the only person brave enough."

For a moment, I felt omnipotent. Swallowing hard, I walked to the nuns' end of the walkway. I turned the knob and stepped into a library—a disappointingly ordinary room, if somewhat shabby. The couches gave off a musty smell, one withered violet plant sat in a corner, and the walls were bare. Over a door hung a piece of redwood with the word "*Veritas*" carved into it. I stood in front of that door for several minutes, unsure of what to do.

My desire to uncover the secret life of the nuns had suddenly dissipated. I thought of Louella sneaking into my room and reading my diary. There was a difference between privacy and secrets. This was what I had crossed the walkway to discover.

I turned to leave the room, and ran right into Sister Maureen. Drawing a sharp breath, she stared at me before clasping her hands together.

"Well, well. This is interesting," she said. Grasping my arm in a painful grip, she marched me directly to the office of Sister Maxwell.

When Sister Maureen explained where she had found me, Sister Maxwell flushed crimson.

"What am I to think, except that you do not want to be here? Are you stupid, or are you just terribly obstinate?" She sat erect in her swivel chair. "Explain yourself, young lady, or this will certainly mean a D card for you."

I felt cornered and frightened, like a hunted fox. I loved Dominican: the cherry blossoms that burst open each spring, the plays and concerts, the secret forest walks. I loved my friends, my visits to the chapel in the early morning, and most of all, I loved Sister Caroline. I could think of no excuse for what I had done.

Yet the satisfied expression on Sister Maureen's face filled me with defiance. I was determined not to show shame or remorse. "Maybe I don't want to be here," I said to Sister Maxwell, countering her steady gaze. "I didn't want to come in the first place. My parents made me. Besides, nobody cares about your stupid secret rooms."

Sister Maxwell burst out of her chair and towered over me. I could see the blood vessels in her face turning scarlet.

"How do you think I should manage you? Should I keep a ruler in my drawer to use on your defiant backside?"

I gasped, never having heard her speak like this, but I was quickly overcome by an urge to laugh. It gave me a twisted pleasure to see her so frazzled. I hammered the final nail into the coffin of my life at Dominican Convent.

"That's not my problem, is it?" I said.

"You are dismissed." she bellowed.

I returned to my dorm room, shocked at what I had done. Throwing myself on my bed, I began to cry, despairing at the mess I had made of my life.

Sister Caroline came into my alcove. All business, she asked me directly, "Do you want to stay?"

Contrite now, I answered without hesitation, "Yes, I want to."

She patted my arm, but her words were not reassuring. "I'll see what I can do," she told me, "but it's bad, really bad." She left for the office where the three nuns were to decide my fate.

Across the room, I spied my notebook lying open. I could plainly see the word I had written: *Veritas*. I grabbed the notebook and began to cross it out. By the time Sister Caroline came back, there was nothing but black scribbles where the word had been. I saw by her expression that my life at the convent was history.

CHAPTER 11

"What are we going to do with you?" Louella moaned.

"Let me go to a public school," I said. "I promise I'll do better."

Jack was vehement that he didn't want me in school with boys, and enrolled me in a private girl's school in the city, which I attended for three miserable months. I complained vigorously every day about the uniforms and the boring classes. "I'm not learning anything," I said.

After a semester, Jack gave up his position and enrolled me at a prestigious public school, Lowell High, starting in the spring term.

"How fitting," I told Judy as we shopped for Christmas presents. "As we enter a new decade, I'm going to start a new life."

A FEW DAYS later, Louella and I heard the front door open.

"Come into the living room," Jack called. "I have something to show you."

We went to investigate. Jack stood beside the brightly decorated tree. "I bet you'll never guess what this is," he said to Louella, holding out a box wrapped in silver paper with a red bow.

She wasn't in the mood to play along. "Oh, whatever are you up to, Jack?" she asked. "Put it under the tree. It'll have to wait until Christmas."

He set the package down and grinned. "Will you ever be surprised," he said.

On Christmas Eve, we sat in the living room, drinking eggnog and enjoying the fire. Louella forbid use of the fireplace except on special occasions, fearing it would damage the expensive carpet. When it came time to open gifts, Jack and I turned to her. She frowned at the box. "I'm nervous about what you've gone and done," she said. "It better wait until tomorrow."

"Oh, no," I pleaded. "I can't bear to wait another day."

"Go on, honey," Jack agreed. "Open it now."

"Well, I suppose."

Jack placed the package in her hands. She slowly untied the ribbon and undid the wrapping paper, then paused.

"Open it!" we hollered.

Louella took the lid off and pulled a full-length mink coat from the brown box. Both she and I gasped, leaving Jack to bask in our amazement. He knew that he'd delivered the goods.

"Oh, Jack," Louella purred. "It's stunning."

"But that's only part of it," he said. "Go on, look in the pockets."

She slipped her hands down the length of the fur into the pockets, and pulled out two wads of hundred-dollar bills. I counted five in each hand. Louella closed her eyes and slowly stroked the soft fur, murmuring "Oh, Jack" many times over. When she opened her eyes, Jack was on his feet, shoveling wrapping paper into the fireplace.

"Oh, for God's sake, Jack," she yelled. "Leave it be. Look at me, honey. Look at your wife. I feel like a million dollars." She stood and modeled the coat. Jack quit stoking the fire and we watched her parade from one gilt-framed mirror to another. She gazed at her reflection from every possible angle.

"It's just right!" he said as she pranced.

She offered to let me try it on. Though taller than her, I slipped easily into the satin-lined fur and posed in front of one of the full-length mirrors. The fur was golden brown, darker than my sandy blonde hair. "So beautiful," I murmured. Jack and Louella, who had moved to the couch to enjoy after-dinner cigarettes, smiled at me.

I was moved by the warmth of the moment. For just that instant, the hollowness of our lives together had been filled, and we were a true family. Yet looking at their lined faces, I felt sadness welling up. Somehow I knew their hour was ebbing along with the decade.

"Let's have coffee," Jack said.

In the dining room, I slipped the fur onto an empty chair. Jack downed his cup, then started to rub his hands together anxiously.

"Well, go ahead," Louella said, eyeing him with a smile. He hurried off to take care of the discarded wrapping paper. A moment later, Louella stood up. Draped over the Queen Anne chair, her coat looked like the slinky animal it once had been. As she gathered it up, a look of concern crossed her face. "Where's the money?" she asked. "It's not in the pockets."

"I didn't see it again after you counted it," I said.

"It must've fallen out on the floor somewhere."

We knelt down to search. I found nothing but a linen napkin under the table.

"Well, it's got to be somewhere," she said.

We proceeded into the living room and began turning over the sofa cushions.

"What's the matter?" Jack asked from the fireplace.

"The money's missing," Louella said.

"What? That's crazy," he said. "Wait a minute. I'll find it."

The three of us hunted for the hundred-dollar bills under chairs and tables, on the mantelpiece, in far corners, in the gift box.

Suddenly a shriek erupted from Louella, who stood beside the fireplace. "Oh, my God. Oh, my God. You burned the money, Jack."

"I did not."

"Yes, you damn well did," she screamed. She pointed to the remains of the fire that had died down during our hunt. Tiny flecks of green paper smoldered in the embers.

"You can't wait a goddamned minute, can you. You have to burn everything. Fancy present, Jack! You might as well burn the fur coat, too."

"I didn't do it, I tell you, Louella, I didn't do it."

I left them there, Louella crying and Jack pleading his innocence. By the time some guests arrived for dessert, they were making polite conversation and, after a few drinks, the incident became an entertaining story for their company. But after their friends left, Louella cried again in the bathroom, and the next day I overheard her tell Sugar Spinoza, "The best moment of my life followed by the worst. What's wrong with the man?"

A few days later, Jack came home with ten new hundred-dollar bills. He had brought the charred bits to the bank, and they had replaced the entire thousand dollars. But it wasn't the same money. The moment had passed.

FOR NEW YEAR'S Eve 1959, one of my girlfriends invited me to her cabin at Lake Tahoe. Louella refused to let me go.

"Why can't I? I'm almost sixteen, and everyone I know goes to Tahoe. Besides, it will be 1960, a brand-new decade."

"It's too far away. And we don't know the parents."

"It's about boys, isn't it? You don't trust me."

"Why should I trust you, young lady?"

"You're still mad about your money getting burned up at Christmas," I said. "Don't take it out on me!"

I stomped off to my room, vowing never to speak to her again. A few hours later, the doorbell rang, and I peeked out to see horrible Florence Willard arriving with a bottle of Christmas whiskey. I tiptoed down to the kitchen to make a peanut butter sandwich. Louella had taken Florence into the dining room, where they talked quietly. I went to the door to listen.

"Oh, that child of yours," Florence muttered. "I'll tell you this: if she were in our family, she'd either behave or we'd send her to reform school."

"I get tired of fighting about everything with her," Louella said. "I don't understand her."

"What's to understand? She's boy crazy, belligerent, and she's always been trouble. Dr. Willard thinks so too."

"Just a minute, Florence. That's not the whole story. She may be different from your child, and she has her own problems. But she's funny and interesting, and she has a big heart. I don't want to hear another word from you about her."

My heart seized up. I had never heard Louella defend me like this.

I tiptoed back to my room and called Judy.

"Well, I'm not surprised," Judy said. "She always says nice things about you to me."

"Why didn't you ever tell me?"

"I don't know. I guess I pay more attention to what she does wrong."

"Yeah, like the fact that she never says nice things to my face. Judy, do you think she ever wishes she had a child of her own?"

"Well, she had a real mother, that crazy grandmother of yours in the loony bin! And then there's my mother, who bitches about her job and gets drunk every weekend. I don't know that flesh and blood makes anything better."

"I just don't understand any of it," I sighed.

That evening, I went to the kitchen where Louella was cleaning up. I sat on a stool and looked at her. She smiled.

"Do you ever wish you had a child from your own body?" I asked.

She stared at me for a second. "You ask the damnedest questions. I never know what's going to come out of your mouth."

She was still smiling, though, so I persisted. "I'm not at all like you. You talk and laugh with your friends and nieces in a way you never do with me."

She looked thoughtful. "You're not like anyone I've ever known," she said, sitting on a stool. "I don't understand what makes you tick. My Lord, I don't even know how to find the right kind of clothes or hairstyle for you!" She gave an exasperated laugh and ran a hand through her perfect coif. Then she looked at me with a directness that made me blush. "But you bring so much into my life," she said earnestly. "I wouldn't want to be without you."

Neither of us knew what to do next. We looked away.

"So can I go to Lake Tahoe?" I asked.

We both laughed. She went to the sink to finish the dishes. Too shy to linger there with her, I went to my room and read. Later that evening, I sat next to her in the living room. We watched *Dr. Kildare* in silence.

CHAPTER 12

L owell High School was home to many of the brightest, richest, and most ambitious teenagers in San Francisco. Despite his objections to public schools, Jack found a way to put my name at the top of the waiting list, and in January I began classes there.

On the first day, students filled the halls, reuniting after winter break. Beautiful girls in angora sweater sets jumped into each other's arms, and boys in red and white varsity jackets roughhoused. For the first time, there were no prayers before class or crucifixes on the walls.

As I waited for the eleventh-grade homeroom teacher to open the door, I noticed a group of boys staring at me, including one I recognized as Stevie Kroll from Ewing Terrace. One of his friends swaggered over. His hair was sun-bleached and curly, and he wore a varsity jacket over a madras shirt. He leaned toward my ear.

"I hear you do it for comic books," he whispered.

I jumped back, my face flushing, and saw Stevie and his pack laughing.

"Oh," I called out. "You still need comic books to get girls, Stevie?"

Instantly, his friends redirected their laughter. Now he turned red. I was searching my mind for another snippy thing to say when the homeroom teacher opened the door.

Poetry class followed homeroom. I envisioned an hour spent reading Elizabethan love sonnets, but Mr. London, in his tweed jacket, taught us a medieval ballad instead. Bored by his lecture on meter and measure, I looked at my classmates and found one girl in the class who interested me. She answered Mr. London's arcane questions with confidence and veiled sarcasm. Over the next week, we exchanged several knowing looks, as though we both knew the same truths about life.

During the second week of class, Mr. London called on her as we read *The Song of Roland*. "Katherine, please stand and read the next passage." When she stood, her chic trench coat parted to reveal bare, skinny legs. She was wearing a pair of Bermuda shorts, forbidden at Lowell High.

"Sit down," Mr. London barked, his face going pink beneath his whiskers.

For this violation of the dress code, Katherine—who I'd learned was Kate Bradford, the girl Mickey loved—was suspended for three days. In spite of my long-standing determination to hate Mickey's true love, it was impossible not to like her. We became friends soon after her return.

Like me, Kate had many different faces. In the halls of Lowell, she was the pom-pom queen, who would wear the most outrageous outfits that everyone copied. Louella liked her because she seemed sensible. For me, she was the only friend besides Judy who could talk as fast as I could about so many things at once. She had an on-again, off-again romance with Mickey, but always kept a few boyfriends on the side. We had long conversations about how impossible Mickey was, although I still harbored secret longings for him.

More exciting still, Kate was the first friend Judy was not jealous of. Kate and Judy had met through their boyfriends, and Judy was thrilled when I told her of our newfound friendship. "I'm so glad, be-cause I wanted to be friends with her, but I was scared it would be dis-loyal," she told me. For the first time, we invited another girl into our tight friendship.

The three of us floated on the edge of the North Beach literary scene. On Friday nights, we exchanged our monogrammed sweater sets for black flats and tights and went to folk concerts at a coffee-house called the Fox and the Hound or to poetry readings at City Lights Bookstore. Sometimes we called ourselves "underground intel-lectuals," not quite knowing what we meant, but impressed by the sound of everything we thought was "beatnik."

At Lowell, the bohemians hung out in the courtyard, wearing black sunglasses and reading Pound and cummings. Some days I joined them, and became friends with a girl named Hannah Stein-berg. She looked like a gypsy with her colored skirts, wrinkled blouses, and dark curls falling wildly around her pale face. She wore a moonstone ring and a long amber necklace. Obsessed with death, she carried a dog-eared copy of *The Stranger* in her purse.

We spent nights sleeping over at each other's houses, and I was en-thralled with stories from Hannah's life, how experienced she was with boys and the interesting people she knew. Her mother worked at an art gallery in North Beach, read poetry at coffeehouses, and was a real socialist. I told Jack that Hannah Steinberg's mother had dinner with the poet Allen Ginsberg, and Jack sneered, "Those people are all a bunch of nonconformists."

One weekend, Hannah had a party at her house. I walked into the musty-smelling flat, packed with unfamiliar people. The boys lining the hall looked broody, with slicked hair and Pall Malls hanging from their lips. I had never seen so much liquor. One girl was throwing up outside the back door. I looked for Hannah, but was told that she was fighting with her boyfriend upstairs. The scene was depressing, so I decided to leave. As I was making my way toward the door, I heard screaming. Someone shouted, "Call an ambulance!" People scattered, but I stood frozen until the ambulance arrived. Three medics ran upstairs and carried Hannah down on a stretcher. She was crying and her wrists were loosely bandaged, blood seeping through the white cloth.

A week later, she was well enough to spend the night at my house. "Hannah," I asked, looking at her bandaged wrists as we lay on the bed, "why did you do that to yourself?"

"I never feel more alive than when I'm cutting myself," she told me. "I've slit my wrists three times since I turned eleven."

"Why would you do something so horrible to yourself, when you are so kind to everybody else?" I asked, lying next to her on the bed. "I've never wanted to do that, no matter how awful things were."

"Listen, sweetie," she said, placing her small hand on mine. "It's my own life."

She took off her necklace and twirled it around.

"Where did you get that?" I asked.

"My father gave it to me before he left for good. He said that amber was made of sun rays and would always protect me," she said, examining the golden stones. She handed the necklace to me, and I inspected each of the gems. One of them looked like it held a frozen insect.

"My God, this looks like a bug!"

"That's part of the magic, Linda. Nothing ever dies—it's transformed. That's why I'm not afraid of death. I'm not afraid of anything, not even my mother."

"Why should you be afraid of her?"

She bent her head down and combed her hair apart with her fingers. Near the nape of her neck was a bald spot. Her mother must have pulled her hair out, I realized. Seeing my expression, she smiled and said, "I hit her back, hard."

"Maybe you should come live with me," I said. "We have two extra bedrooms."

Hannah shook her head. "You couldn't pay me to live here. At least my mother smiles and laughs sometimes. Your parents just slink around. They hardly even talk to you, except to bitch. Your father hangs outside your bedroom door like a park pervert."

I was embarrassed, but she was right. Jack no longer came into my room, but when my friends slept over, we often heard him outside my bedroom door. One night Beth was staying with me during a holiday break from St. Mary's. We were lying in bed talking when we heard his breathing.

"Beth," I whispered, taking courage from her presence, "keep talking like I'm right beside you."

I got up from the bed and tiptoed as quietly as I could to the door. I stood for just a moment, quietly placing my hand on the doorknob. Suddenly I swung the door open and there he stood, wearing a white terrycloth bathrobe which was wide open, exposing his nakedness. "Leave me alone," I yelled. He slithered off without protest. Beth and I stared at one another for a moment, silent. Then we started talking again about her older sister's wedding.

I MADE OTHER friends at Lowell besides Hannah and Kate. We talked incessantly on the phone, or we curled up on one another's beds musing about boys and sex and parents. Groups of us drove our family cars scouting for parties with the radio blasting "Only the Lonely" by Roy Orbison or "Beyond the Sea" by Bobby Darin. I was attracted to thin, jeans-clad bad boys who chain-smoked and led mysterious lives. They cut class and smiled sexily when they weren't sulking. My fantasy life soared with possibilities, but I was too guarded to do much more than dream.

Besides, I'd rather be with Judy.

One Friday night she smuggled three banned books into my house in her black purse, and we spent the whole weekend sprawled on my bed reading to each other.

"Listen to this," she said, when she saw the opening lines of Vladimir Nabokov's *Lolita*. "Lolita, light of my life, fire of my loins. My sin, my soul." Then she pulled out *Lady Chatterley's Lover,* available for the first time in unexpurgated form. "An entire novel filled with adultery," Judy promised. Radclyffe Hall's *The Well of Loneliness* awed us. We quoted the line, "And that night they were not divided." We quoted the line to each other whenever we saw a young couple holding hands. When Judy begged me to tell her what happened with Mickey in the backseat of his car, it was that line I threw at her. Sex was everywhere that year, in the conversations we had, our dreams, the songs we listened to, and in every book that mattered to us. But no hero compared with Howard Roark, the man who stood naked on the edge of the cliff in Ayn Rand's *The Fountainhead*. For sheer eroticism, that image leveled us.

One night as were getting ready for a dance, she stood looking at herself in my full-length mirror. Her short skirt, tight gray sweater, and high heels showed off her shapely figure. Her blonde hair curled at the ends, slightly back-combed on top. It wasn't just me—everyone who saw her said she was beautiful. But that night, I noticed her tight mouth and knew there was trouble brewing.

"What's wrong?" I asked. "You look gorgeous."

"All I see, no matter how thin I get, is that fat kid called Rollo," she lashed out. "That's who I am, no matter what I do."

No matter how much I reassured her, she was still angry when we got to the party. We sat down on the folding chairs in the darkened room and, as usual, the cutest boy came up to her immediately.

"You want to dance?" he asked, smirking confidently.

"What's wrong with you?" she spoke loudly enough that people around us could hear. "Can't you see I have no legs? Can't you see I lost them in an accident? God, you are so insensitive!"

The room was dark enough that he wasn't sure if what she was saying was true. He backed up, mortified, and disappeared. Then she whispered to me, "Let's get out of here."

We left the party and I asked her why she did it.

"I hated his cocky smirk. Let's go to Aquatic Park and walk barefoot in the water."

We ran all the way there, holding hands, laughing at what she had done.

Yet, like her mother Patricia, Judy could turn from outrageous to righteous without a warning.

"Listen," I said to her one day after school. "Susie Levine's mother taught me the difference between lingerie and underwear. And now she's given me the key to a better life."

Judy looked bored. "Go on," she said. "Tell me."

"Honey," I began, mimicking Mrs. Levine, "when you get to be my age, you understand one thing. The difference between poor women and rich women is the state of their skin. You need to start today with the best skin cream."

Judy glared at me, folding her arms across her chest.

"What is it?" I asked.

"Honestly, do you think your idle thoughts are going to make you a good Catholic woman?" I was startled at her sanctimonious tone.

She rose and, as if withdrawing a sword, took an envelope from her bag and handed it to me. Then she walked out the door, her head high. I opened the letter.

April 20, 1960
Dear Linda,

Sometimes I just hate the people we are both becoming. Tactless. Selfish. You are always having the same problems. Mickey dumped you years ago and still you complain. Then there are all the new boys you like but won't talk to, and your rich empty friends, your critical mother. I'm not any better. I wait for Andy to call each night, another self-centered boy I've fallen for.

Sunday Mom and I went to Mass and then Nannie came over. Daddy wasn't drunk, and we all had a great meal. But then yesterday it began again. My mother was drinking, and she screamed and raged about your depraved father and snobby mother for an hour. Saturday night when we were at the Hungry Eye with your new Lowell friends, I couldn't believe how shallow you were. Your friends were horrible. You are becoming as phony as an 8-dollar bill with them, and so is Kate. I worry about what is ahead for both of you. Will you lose your faith? Your virginity? You don't talk about anything that matters anymore.

I just read a book called The Ugly American. *Linda, do you have any idea of the state of our relations with other countries? And all we do is worry about Love. Will He call or won't He. And our nagging nasty mothers: mine's drunk and yours is the coldest fish in town. Our fathers aren't even alive except when mine is bashing the door down or yours is creeping into your bedroom. That's our life.*

I went to early morning Mass. It was so beautiful: the choir, the singing, communion, and the beautiful day.

We have shared a lifetime of heartache, disappointments, and joys, and I know we will always be friends, but we are not prepared for womanhood. We need to change ourselves if we want to live a life of higher purpose.
Your Friend Always,
Judy

I sat stunned, reading and rereading her words. I could feel the truth in them. I ran out of the house and caught her at the bus stop.

"Let's talk, Judy."

She agreed. We sat down at a donut shop and went over her letter. I accepted some of her criticism and promised to go to Mass every day before school. We pledged to do things to remind ourselves that the world was bigger than us.

"Do you ever wonder who you are?" I asked her before we left.

"Isn't that the whole egotistical question of our era?" she answered. "It doesn't matter who we are. It matters what we put into the world."

Maybe Judy was right. Every time I looked closely at who I was, I would hit a barricade I couldn't cross. I wondered how I would ever become the person I wanted to be. Perhaps the mistake was to spend so much energy trying. Instead, I thought, I'll apply myself to something that really matters.

During the summer of 1960, Judy and I became "Kennedy Girls," despite my father's objections. We wore red, white, and blue KENNEDY FOR PRESIDENT buttons, which showed his profile surrounded by stars, and we ushered people into a large auditorium in San Francisco to hear him speak. After his speech, I shook his hand, and he looked right into my eyes. Judy and I were swept away by his charisma and good looks, and were excited to be a part of the "new generation," which would abolish war and poverty.

In spite of my promise to attend daily Mass, in my senior year of high school I stopped going to church. Around us, people were talking about changing the world, while every Sunday my priest listed the ways I could be eternally damned. The more I thought about it, the less Catholicism made sense to me. But what finally drove me to quit was being forbidden to attend my cousin's wedding at an Episcopalian church. My priest told me that other churches were filled with heretics, and that attending one would be grounds for excommunication. For the first time, I knew a priest was wrong. God would not condemn me for going to a wedding.

The winds of social change were blowing through our Wonder Bread lives. Although copies of Louella's *Good Housekeeping* magazine carried the same old cleaning tips and recipes for meatloaf, several hundred protesters, including Hannah Steinberg, were fire-hosed down the staircases of City Hall by angry police. I found this out when I met her in the girl's bathroom one Monday.

"I missed you in class on Friday," I said. "Where were you?"

As she turned toward me, I saw her face and arms were swollen and badly bruised.

"My God, Hannah."

"No, no," she shook her head. "It's not what you think." Her laugh was sharp. "The police did this to me, the pigs."

As alarmed as I was by her injuries, I was more surprised by her anger.

"We were picketing HUAC—the House Un-American Activities Committee. There were a few hundred of us singing a protest song. One of the policemen took a fire hose, aimed it at us, and shouted, 'You want some of this?' He turned the hose on full blast and knocked us down the steps."

"That's terrible, Hannah. But why were you there?"

"Linda, there's a lot you don't know about me. I care about social justice. My mother's parents were killed in a concentration camp, and nobody stood in the way. That's why my mother became a socialist, to try and make a difference. If we don't stand up to injustice, nothing will change."

I felt ashamed to be so frivolous, but as Hannah spoke, all I could think about was the boy I was meeting for lunch, and not having eyeliner on.

"You were so brave to go down there," I told her, opening my makeup bag.

"There are lots of us meeting all the time," she said. "Trying to ban the bomb, planning marches for civil rights, making this awful government tell the truth!" She was breathless. "You should join us, Linda."

"Yes, I should do something," I agreed, blotting my lipstick with a tissue.

At dinner I told Louella and Jack what had happened to Hannah. Louella seemed concerned, but Jack got angry.

"Those commies are whining all over this country," he said. "If they don't like it here, why don't they go live in Russia?"

Jack was angry, Hannah was angry, Judy was angry. I wondered why I didn't care enough to be angry. I just wished my hair wasn't so straight, my chin so pointy, or my grades so bad.

RUSHING THROUGH THE hall a few months before graduation, I bumped into Miss Madison, the dean of girls. I dropped my things on the floor. As I apologized, she bent to pick up my books.

"*Love Sonnets* by Elizabeth Browning. Wonderful," she said. "And *Dr. Zhivago*, which is just the best. Tell me, do you like it?"

I wondered if she was asking me to explain why I was carrying around a book forbidden by the Catholic Church.

"Do you want me to tell you what I think of them?" I asked her.

"Yes, that's what I'm asking."

She invited me into her office, where I sat across from her. She leaned in toward me. "So, what do you think of *Dr. Zhivago*?"

"Yuri is my ideal man," I said, flattered by her interest. "So idealistic and romantic."

"Yes, but he's weak in a way, too, don't you think? He leaves his future to chance."

"He's too busy living his life, Miss Madison!"

She smiled, encouraging me to continue.

"I wish I was like him, to be overcome at the sight of cherry trees, the beauty of life. Instead, I'm always worrying about what's going to happen to me and my friends. Yuri is a man who believes in destiny. Listen—" I fumbled through the book until I found a passage I had underlined. " 'Never, never, even in their moments of richest and wildest happiness, were they unaware of a sublime joy in the total design of the universe, a feeling that they themselves were a part of that whole, an element in the beauty of the cosmos.' "

"That notion is beautiful," she agreed, "but do you really believe the universe has a design?"

"Yes, yes, I do," I said. "I just don't understand how it works. What about when he sees the candle in Lara's window and knows it was lit to signal someone? He writes a poem about that candle, and he hasn't even met her yet. Everything is related in ways none of us understands."

Miss Madison studied me, a look of affection on her lined face. "You are a very smart girl. You know so much."

I froze, steeling myself for the "if only you would try" sermon.

But she surprised me again. "We are failing you here. I don't know why. I suspect that you learn in a different way. Have you thought about what you'd like to do after high school?"

"My grades aren't good enough to get into college," I said, then blurted out, "but I want to be a writer."

She nodded. "I think you are a people person," she said. "Work with people, make them laugh. Watch them, learn from them. And one day you'll find you have a whole lifetime to write about."

GRADUATION MORNING IN June 1961, Kate and Judy arrived at my house in Kate's VW Bug. Then the three of us drove across the Golden Gate Bridge as the sun rose over Sausalito. We parked at Juanita's, a bohemian restaurant perched on a creaky barge. Juanita, the notoriously cranky owner, stood bantering with the customers drinking coffee. She led us to a table with mismatched crockery and brought us orange juice in Mason jars.

"We're graduating from high school tonight," Kate announced.

"Well, that calls for a celebration," Juanita said, walking toward the kitchen.

She returned to our table with champagne. "On the house," she said, setting down three glasses and winking at us.

"Let's make pledges for our life ahead," Judy said.

"I'll start," she continued. "First, let's promise never to have sex with a married man." We tapped our glasses.

"Never," I said, "under any circumstances, will we have an abortion." We toasted again.

Judy lifted her glass. "We'll never stop searching for the Truth," she said.

Clink clink, clink clink.

Kate's pledge came last. "And above all, we'll always be friends."

We were silent as we drove back to the city.

CHAPTER 13

"Now everything starts!" Judy announced the night we graduated from high school, reminding us that a commencement ceremony was a beginning, not an end.

It didn't feel that way to me.

Kate went to Europe, Judy went to summer school at Berkeley, while I stayed home with my parents on Jackson Street. I spent most days in my room, listlessly reading novels. I had no plan for what to do next.

I found the house quiet that summer. Jack and Louella were relieved that I had graduated, considering all my misadventures, and they paid little attention to me. In the two years since the gift of the mink coat, they had aged a great deal. Full of physical complaints, they rarely entertained anymore, and often spoke about moving to a smaller, more manageable place.

I knew I had to find my own life. But how? In school, I had always been so bold. It helped to have a system of rules to question and an audience of friends to suggest and admire my daring actions. When

I wasn't rebelling against something, I found it difficult to chart my own course.

Reminded of Judy's saying that a good life was what you gave back, I found a job in a children's hospital. But the suffering I saw there only made me feel more helpless. I did my job dully, counting the minutes until I could go home and finish whatever book I was reading. Where was my spirit, my fight, the sense of passion that would push me in the right direction? I was reminded of a dried-out gourd I had seen once in a museum, hollow except for a few seeds.

There was a Catholic church across from the hospital. I went inside one day after work. As I walked through the old wooden doors, I was comforted by the familiar smells of incense and wood polish, and the statue of the Blessed Virgin surrounded by flickering candles. Maybe grace was hiding here, waiting to appear. I noticed two lit confessional boxes along the far wall and, lulled by habit, I ducked inside. I could hear the priest breathing though the screen as I began my rote litany.

"Bless me, Father, for I have sinned. It has been one year since my last confession. A year since I've been inside a church."

But before more words came, fury overtook me. Who was this priest to forgive me? Why did I need a man to tell me how I should make peace with God? I couldn't believe I had come here. Suddenly it seemed more absurd than believing in the Easter bunny. My anger felt good, cleansing, and for the first time in months, I felt alive. I rose to leave.

But the priest startled me with a question: "What happened a year ago that upset you?" His voice, with its soft Irish accent, sounded genuinely interested.

I hesitated, then the words came rushing out.

"It seemed like a lie, and Mass felt like a charade. But without something to believe in, I'm lost," I said. "The world is changing so fast, and I feel like I should be doing something important with my life."

"I know just what you mean," he said. "Sometimes I feel the same way."

We were both silent. I was caught unawares, my anger replaced by curiosity.

"Perhaps we should meet outside of this box," he suggested, as if reading my thoughts. "It sounds like you need to talk, not confess."

I agreed to visit him at the rectory a few days later.

When he met me at the door, his looks surprised me. He was about six feet five, and he was younger than I expected, perhaps around twenty-five years old. His wire-rim glasses framed penetrating black eyes. "Patrick Donahue," he said, smiling as he shook my hand and directed me to a chair. A dim sense that this situation was not quite right flitted at the edge of my thoughts, but I brushed it aside as he sat behind his desk to face me. *He's a priest, not a regular man*, I thought.

"I was enchanted by you when you came to confession," he said.

"I didn't think priests went in for enchantment."

He burst into laughter. "Oh, what would life be without it?" Then he leaned in toward me, resting his chin on his folded hands. "What's your name? Tell me all about you."

Feeling shy under his steady gaze, I started to talk about recent world events. Protests on the steps of City Hall. Freedom fighters in the South. Before long, we were engrossed in conversation about social justice and civil rights. He was fiery about his values and listened with interest to everything I said. Three hours passed before I realized it, and I got up to leave.

"Will you come back?" he asked. "We've hardly started our conversation."

I couldn't believe I'd found someone in the Church with whom I could be honest about my questions and uncertainties. I felt sure he had the answers I was seeking.

Over the next weeks, we met many times. We talked about our favorite books and poems, Ray Charles's voice and the elegance of Harry Belafonte's songs, and we shared our worries about the threat of nuclear war.

"Sometimes I feel like I'm wasting what little time I have before the world ends," I told him.

He hesitated a moment before admitting his own frustration. "I wonder," he added, "if I'm hiding out in this church rather than helping people, like going on marches and doing sit-ins."

I was surprised. "But isn't that what being a priest is all about—helping people?"

"In its best moments, yes. But I often feel like I'm not doing any good."

"You're helping me," I said.

"How?" he asked, a note of urgency in his voice.

"I don't know—you remind me about all the good in Catholicism. I feel like you understand me and all my questions and doubts."

"I try to, Linda," he said, gently touching my arm.

I moved my arm away. "What made you decide to become a priest?" I asked.

He described his childhood in Ireland and how his alcoholic father forced him to kneel on broomsticks for hours as punishment for minor infractions. "Becoming a priest was the only way out of my father's house," he said.

"That shocks me," I said. "I thought men became priests because a beam of light shone in their eyes at midnight or something."

He laughed and said, "There are a few things you don't know."

You couldn't be more right about that, I thought.

ONE DAY, WHEN I turned into the rectory driveway, I found him waiting for me. As I got out of the car, he took my hand and led me to a side garden where he had prepared a blanket on the grass. It was still early spring, and I shivered in my light coat.

"What's this?" I asked, seeing a wrapped package on the blanket.

"For you."

I opened the gift nervously and read the cover: *Leaves of Grass* by Walt Whitman.

"Let me read to you," he said. "This is my favorite part.

> *I have heard what the talkers were talking, the talk of the beginning*
> *   and the end;*
> *But I do not talk of the beginning or the end.*
>
> *There was never any more inception than there is now,*
> *Nor any more youth or age than there is now;*
> *And will never be any more perfection than there is now,*
> *Nor any more heaven or hell than there is now."*

The poem filled me with joy. This was just what Sister Caroline talked about. *Everything is happening right now,* I thought, *and I have to make myself a part of it.* I started listing possibilities in my mind—volunteer, write more often in my journal, recommit to my work at the hospital—when I noticed he had stopped reading. I opened my eyes as if coming out of a trance.

"Do you like it?" he asked. He was leaning so close I could see the irises of his black eyes. His hand had encircled my wrist.

"Yes, a lot!" I answered a bit too brightly. His intensity felt too strong, and I moved my hand. The excitement I felt over the poem and the possibilities it promised withered away.

A few days later, he called me. His voice was unsteady.

"Linda, I have to face what's happening. Every night I have nightmares. Unless we cut ourselves off from one another, I'll have to leave the priesthood."

"Leave the priesthood? You can't do that." I sounded calm, but my hands were trembling.

"Yes, I can," he insisted, speaking quickly now. "Look, I have a friend who lives in New Orleans. We could go stay with him for a little while," he suggested. "We could make a life together."

Suddenly I felt sick to my stomach. I had wanted him to guide me, but he was more lost than I was.

"I have to go now," I said, and hung up.

"Wait, Linda," I could hear him protest as I put down the receiver. In some small part of me, I felt betrayed. But mainly what I felt was a powerful wave of guilt. *I had somehow led him on,* I thought. *I'd pushed him into this.*

I knew then I couldn't turn to the Church for help with my questions. I felt so ashamed of what had happened, I didn't even tell Judy about it. When she asked about "The Priest," as she called him, I told her that he was having doubts about the priesthood, and had gone on a retreat to think things through.

She said, "I can't think of anyone who would feel more doubt than a priest."

"What do you mean?"

"Maybe there's no God at all."

She reached into her purse and pulled out a copy of Bertrand Russell's *Why I Am Not a Christian.*

"I'm reading this in philosophy class," she said. "It's making me doubt everything we were taught."

"Wow, Judy, that's a pretty big leap for someone who was such a self-righteous Catholic a few months ago!" I studied the old white-haired man on the book jacket. "Why would you believe some old professor?" I asked.

"Because what he says makes sense," she said. "He just led an anti-nuclear march. I'm beginning to think that's what spirituality means, more than saying prayers."

Judy discovered more than ideas in her philosophy class that summer—it was there that she met "Wolf," a short, blonde German whose real name was Wolfgang. "He's had many lovers," she confided with admiration. "And his name—well, you have to admit it's fantastic!"

One night in late August, she called. "Oh my God, I have to see you," she whispered. "I'm taking a taxi over."

A few minutes later, she rushed into my room.

"Watch me walk," she said.

Long ago we had been told that you could tell if a woman was a virgin by the way she walked. Sex, the rumor went, made you bow-legged, and it was especially obvious after the first time. I watched her cross the pink carpet.

"You did it!" I cried.

"I was afraid of that. If Ma finds out, she'll kill me."

"Judy," I reminded her, "your mother is too drunk these days to notice anything."

She sighed. "So what do you want to know?" she asked, kicking off her high heels and lying down on my bed.

"Everything! My God, I can't believe it. You've been *deflowered*!"

We talked all night and I hung on every word.

"Will you use birth control?" I asked. "Remember, you took the pledge."

The federal government had approved the pill in 1961, and many newspapers were filled with upbeat speculation about how women's lives would change. From their pulpits, priests sounded a darker note, warning that all birth control was a sin. They urged Catholic women to pledge never to use it.

"Why do you sound so spooked?" she replied. "You don't even go to church anymore."

"But what if it's true?" I said. "What if God punishes women who take birth control or who have sex outside marriage?"

I felt self-conscious about how old-fashioned I sounded. In school, not that long ago, I had thought nothing of challenging religious doctrine, and would have been the first to question why God seemed to punish only women when it came to sex. But now here I was, feeling I should be looking over my shoulder to make sure no one heard our conversation, wondering if perhaps, even as a bystander, I was committing a sin. My lack of direction, combined with my experience with Patrick Donahue, had made my bravado disappear entirely. Fear was all that was left in its wake.

I spied a new pack of Winston cigarettes poking out of the black leather handbag Judy had set on the floor. I was ready to change the subject.

"Could I have a cigarette?" I asked.

I brought over an ashtray as she tore off the cellophane, tapped out a cigarette, and lit up. Inhaling deeply, she closed her eyes, and a look of ecstasy passed over her face. Then she exhaled, and her body relaxed. Still she made no effort to offer the pack to me.

"Why are you torturing me like this?" I said.

She opened her eyes. "You have to stop smoking like a Catholic schoolgirl. You look so guilty and awkward." She modeled how to hold a cigarette nonchalantly, how to inhale with languor, how to blow a smoke ring.

"Okay, now you're ready."

"Ready for what?" I asked.

"For true womanhood."

I laughed, but she looked serious.

Sex had changed Judy—it made her more self-assured, more grown-up. Maybe it could change me too. As I practiced smoking with sophistication, I tried to imagine myself "doing it" with a man like Wolfgang. But I couldn't imagine a thing.

———————

LATE IN THE fall of 1961, I played matchmaker for one of my best friends at Lowell High, Tony Rossini.

"You have to meet my friend Beth," I told him. "You're perfect for each other."

My instinct proved right: the two hit it off. When Tony joined the Navy after graduation and came back to visit from the San Diego naval base, he brought a friend of his named Randy Ryan, "to return the favor." Randy was a sailor from Pueblo, Colorado, with a wiry frame and blue-gray eyes. He was nice enough, and we began dating, but when he held my hand, I felt no excitement.

Over the next few months, Beth and I drove to San Diego on most weekends, navigated through the sleazy part of town filled with tattoo parlors and pawnshops, and met Tony and Randy at Denny's for dinner. We spent the weekends going to amusement parks with them and making out on beaches. Then we returned at night to the Best Western, where we shared one room and the men another.

One weekend, the pattern changed. Before dinner, Beth took me aside. "Tony and I want to share a room tonight," she said. "Is that all right with you?"

"It's got to happen to me sometime," I said, trying to sound matter-of-fact. But inside my stomach did a somersault.

Later, Tony and Beth got up from the table, leaving Randy and me alone in the orange vinyl booth.

"I guess we're roommates," he said slyly. I willed myself to smile as I followed him out of the restaurant.

Our room was small, with a stained brown bedspread. The smell of disinfectant didn't mask the odor of stale cigarette smoke. We sat down on the bed, and Randy put his arms around me and began to kiss me. As his kisses grew more passionate, I felt frightened, then ashamed.

Stop being such a prude, I said to myself.

Randy touched me. I touched him. He whispered how good it felt. I repeated his words, trying to generate some remote sense of pleasure. But the whole time I felt detached, as though I were watching myself from the ceiling above.

Mickey's face floated to mind and then disappeared.

Afterward, Randy lay back against the pillows. Anxious, I watched as he fished for the cigarette pack on the nightstand.

"How did I do?" I asked, as though I had just taken an exam.

He smiled. "Like a duck to water."

Later I lay in Randy's arms, repeating the cliché to myself. I kept hoping his approval would help me shake off the numbness I felt.

A few weeks later, Randy went to sea. We wrote short, steamy letters, and I clung to the idea of him. This was love, I told my friends, trying to convince myself.

WITHIN WEEKS, I noticed something strange was happening to my stomach. My period was light and I had terrible cramps. I was tired all the time, and my swollen abdomen hurt more each day, but I told myself it wasn't anything important.

I had learned to separate my mind from my body, and this split was only reinforced by my religious training. Most of the time, I ignored my body's symptoms and messages. So even after all the conversations about sex I had had with my friends, the possibility that I was pregnant didn't cross my mind.

One Friday, Beth and Tony came to visit. We were sitting on the couch chatting when a powerful wave of cramps hit me. I tried not to pay attention to it, but the pain was searing. Excusing myself, I hurried to the bathroom and doubled over as another wave hit. I found I was bleeding heavily, and knew this was something more than a period. I tried to clean myself up, and had a glass of water to calm down, but I was terrified. As I walked down the hall, another cramp hit me. It was so excruciating that I fainted.

I woke up in a hospital. A bandage covered my stomach, and a doctor stood over me. I felt a blinding pain as I struggled to sit up.

"You had an ectopic pregnancy that ruptured, and we had to remove some of your organs," he said, glancing at my chart. "You almost died. If it had been another twenty-four hours, we couldn't have helped you. You'll be okay, but you may not be able to get pregnant again."

Woozily I lay back down. Not have children! I was going to be like Louella. This must be God's way of punishing me for having sex before marriage, I thought.

Before long, Jack burst into the room. I had never seen him so angry.

"You cheap tramp," he spit out. I turned my face away.

"Don't you look away from me," he said. His eyes looked bulging and wild. "You've disgraced your mother. You've ruined me. Everyone will know what you did."

Through the fog of painkillers, I watched him pace at the foot of the bed, growing angrier with each step. "And I'll tell you something else," he said, jabbing the air with a finger. "You won't see that boy again who did this."

Two nurses came in and told Jack to leave. Eventually, I drifted off to sleep. I woke up several hours later when the doctor came to see me again.

He pulled his chair close to my bed. "How are you feeling?" he asked. "You have been through a lot."

"My stomach hurts so much," I said.

"You had a lot of stitches," he told me. Then he leaned toward me. "Tell me, dear, did you consider preventing this from happening? You know, not getting pregnant?"

"My religion is against birth control," I said, feeling foolish at the inadequacy of my answer.

"I see," he said, with a slight frown. "I understand the nurses had to make your father leave the hospital room."

"I don't want to talk about him," I answered, looking away.

"Linda, have you ever thought about speaking to a psychiatrist?" he asked gently.

I nodded. "During my second year at boarding school, the nuns arranged for me to see a woman doctor."

"Did you find her helpful?"

"I liked talking to her, but my father didn't want me to keep going. He said she was a troublemaker, getting into our family business."

The doctor suggested I try again. "After what you've just gone through, it would be good to talk about it with someone."

Louella picked me up from the hospital the next day. I left with one fallopian tube and one ovary. We drove home in silence. Still weak, I went straight to bed, and Jack soon came to the doorway. "I was wrong to talk to you that way," he said, looking down at the carpet. The pregnancy was not mentioned again.

Jack was true to his word. I never heard from Randy again. Long afterward, Tony told me that Jack had made an arrangement with him not to contact me. When I found out, I was furious with both of them, but at the time, I barely noticed Randy's absence.

WHEN I WAS well enough, I went to see Dr. Tarnoff. Short, bald, and attentive, he looked just as I imagined a psychiatrist would. I spoke to him of the numbness I felt and my inability to make decisions in recent months. I had the sense, I told him, of feeling unreal, unmoored, just drifting through life. Some of his questions made me uncomfortable, especially when he asked me about my relationship with Jack. At first I made a joke of it, as my friends and I had done, describing his sneaking around outside my door when Judy or Beth slept over. But Dr. Tarnoff didn't laugh. He kept asking questions, and listening to my answers, though he seldom offered a response.

He surprised me one session by suggesting a link between my feelings of disconnectedness and my childhood. Although I was always keenly aware of my status as an adoptee—second-rate—I had never explored the effects my adoption and my adoptive parents may have had on me. He told me he had adopted children himself, and that it wasn't being adopted that made me feel unreal. It was being told not to look back. Even my birth certificate had been amended, as though where I had come from, the identity of my original parents, counted for nothing: all erased. And Louella and Jack wouldn't even fill in the blanks about their own lives: their family histories were kept secret, hidden from me.

"How can you look ahead if you don't have the past to help you understand who you are?" Dr. Tarnoff asked.

Near the end of our seventh session, Dr. Tarnoff was called out of the room by his nurse. He had left his chart open on his chair and, unable to resist, I moved closer and began to read his notes.

November 15, 1962
Linda is a pretty eighteen-year-old girl with long, blonde hair. Her nose is rather large, her eyes blue, and her figure slim. Her behavior is quite dramatic, as is her leaping style of speaking, jumping quickly from one topic to another, but always with some logical sequence. No abnormal mental trends noted. Intelligence above average. Insight excellent. Wit socially appropriate. Judgment questionable.

The referring doctor provided a brief family history. The girl was given up for adoption immediately following delivery. The adoptive parents were quite ambivalent about taking her. He and she were both older, forty and forty-five, respectively, when she was born. Adoption not talked about. There appear to have been years of inappropriate sexual behavior by the adoptive father. She has been in active rebellion since leaving her church and is "seeking meaning" in nonconformist ways. Now she has become sexually promiscuous. She describes herself as a "semi-beatnik" who wants to understand herself. Depression likely.

My face burned with shame. I returned the chart to its original position before Dr. Tarnoff came back. I didn't make another appointment when I left his Fortieth Avenue office. Instead I briskly walked the eight blocks to the Pacific Ocean. I crossed the windy Great Highway and found some stairs down to the sandy shoreline.

Winter fog and mist swirled over the crashing waves as I looked out to sea, feeling shaken and angry by what I had read. Dr. Tarnoff had said such kind things to me in our sessions; he told me I was smart and interesting. Yet he had written about me in a way that made me feel ashamed. It was his superficial comments that I dwelled on the most, his description of my personal traits: my large nose, my dramatic behavior.

And yet, for the first time, I had seen on paper some very important facts about my life: Jack and Louella's ambivalence about adopting me and their reluctance to speak about it, "years of sexually inappropriate behavior" by Jack, and the depression that rendered me so full of helplessness. But I wasn't yet ready to face how my childhood had shaped me. It was all too big, too unfathomable to confront.

So instead I thought about the story I'd tell Judy about discovering the chart, and how he'd described me as a "semi-beatnik." By the time I got home, the experience had turned into an anecdote I could joke about.

———————

JUDY AND KATE had saved up for a six-month trip to New York. During that time, I was going to keep working and save enough money to join them. Then the three of us would fly to Europe, where we'd travel until the money ran out.

"Promise you'll come?" Judy asked as she boarded the bus at the Greyhound terminal.

"Of course," I said as we hugged good-bye. Part of me meant what I said. Yet another part knew I was too afraid to leave. The city's familiarity was something I could cling to, since everything else in my life seemed so uncertain.

Soon I quit working at the hospital and found a job in the center of Fisherman's Wharf at Cost Plus Imports, a store that carried exotic goods from around the world. Every day strange new items, like chocolate-covered grasshoppers and Madras bedspreads, appeared as merchandise. Within two months, I had saved enough money to put a deposit down on an apartment that Beth and I could share together on Palm Avenue. The place was ugly and the furniture threadbare. But it didn't matter. It was home.

"Well, child," Beth said, mimicking the little old nun I'd once locked in a telephone booth. "We've come a long way from Dominican!"

Tony came by and took our picture out front. Arm in arm we stood, grinning: two slim, bright-eyed girls, each with shoulder-length ash-blonde hair worn in a flip.

"I feel like my life is beginning," I said, as the shutter clicked.

CHAPTER 14

One winter morning in 1963, I walked through the door of Liberty House, a civil rights organization started by students at San Francisco State College. It was in the heart of the Fillmore District, next door to Jumbo's Bop City, an old chicken shack that had become a haven for black musicians. The area was poor but considered cool, and the decrepit building that housed the organization was made more hopeful by the colorful political posters taped to the windows and walls. Inside, I encountered a thin black woman with an enormous Afro and a brightly patterned caftan sitting behind an oak desk.

Glancing up at me with an annoyed look, she asked, "Yes?"

"I'm here to volunteer," I said.

Her expression softened. "Sister," she exclaimed, "do we ever need your help!"

She pointed to an empty desk. I sat down, smiling at being called "sister," and looked around. Pictures of Martin Luther King, Jr., and Medgar Evers hung on the walls. I could hear Billie Holiday's sweet voice singing "God Bless the Child," wafting down the hall from someone's radio. Several people were bagging clothes and answering phones. I waited for instructions. The woman gestured to one of the ringing phones and said, "Answer that!" I grabbed it. Later, when the phone stopped ringing, she added, "By the way, I'm Ida Pauline, if you want anything."

Calls came in to relay information about meetings, to organize car pools for rallies, and to find rides to demonstrations in the South. I was doing my best to take messages when a call came in from a frantic-sounding woman. A family of nine had lost everything they owned in a fire at Hunters Point, the poorest black section of the city. No clothes, no furniture, not one baby bottle left. Could we help?

This will be easy, I said to myself, thinking of the overflowing collection baskets, the huge fund-raisers at our family church, the gold and silver on the altar.

I called my old rector and told him about the tragic fire.

"Hunters Point?" the priest said with a little cough. "Oh, we can't help those people. They don't belong to our parish. Contact the diocese or, better yet, try the Red Cross."

When I told Ida, she said, "Don't you know it's the poor people who take care of each other? The rich don't think other people's troubles are their business."

Chagrined, I called a Baptist church in the neighborhood. It had peeling paint and a broken window. The preacher thanked me and said he'd see to it the family was cared for.

A few days later, Ida Pauline came into the office with a newspaper under her arm. She slapped it down on my desk. From the front page, Alabama Governor George Wallace stared brazenly out at me.

"Now that's one evil son of a bitch," Ida said. "He looks just like a bulldog!"

"You know, he doesn't bother me nearly as much as the priest who wouldn't help the Hunters Point family," I said. "George Wallace doesn't try to be anything but what he is. The priest pretends he's something else."

"I know exactly what you mean," she said.

"But listen—I don't think you should say George Wallace looks like a bulldog," I added. "Bulldogs are sweet. It's mean to compare them to him."

For a moment she just stood there. Then she said, "Girl, you say the damnedest things."

JUDY CALLED ME early one June morning from New York City. "When are you coming?" she asked.

"I have to save more money," I said.

"Why do you sound unsure?"

My saving had slowed, now that I had to pay rent, but it was also true that I rarely thought of New York.

"Judy, my life is so good. And the whole city is changing. People are becoming freer by the day."

"Free of what? What are you talking about?"

I could hear the skepticism in her voice, but I continued. "Free of uptight morality, racial prejudice, being sheep! It's all happening right here, and I feel like I'm in the middle of it."

"Yeah, well, what about Bull Connor, that racist monster in Alabama, turning dogs on peaceful marchers? That's not so free. People die. That's the only way they get free."

After an awkward silence, our conversation shifted to easier topics. After we said good-bye, I wondered why Judy was so cynical. I had been volunteering at Liberty House almost every morning for months. I loved the people, the jazz and blues excursions to Bop City after work, and the belief I was working to change the world. We were the generation who would get rid of poverty and bigotry, and I was helping make it happen. I lit a cigarette, poured myself a cup of coffee, and worked my way through the phone calls that Bill Price, the Liberty House program director, had assigned me.

Bill taught history at City College of San Francisco. He was the only person in the office who dressed every day in a sports jacket and slacks. He had an easy smile and a mischievous sense of humor. We would crack jokes to lighten the mood, and sometimes our eyes would linger on each other a beat too long. I found him very attractive, but I knew he was married, with a child.

On this particular day he was not smiling, though. Soon after my conversation with Judy, he announced that civil rights activist Medgar Evers had been assassinated in front of his house in Mississippi. Evers's wife had found him dying in a pool of blood. The office erupted. People began sobbing, swearing, and talking heatedly in tight clusters. All the whites seemed to withdraw into private shame, while the blacks grew more and more angry. By evening's end, everyone's emotions were spent, and one by one people left, until only Bill and I remained.

We finished our work in tense silence. I was getting ready to leave when Bill said, "Linda, I could use a drink. Would you join me?"

I felt relieved to hear his invitation. A drink might relax me. And it was a sign that I was still accepted, even though I was white. "Of course," I said, smiling.

We closed up the office and went to a nearby bar, where we talked about the day's events and the status of civil rights in America.

"I just wonder," he said, "when we're going to stop asking and start demanding."

"Demanding what?" I asked.

"Justice. Rights. I'm ready to be angry, instead of asking *please* all the time."

Bill looked fiercer than I had ever seen him. Once again, I was filled with shame at all my skin color stood for.

"I'm sorry," I said.

"Why?" he asked, his eyes still angry. He stared out the window.

"That I don't have the right answers. That I can't change things."

He looked at me. "I don't need your apologies," he said softly.

The conversation switched gears, but the undercurrent of tension remained. We made steady eye contact, and our arms touched across the table as we paid the bill. We walked outside and stood on the curb, an awkward silence again filling the air.

"I don't want this night to end yet," he said, looking at me with a serious expression.

"I don't either," I replied. He touched my face with his hand, and his gold wedding ring glinted in the dark. Seeing it, I was filled with guilt. I had been flirting with a married man. I remembered the pledge Judy, Kate, and I had made on graduation morning. What a terrible sin adultery was. What a mess sex had already made of my life. I thought of Bill's pretty wife and young son, who often visited the office. As Bill leaned in to kiss me, I quickly moved my face away.

"I don't think we can do this," I whispered. "You're married."

He looked hurt, then angry. "I think I know why," he said icily.

"No," I said, reaching out for his arm. "It's not—that. It's because you have a wife and son."

Bill backed away, glaring at me. "Hanging out with Negroes to salve your racist conscience, is that it? I thought you were different, Linda." Then he hailed a cab and climbed inside. The cab sped away, leaving me stunned on the curb.

I felt, standing there, that I had again reached a dead end. *I belong nowhere*, I thought, waiting for a bus to take me home.

The next morning, I went to Tro Harper bookstore and bought *Europe on Five Dollars a Day*. At least now nothing stood in the way of my traveling with Kate and Judy.

———

THE NEXT NIGHT I told Beth about Bill Price.

"Don't take it personally," she said. "It's the sixties! Everyone's looking for free sex these days, and they'll use anything to get it."

She and I were headed to a party at a creaky Victorian house on Stanyan Street. Inside, we made our way through clusters of chattering people. Cigarette smoke and the smell of patchouli filled the air. A man sitting cross-legged on the floor amidst a rapt audience caught my attention. He reminded me of a professor giving a lecture to young beatnik types. From their enthralled gazes, I assumed he must have been saying something compelling. He wore an Irish cable-knit sweater, its wool the same brown as his hair. I thought he looked like a scarab beetle: heavy-bodied and oval-shaped, with glittering eyes.

Drawing closer, I heard him talking about his job as a psychologist and his years studying esoteric literature. He claimed he had "occult wisdom," knowledge that could save the world. I was drawn in. I sat at the edge of the circle and someone tapped my elbow to pass me a joint. I inhaled and coughed loudly, never having smoked before. The man in the brown sweater stopped speaking and smiled at me. I was flattered that he had noticed me, even in the midst of my embarrassment at being an obvious neophyte. "Let me show you how," he said.

Following his instructions, I kept the smoke deep in my lungs until I felt I would pass out.

"That's right," he said approvingly.

Soon I felt euphoric. The floral wallpaper shimmered and the music washed over me in waves. The man was talking again, and each sentence seemed more fascinating than the one before. I believed he was directing his words toward me, and I drank them in. I learned his name was Hank. *He knew things*—he said so—and others seemed to think so too. I wanted to know what he knew. Little by little, the others in the circle drifted away, and then he was talking just to me. By the end of the night, we had plans to see each other again.

We met up a few days later at a bar in North Beach. As I walked in, Hank was chatting animatedly with two men playing chess in the corner. He called me over, smiling. I noticed that he was friends with virtually everyone in the place. He was soon engrossed in a conversation with the bartender about Sufi mysticism. Hank seemed able to talk about any subject with confidence. I soaked up his ideas admiringly, grateful for his generosity. After our night out, I found myself spending a lot of time with him.

"Alan Watts understood faith most of all," he said once, as we walked down Columbus Avenue toward Caffe Trieste.

"Why? What did he say?" I asked.

"He said faith needs to be open and dynamic, not passive. Religion keeps people from the truth. You're lucky you were clever enough to figure that out."

Hearing him say that, I felt glad that leaving the Church was a sign of how smart I was. Until then, I had seen my departure from the church as a failing.

"Miles Davis is the most brilliant jazz musician alive," Hank told me after a jazz concert.

"What makes him so great?" I asked.

"Well, for one thing, he introduced at least three new movements in jazz. Everyone who works with him becomes a jazz musician in their own right: Coltrane, Mingus, Bill Evans. You know, the masters."

I didn't know, but I desperately wanted to. So I continued to see him. Hank was a good teacher, patient and encouraging, and I was a good listener, excited by his ideas, flattering to his ego. His favorite topic was William Blake's idea that our social conditioning blocks true perception. If we could remove this block, we would understand life's meaning.

"Look, there's this amazing new substance around called LSD-25. Man, I can't believe what it turns people on to. It's like the layers get peeled back and people can finally understand this whole trip of life!"

"I've always thought drugs were a way to escape life," I said.

"This isn't a drug—it's a sacramental medicine," he said. "Indigenous people have always used sacred plants to help them see beyond all this." He gestured to the people scurrying along the street, as if their lives were trivial.

I was fascinated by the idea that "the real world" might be just an illusion. That's how so much of my life had felt to me—phony, illusory. Hank seemed to have a way to pierce through to something more real. He described the psychedelic drug as if he were both its creator and its priest.

Everyone was talking about LSD at the time: articles about it appeared frequently in newspapers and magazines, and many of my friends had tried it.

"One trip is equal to four years in art school," Wren, a writer friend, told me one day as we sat drinking coffee. "Psychiatrists say it opens people to their creative side."

"But isn't it dangerous?" I asked, trying to dampen my own interest.

Wren shook his head. "People have been experimenting with it since the forties. There are no serious side effects."

"I want to try it, but I'm scared."

"What will happen is your narrow, sanitized view of reality will open into something sublime. You'll feel alive in a way you've never imagined, more enlightened than you ever do reading books," said Wren. "Then again, you might be the type to shy away from mystical experience."

Wren's attempt at reverse psychology did not escape me, but I decided to try the drug anyway. Hank and some of his friends planned to take it the following Saturday, and they invited me to join them.

That morning I met up with Hank. We each took a tab of LSD, and I swallowed it before I could change my mind. We were on our way to Haight Street to meet Phil Lesh and a friend of his named Jerry

Garcia. The two of them had formed a band with some friends called the Warlocks. Hank said he was going to be their manager.

Phil seemed otherworldly. His eyes were always cast upward, lost in thought while he dreamed up a new idea more brilliant than the one before. But his dreaminess didn't prevent him from connecting with people. Jerry was more aloof. There was something raw about him, and his nervous restlessness made me uneasy. He talked a lot, but mostly gazed past the person he was talking to, as if looking for something just beyond reach.

Inside the dirty apartment where we met up, people with long hair and bare feet lounged around. A Ravi Shankar album played on the stereo. I sat down in an overstuffed chair, excited and apprehensive. The walls slowly began to pulse to the beat of the ragas. Near me, a man sat down at an old lift-top school desk. He opened it up, took out a hypodermic syringe, mixed up something powdery, and filled the needle with it. Then he squirted it in the air until a tiny drop came to the tip. He laid his left arm on the desk and poked the needle in a vein. Moments later, he gave a slow moan of pleasure.

I watched with horror, the revulsion intensified by the drug I'd swallowed. I felt sure he had just summoned his own death. In the corners, shadows began to take sinister shapes: teeth, bones, and then fully formed skeletons rattling round the room. The man with the needle stared at me as he slowly caught fire. I cried out loud as the flames that swallowed him got sucked up into one of the ceiling tiles.

Hank's voice brought me out of the nightmare. "Hey Linda, let's get out of here," he said, grinning. We walked outside, where we met Phil, Jerry, and his girlfriend. Soon we found ourselves in an orange Mustang, Jerry behind the wheel, at the base of Lombard Street, the twistiest road in the city. Our car faced the "Do Not Enter" sign planted next to the street.

"I'm going up—it's how the crow would fly," Jerry said to nobody in particular.

He looked like a crow, with his bushy black hair spread out like feathers in every direction. We sat, entranced while he drove the wrong way up the street. As the car careened around the eight switchbacks, Jerry played the wheel like a ship's captain, and we swayed and rolled into each other. If a car had happened to come down the street, we would have collided head-on, but for the moment we had Lombard to ourselves. At the top, we exploded into cheers.

Jerry parked at the large square across from St. Peter and Paul's Church in North Beach. I curled up on the lawn and he came over. His bushy moustache and curly goatee seemed alive, each particle of hair bristling with vibrant molecules. I held up a blade of grass. We both marveled at it, a single strand of life effervescent with pure light. Then the blade turned to water. We laughed until the laughter made waves through the air. The world—people, trees, streets, sounds—was coursing with energy, all flowing from a common source. Everything was God.

Together, the five of us wandered through the park, into and out of the church, and past the colorful stores and cafés along Columbus Avenue. At dusk we reached Vesuvio Café. The golden glow had begun to fade as the colors of day were transformed into shadow, but my trip hadn't ended. The people sitting on stools, in work shirts, black sweaters, and flowered dresses, wore the heads of reptiles and insects. With the long scaly head of an alligator, one creature stared forlornly at me with yellow eyes. Sharp, uneven teeth studded her monster jaw. I heard a voice say, "Your mother." I was aghast. My birth mother could be any of these creatures. Was she? As quickly as the question came, it disappeared.

Evening enveloped us in the bar, my body now tired. The scent of food was strong and the lights bright, but the intensity of feeling had vanished. Disappointed to touch down again in the real world, I knew already that I wanted to take LSD again.

———

THE PSYCHEDELIC EXPERIENCE convinced me even more that Hank had access to a new way of life. He was opening doors, helping me break down all my years of uptight religious and social training—"brainwashing," he called it. His company filled a void that had opened up in my life since graduation. Kate and Judy were living in Greenwich Village, a world away. Beth was getting ready to leave for college, which didn't seem to be an option for me. My parents were tired and preoccupied. I couldn't go back to Liberty House after the incident with Bill, and the comforts of Catholicism were long gone. Spending time with Hank seemed like the only possibility.

Yet I began to see glimpses of other sides of him. I caught him lying: bragging about knowing someone he didn't know or about having a job I knew he never had. He rarely carried cash, and he let other people buy him coffee, meals, or tickets to events. "Money is coming" was his mantra, and usually the money came from me. He stole, too, from the homes of friends, at parties and get-togethers: ashtrays, knickknacks, and spare change. Once, after we had visited friends of Jack and Louella's, they reported an antique vase missing. When I noticed it in his apartment later, he rolled his eyes. "Those damn rich people! They won't miss one little vase."

I never confronted him or called his bluff. At some level, I sensed his anger would be too powerful for me to face. I saw how enraged he became when he spoke of people who had "fucked him over": teachers, employers, past friends and lovers. In those moments he looked fierce, his face red and his voice thunderous.

Over time, I began to feel more frightened of him. He played by other rules than I did, and I realized it was time to break away. I just had to wait for the right moment to tell him, whenever that might be.

One afternoon, Hank invited me to visit his father, who lived in Oakland. I agreed, planning to end things on the car ride back to the city. As he drove, he angrily described how "tuned out" his father was, but the reality was worse than I expected.

His father was a retired physical education teacher who lived on a block of shabby apartments. The man was shirtless when he answered the door, wearing only a pair of tight swimming shorts. He looked like his son, only shorter and with bigger muscles. What I noticed immediately was the deadened expression on his face. He seemed to have no reaction to Hank at all. After mumbling hello, he led us through dark, cramped rooms out to the apartment pool. He immediately went for a swim, leaving Hank and me to sit on uncomfortable plastic chairs. When he joined us, he barely spoke a word. Hank tried to ask him some questions, but his father offered terse responses, and never looked at Hank or asked him a single thing about his life. He ignored me entirely.

Sitting there, I felt so sorry that Hank had to grow up with this man, and I was filled with a sudden gratitude for Louella and Jack. No matter how hard our relationship had been, they were always gracious to my friends and me. I realized I had taken their generosity for granted.

On the drive home, Hank's shoulders were slumped and his knuckles were white on the steering wheel. I could tell he was upset by the way his father had treated him, and I decided this was not the time to talk about ending our relationship. I tried to be sympathetic. "It's not your fault he's so cold," I said, but he shrugged me off. We drove in silence.

We went back to my apartment. I walked into the bedroom, with its two single beds, and put my coat in the cardboard closet. "I'll make you a cheese sandwich with mustard," I called out to him.

Hank and I have different recollections of what happened next. I remember it this way.

Hank followed me into the bedroom. He pulled me down onto my bed and began to cry, holding me close. I tried to comfort him. He groped me. From the beginning, I had told him that I was still recovering from my last sexual experience, and that the idea of sleeping with him didn't feel right. I pushed him away and asked him to stop.

"I'll drive to Big Sur," he said calmly. "I'll sit under a tree, put a gun in my mouth, and shoot myself. I can't take any more rejection."

His threat paralyzed me. He rolled over on top of me, kissing my neck. Inside, I was thinking, *I need to get the hell out of here. Or scream.* But I didn't move. I didn't want to be responsible for him killing himself. And, I thought, hadn't the nuns and Jack warned me about leading men on? It was my fault. I had spent time with him. I had led him to expect this.

I drifted off to the old foggy, detached place, no longer protesting. My body wasn't there, I was staring at the ceiling, thinking about the new Mexican lamps at Cost Plus, trying to remember how many panels of colored glass each one had. Then it was over, and I was back in the room, looking at myself in bed with this man I had decided to stop seeing.

THE FOLLOWING MONTH, my period didn't come and my breasts were beginning to swell. Without telling Hank, I visited Dr. Morton Henry, whom I had known most of my life.

He came into his office, stethoscope swinging, and peered suspiciously at me through his bifocals. "Yes, Linda? Now what's the matter?"

"I haven't had my period for two months," I said, avoiding his gaze.

"Could you be pregnant *again*?" he asked, his pencil poised like a dagger above his pad.

"Yes—I guess I could be," I said, fidgeting with my hem.

"Well, we'll have to do a rabbit test. I'll collect a urine sample from you, and we'll learn the results in two days." He cleared his throat sternly, and I fixed my eyes on his ludicrous dotted bow tie. "Yet another thing your poor parents will have to deal with, Linda. Let's hope it's not true."

A rabbit test was the standard way to determine pregnancy then. A woman's urine was injected into a rabbit, and if the rabbit died, the woman was definitely pregnant. I waited anxiously for the results, but inside I knew what they would be. Sure enough, the nurse called three days later to say that my test rabbit had died. I was carrying Hank's baby.

So many emotions washed over me as I hung up the phone. Unmitigated joy in knowing I could still carry a child, that the doctors had been wrong. Fear about a future with Hank if we shared a child. Embarrassment that I had gotten pregnant again, not having learned anything from the first time. And complete uncertainty about what to do.

I remembered a girl in high school who had gone to Tijuana for an abortion. She came back looking relieved and had gone on with her life. I could do the same. I was certainly not in love with Hank, he had no job, and my job at Cost Plus Imports couldn't support a family. There was nothing to grasp on to in our lives, no firm foundation from which to raise a child.

It seemed obvious. When I told Hank, we agreed that abortion was the best option, and he helped me find two hundred dollars to pay for it. On a dreary October morning, he dropped me off at the Greyhound station. The building was as cold, smelly, and unwelcoming as it had been when Judy and I had gone there to gawk at people in distress. Now I was one of them.

As I waited for the bus, I unfolded the piece of paper with the clinic's address and studied it. I thought of Judy and Kate waiting for me in New York. Once I got back from Tijuana, I would leave Hank and join them. The station slowly filled with people. The trip to Tijuana was announced over the PA system.

My thoughts picked up speed. I remembered the pledge Judy, Kate, and I had made on graduation morning never to have an abortion. I had been told I might never be able to get pregnant again and, here I was, given a second chance. I thought of the woman who had given birth to me. Louella had once told me she was eighteen, just my age, when I was born. What if she had made this choice? I wouldn't be alive today. An abortion suddenly seemed like an indictment of my own life. The presence of this child in my womb—I just knew it was a girl—was a gift that had been mysteriously bestowed. For the first time I imagined her growing inside me, a tiny living creature. Somehow, we both would be all right, whatever happened with Hank. I smiled, hearing myself think: "we."

I called Hank from a pay phone. "I can't go through with it," I said. "Do you have any other ideas?"

He suggested we visit his mother for advice. He met me at the station, and together we boarded the bus for Sacramento. I had never met Emma, but the instant I walked into her house, I felt comforted by the aroma of fresh coffee and the warmth of her greeting.

"Linda, I'm so glad to meet you," Emma said, touching my shoulder. I couldn't believe Hank had such a kind mother. I was drawn to her maternal presence, feeling almost sleepily secure. She was nothing like his father. *This has to be a good sign*, I thought.

"She's pregnant, Mom," Hank announced within moments of our arrival. Then he left the room to make a phone call.

Emma turned to me sympathetically, no trace of judgment in her brown eyes. "Oh, honey. What are you going to do?"

"I don't know," I said, relieved to have someone other than Hank to talk to, grateful he had brought me here. "I just know I want to have the baby."

"Will you two get married?"

"We aren't in love," I answered truthfully. "Besides, there are some things about him that scare me."

Emma didn't flinch. "I know he has problems, but he is good inside, and the baby will need its father's name. You can always get out of it later, though this baby may be what you both need."

With a mother like Emma, Hank had to have a lot more good in him than bad, I thought, *whatever his troubles.* He and I sat on her couch that day and made a decision: we would get married and have the baby together.

As we boarded the bus to Reno, I trembled.

"What's wrong?" Hank asked. "You look so down."

"Morning sickness," I murmured, shaking with fear.

We spoke no more during the trip to Reno. Once there, we found a motel, and the next morning we walked down the strip until we found a sign that read WEDDINGS. We walked into the office and rang a bell. A tired-looking bald man came to the desk.

"Can I help you?" he said.

"We're here to get married," Hank said. Neither of us looked at the man.

"Congratulations," he said, before hollering into a back room, "Martha!"

A woman emerged, tying a red kerchief around a head full of rollers. She was to be our witness to the two-minute ceremony. The bald fellow briefly mentioned love and eternity before he signed our license. We paid him and went back to collect our things from the motel.

It wasn't until we got to the bus station that I realized I had lost my purse somewhere that morning. Money, identification, glasses—all were gone. What upset me most was losing my copy of *Europe on Five Dollars a Day.* The loss was a sign, a sentence: all doors were shutting, except the one leading to a life with Hank.

CHAPTER 15

On the bus ride home, Hank and I sat morosely in our seats. We had not spoken about anything other than practical arrangements. I stared out at the snowy Sierras, thinking about the daunting task of telling my parents what I had done. Although that conversation was an unpleasant prospect, it was a distraction from the more disturbing thought that I had just joined my life with Hank's. Telling my parents would give me perverse comfort, harking back to all the times I had witnessed their disappointment in me. I knew, at least, how to face that down.

I called them as soon as I arrived at my Palm Avenue apartment. Louella answered. "Where've you been? I've been calling all week!"

"To Sacramento," I said. "Hank's mother lives there."

"That man has the mark of a criminal. What on earth are you doing with him?"

"You don't understand how interesting he is, how much he knows about life," I told her halfheartedly, trying to convince myself as well. "It's not just me. Lots of people think he's amazing." Afraid to stop now, I took the leap. "Anyway, I have news. I'm pregnant."

"Jack, get on the extension right now!" Louella shouted. "She's gone and gotten herself pregnant by that scoundrel."

"It's worse. I just married him."

I waited through a long silence, fighting the humiliation that threatened to blow my flippant cover.

"This will kill your mother," Jack said.

"I'm sorry," I muttered, and hung up. As I lay on my bed, my stomach hurt, but I didn't cry. I was too numb. Ten minutes later, the phone rang.

"Hello," I answered, dully.

"This will not kill me," Louella said, her voice steady. "This is not what I wanted for you, but we will certainly stand by you." She hesitated, then added, "And, despite the circumstances, we're happy about the baby."

I was surprised by how much her words meant to me. When I spoke my voice was no longer confident. "Thank you—that means so much," I said, choking up, and quickly got off the phone.

Later, when Beth came home, I told her I was pregnant. She took my hand and squeezed it. "Child, I'll help you through this. I can put off going to college. You don't have to do it alone."

"I won't be alone," I said. "I just married Hank."

When I saw Beth's stunned expression, my tears came in a rush.

I CONTINUED TO work at Cost Plus, and Hank and I found a tiny apartment in the Haight district, the emerging Mecca for those soon to be labeled as hippies.

A few days after we moved in, Louella dropped by unexpectedly. I found her waiting in the drab lobby, dressed in a silk suit. When I kissed her cheek, I caught the scent of her Arpege perfume, blending with the waft of marijuana from a neighbor's open window. I ushered her down the long staircase to my new home in the basement. With a quick glance, she took in the grimy Formica surfaces and lumpy daybed. Her mouth tightened and I heard the quiet *tsk* she made when she was upset.

"I can't stay," she said, as if she had held her breath since entering the tiny room. I listened to the retreat of her heels on the stairs. She had brought a Gump's bag stuffed with some things I had left when I moved out. Inside, I found clothes, my senior yearbook, a photograph album, and a picture postcard of Judy and Kate feeding pigeons at St. Mark's Square in Venice. "Just come, as fast as you can get here," they had written. I dropped the picture back into the bag, and stared out at the bleak November sky.

ALL HANK AND I could do was fight. I was furious at myself for marrying him. Hank was fuming, too, always stomping around the apartment and speaking in argumentative tones. But I could see no way out of it.

One day, we argued in the stairwell.

"You stupid bitch," he spat out. I thought his eyes held a look of manic glee.

"I'm sorry I made you mad," I said, carefully measuring my words. "I won't do it again." I felt dizzy, looking down at the floor below.

He stopped ranting then, and I smiled up at him, willing myself not to tremble. We walked down to our apartment, and I cooked basmati rice and vegetables for dinner as if everything was fine. I had a sense that I had to take care of this myself, that I was isolated in my fight to protect my baby. And underneath, I felt I deserved all of this for getting myself into this mess, that I was being punished for the bad choices I'd made.

Later, Hank fell asleep on top of the threadbare chenille bedspread. I lay awake beside him, allowing myself to seriously wonder, for the first time, how I'd landed here. After the scene in the stairwell, I was shaken enough to imagine ways to get out. When morning light slanted through the windows, I dressed and slipped out into the San Francisco dawn. Outside, sunshine melted the fog, and a yellow taxi whizzed past. Even the clanging sound of garbage trucks was a sweet relief.

Craving familiarity, I caught a bus to the Marina. At Charley's restaurant, I took a booth where someone had left behind a morning paper. On that November day in 1963, the pages were filled with stories about the "New Left," civil rights sit-ins, and police brutality.

Glancing up, I spotted Mickey Malloy seated at the counter. I had seen him just a few times in the past six years, and he had always seemed chilly and distant. He was handsomer than ever, reminding me of Paul Newman in *The Young Philadelphians*. I rose without hesitation and walked over to him.

"Hi, Mickey."

"Hey, Linda," he said, barely lifting his eyes. "How's it going?"

"A lot has happened to me," I stammered, leaning awkwardly against a steel-ribbed stool. "I'm married. I'm having a baby in July."

He looked up quickly. "How is it?" he asked, speaking genuinely to me for the first time in seven years.

"I'm excited about the baby, but everything else is a mess."

"I'm sorry, Lulu." He said it in a whisper, leaning toward me. He touched my arm, and electricity sang through me. My heart pounded, my face flushed, my breath got shallow. I ached to be the cigarette he was smoking, the coffee he was drinking.

But, as if he suddenly recalled something, Mickey turned away from me and studied the menu. "I'm sorry to hear that," he repeated, but this time the words came from far off. "Well, I'll see you later," he said, closing the conversation.

A blush streaked across my face. The rebuff felt as painful as it had when I was thirteen. I mumbled a quick good-bye before rushing from the restaurant, fighting back tears.

Everything seemed so botched up, I couldn't see how it would come right. But as I walked to work, I noticed the city's familiar morning scents: roasted coffee beans and Italian bakeries, diesel from the delivery trucks mixed with salty wind off the sea. The streets roared with cars, motorbikes, and buses carrying people to work. I could imagine my child growing inside me, a part of this buzzing energy. Amid all this bustling life, away from Hank, my problems started to seem less overwhelming. I might never have Mickey, but I had a sense that I could make a good life for my baby. I could show her the amazing things in the world I knew—love songs from *West Side Story*, French perfume made with rose petals, hot glazed donuts from the Chestnut Street Bakery. I would give her every ounce of love I had in me.

I walked through Fisherman's Wharf until I came to Taylor and North Point, where the Cost Plus import store filled a city block. Inside, I got to work. I had just finished arranging Indian print tablecloths and was stacking mounds of Ghirardelli chocolate when the manager's voice came over the loudspeaker.

"May I have your attention, please?" Mr. Parker rarely made announcements, so everyone stopped to listen.

"Ladies and gentlemen. We have just learned that John F. Kennedy, the president of the United States, has been shot. We will update you about his condition as soon as more information becomes available."

Employees and shoppers let out a collective gasp. In just seconds, the façades that protected people from each other crumbled and raw emotion took their place. All around me, strangers were hugging each other and weeping.

Minutes later, the loudspeaker came on again. This time Mr. Parker's voice sounded muted, as though he'd been crying. "Ladies and gentlemen, the president of the United States has died from gunshot wounds suffered a short while ago in Dallas, Texas."

Dazed, people gathered at the front of the store. I stood off to the side, Judy's cynical remark about the civil rights movement echoing in my mind: *People are going to die. That's the only way they'll be free.* JFK had been a symbol of the hope and freedom I thought was right around the corner. Now I wondered if Judy was right—if freedom from life's injustices only comes with death.

I expected the store would close, but Mr. Parker told us that closing would be bad for business. My distress turned to outrage. Here it was, soulless capitalism, just like the Berkeley students were saying. I followed him back to his office.

"Mr. Parker. You have to close the store."

He turned toward me. "A decision like that costs money," he said, staring me down. "I have to worry about the bottom line, not some beatnik ideal."

As he spoke, he tapped out his words with one foot. For a moment, I stood mesmerized as his polished wing tips clicked rhythmically. Then I looked him straight in the eye.

"You're exactly what's wrong with this country," I said, not sure what I meant, but full of righteous anger. Not waiting for his reply, I marched out of the store.

Without any plan for what to do next, I took a cable car to Jack's optometry store on Post Street. I kept remembering how Kennedy had looked at me when he shook my hand. It seemed impossible that he had just been murdered. Jack greeted me with a sad smile. He was almost as upset as I was, even though he had voted for Nixon.

"I know how much you liked him," he confided. "And, well," he hesitated, "at least he was a Catholic. It's a terrible, terrible thing."

"Are you closing your store?" I asked.

"Of course. He was our president."

I gave him a quick hug. As I pulled back, I caught surprised embarrassment in his eyes. Many years had passed since I had shown him any physical sign of affection.

He invited me upstairs to the office, where we stood in front of a red Coke machine that boasted ICE COLD. He handed me two dimes, and I pulled out two of the green glass bottles. For an hour we sat, drinking Cokes and talking over the events of the day. I got up to leave.

"Come here anytime you want," he said. "Come for anything at all."

I knew he meant it, and for a moment I felt a surge of affection for him. But the old alarm shot through me, mixed with pity and guilt.

In that moment, I thought of two photographs of us I had found in the photo album Louella had brought to my apartment. The first was taken when I was two: in it, I am sitting on his lap and leaning against him. My blonde hair looks windblown and my smile is easy. The second photo shows us at the beach when I was four. We are both in bathing suits and he holds me in his arms. I am pushing away from him; I look angry and scared. Standing there facing Jack, I felt like the little girl in both those pictures, seeking comfort but also ready to run away.

"Thanks for the Coke," was all I managed, and darted out the door.

As I walked home through the city streets, I felt the grief in the air. Something had been forever broken. Back at Frederick Street, Hank had lit a candle in the window of our basement apartment. Seeing the tiny flicker, I felt hopeful about our prospects for the first time since marrying him.

For three days we sat glued to the television, listening to the news, and all that time Hank kept a candle burning. Near the end of our vigil, his friend Phil Lesh dropped by to see us.

"It's the professor," Hank said, laughing at his own joke.

"Professor," I repeated. "Professor of what?"

"Of everything," Hank said. "He's the most fucking brilliant man on the planet."

We all laughed, and Phil told us he'd been listening to Beethoven all day. He said music was the only light left in the world.

"Yeah, man, yeah," Hank said, like a backup singer.

"The world hasn't seen the last of Phil Lesh," he said, after Phil had left.

As I had done with the candle he had lit in the window, I told myself that Hank's appreciation of his friend was a sign that Hank was good beneath it all. He cared about Kennedy's death. He had interesting friends. If I could just be nicer to him, he would change.

ON APRIL 7, 1964, I turned twenty. To mark the occasion, Jack and Louella gave me the money for a down payment on a small two-story house near City College. Hank and I filled it with furniture from thrift stores, and Hank hung some of his paintings on the walls. He was an abstract expressionist, he told me, and had shown his work in art shows.

"I never needed lessons," he explained. "My intuition is so good I can just take a canvas and splatter paint like Jackson Pollock." The canvas he displayed in our living room was about six feet square, with a bright red and yellow background, and a blue hieroglyph in the middle that reminded me of a swastika.

"Why did you paint a Nazi symbol?" I asked him the day he put it up.

"No, not Nazi," Hank corrected me. "It's Hindu and very ancient. Think of it as a symbol of magic."

Although the painting gave me the creeps, I found it easy to doubt my own judgment. Hank had an uncanny ability to take a tidbit of information he'd picked up somewhere and turn it into a full-blown discourse, sounding so expert that it was difficult to separate fact from fantasy. For a time, he turned our house into a beatnik salon, drawing people for long, fascinating conversations. Playwrights came. Poets. Musicians. Professors. People who had done time. Hoodlums who spoke about philosophy. Activists who made things

happen. Listening to talk of mysticism, alchemy, and Jungian arche-
types, I would forget my desperate sense of being trapped. The conversations reinforced my growing certainty that Truth dwelled in
places other than the Catholic Church. I saw possibilities for a new
kind of cosmology, one where the ladder to heaven didn't have men
standing on the top rung, where God's house was big enough to hold
pagan babies, ancient Tibetan texts, and gods by other names. The
conversations gave me a way to talk, for the first time, about the
awakening I experienced at the chapel at Dominican, and my feelings
while on LSD—the sense I had that everything was interconnected,
full of God's light.

But my spiritual optimism would fade after everyone left, and our
home life continued its downward slide. Hank no longer cared what
I thought of him, and began to tell me disturbing things about himself. He'd been married before. He'd been arrested. He had "paranoid
tendencies" but was in therapy now. I was shocked that I could have
married someone without knowing any of these things. Why had I
not asked any questions? Hank fumed, threatened divorce, and
hinted at romances with students he met at San Francisco State College, where he was taking classes. Sometimes I fought back, but
mostly I stayed silent, withdrawing inside myself.

Despite the connections and talents he boasted about, Hank could
not maintain most of his friendships or find a job. Worse, his history
of bad debts began to catch up with him. Former acquaintances
called demanding money they claimed he owed them, and threatening letters arrived from collection agencies. As our financial worries
mounted, I took them on myself, not knowing how to make Hank do
anything to help.

In search of work, I went to an agency downtown that hired temporary employees. There I was greeted by a middle-aged woman with
a vivacious smile holding a Gauloise cigarette. Her camel-colored
sweater set matched her gold necklace and earrings. I worried that my

blue seersucker dress was not up to the standards of the agency, but she quickly put me at ease.

"What a nice dress, dearie," she said, beaming.

Not until she got up to fetch me coffee did I see the crutches she used and the braces on her legs. Later I learned that she had been crippled by polio when she was sixteen.

Sally Courtney was nearly forty, and had a wicked sense of humor, a love of life, and a resiliency I admired. We quickly became friends.

"Look, if I could endure polio and this godforsaken wheelchair, you can survive one lousy marriage," she said to me after I told her how desperate I felt. "I've survived two rotten ones myself!" she confessed. "When do I get to meet him?"

I cringed at the thought.

"Come to my place for dinner," Sally urged.

"No way," I said. "He might eat with his fingers, or steal something from your apartment, or tell you outrageous lies. Worse, he might charm you, and then you won't believe me!"

"Just come," she said, patting my hand.

Reluctantly, I agreed. Partly I wanted to please her, and I also hoped she might tell me what to do.

HANK AND I arrived at Sally's downtown apartment that Friday night. In the lobby, we were faced with two ways to reach her sixth-floor flat: stairs or an ancient, cagelike elevator. Having always had a fear of elevators, I instinctively started toward the stairs.

Hank grabbed my arm.

"I can't believe how many things you're afraid of," he said, pulling me toward the elevator. "Be brave. I promise you'll be okay."

When the door clanked shut, I felt a surge of panic.

"Let me out," I said.

"What's wrong?" Hank asked, pressing the button.

"I can't breathe," I said. "You've got to stop this thing."

A sinister smile spread across his face. Then he began to jump up and down, all two hundred–plus pounds of him. The little cage shook and lurched to one side. I was too frightened to scream.

"Oh, yeah, you think you're scared now. How about this?" he said, jumping higher.

The elevator creaked and groaned. *My baby and I are going to die,* I thought. When the rickety elevator finally stopped on the sixth floor, Hank pulled the door open and allowed me to step out. Breathless and shaking, I headed toward the exit at the end of the corridor.

"Hey, where are you going?" he called after me.

I could barely speak. "I won't go anywhere with you."

Hank rang the bell to Sally's flat. "You always make things worse than they are," he yelled after me.

Sally opened the door. "Hello," she said, looking up from her wheelchair. "You must be Hank. Where's Linda?"

"Sally," I called out from the end of the hall. "I just can't go through with it. I'll call you tomorrow." Without waiting for her to protest, I sprinted down the hall, trailed by Hank's laughter.

I knew he would follow me, convince me to come home, tell me I had overreacted. Frantic to disappear before he could find me, I hailed a passing taxi. I gave the driver Beth's address on Haight Street. When she opened the door, I rushed into her arms and burst into tears.

"Oh, Beth, I'm so freaked out," I said as she led me to the couch. "I've got to get away from Hank."

"I thought he was a little crazy the first time I met him," she said, "but I knew he was sort of a genius too." She gave my shoulder a squeeze. "How about a cup of jasmine tea?" She went into the kitchen. The doorbell rang.

"Please don't answer it," I pleaded.

"Linda, he doesn't have a clue where I live," Beth said.

"You don't know him," I told her. "He's got the power to find me anywhere."

"There's no way it's him," she insisted, opening the door.

Hank stepped into the apartment as though he owned it. He walked to the couch and stood before me. "I've upset you," he said. "I'm sorry I did whatever it was that made you run away. Please come home with me now, without trouble."

He spoke to me like one speaks to a patient in a mental hospital.

"I'm a psychologist, remember. I may not have my license, but I can see you have some huge problems. I'd like to help you—help you move past some of your hang-ups and fears."

Beth watched, wide-eyed.

I took his outstretched hand and followed him out the door in what Beth later described as a hypnotic trance.

Once outside, Hank explained how he had found me.

He had watched me get a cab from the hallway window in Sally's building. All he had to do then was run down to a pay phone and make a call.

"This is Sergeant Harrison with the San Francisco Police Department," he said, reenacting his words. "A suspect just got into one of your taxis: number 6457. Please tell me where the taxi took her."

The dispatcher gave Sergeant Harrison Beth's address.

CHAPTER 16

The baby was due June 16, but that day came and passed. One morning, when I was three weeks overdue and increasingly impatient, I felt a sudden burst of water running down my legs as I stood in the kitchen making coffee. A painful muscle spasm tightened my belly. I called out to Hank, who helped me into his Morris Minor and drove me to St. Francis Hospital. Another contraction doubled me over in the parking lot. Once it passed, Hank led me into the emergency room, where I was wheeled away.

I was taken to a bare, cream-colored room with a large crucifix on the wall. I was unprepared for the contractions, meeting each wave with resistance and screams. One nurse told me to "buck up." After a number of hours, another nurse gave me a shot to help with the pain. It didn't provide relief from the contractions, but it left me too limp to make any noise.

Twenty hours after I arrived, I felt a pressure so intense I imagined the entire ocean behind it, forcing me to push as hard as I could. Nurses yelled, "Stop and wait for the doctor," but it was beyond my control to do anything but push. My bed was rolled into a bright surgery room. My arms were tied to the rails of the bed, my feet placed into stirrups. Dr. Henry came rushing into the room, and someone put a mask over my face.

The next thing I knew she was there, my daughter, eyes wide open, looking at me as though she had known me always. The room glowed with radiant light, as if it were filled with angels, and I wept at her beauty, my heart swelling with a deeper love than I had ever known.

Hank wasn't at the hospital when Courtney was born; he said he was "doing business," his mysterious phrase for activities I knew not to ask him about. Later that day he came to see me at feeding time, and was visibly moved by the sight of his daughter.

"Far out and beautiful," he kept repeating. He lay down on the bed next to mine.

"Don't lie there," I said. "The nurse said there's a new mother coming in. Here's a chair next to me."

"Don't fucking tell me where I can and can't lie down."

"Hank, please. Not now."

Just then a nurse appeared and asked him to move. I thought I would die from mortification when he gave her a defiant look. He got off the bed, leaving dirty streaks on the sheets from his shoes.

"I'll be back this afternoon," he said as he stalked out.

I closed my eyes and drifted off to sleep. When I awoke, it was feeding time again. The nurse brought Courtney to me, wrapped tightly in a yellow blanket.

"Look at that perfect rosebud mouth," she said, "and I just love her name."

I loved both Sally Courtney and her name. Courtney had such a luscious sound—certain, yet gentle, perfect for my child. For a middle name, I decided on Michelle, meaning "she who is like God."

For half an hour, I fed and cooed to my new baby. I was in bliss.

Then the nurse returned, announcing visitors.

"Baby has to come with me now," she said, as she whisked Courtney back to the nursery. I looked up to see Jack, Louella, and a short woman with gray hair and blue eyes.

"Nellie!"

"Well, my dear, this is quite a day." She kissed my forehead and I smelled her familiar White Shoulders perfume.

"Nellie's here visiting her relatives in Oakland," Jack said. "We decided to surprise you."

They went to look at Courtney through the glass. Nellie returned first, her eyes shining.

"Well, she surely is her mother's daughter," she exclaimed. "I declare, she looks just like you."

I beamed. We spoke of easy things: Nellie's children and grandchildren and Jack's upcoming retirement. Then she turned to me, her eyes tearing up.

"Oh my word, to think The Good Lord brought me to you on this very day," she said. "I want to hear all about your new husband."

My heart sank. There was nothing I wanted more than to have Nellie stay and talk to me the whole afternoon, but I could not bear the thought of dealing with her questions about Hank or the possibility of her meeting him. As I did so often in situations where Hank was involved, I made an excuse. "I'm just so tired," I said as Jack and Louella returned from the nursery. "I want to visit, but I'm afraid I'm falling asleep."

AFTER THEY KISSED me good-bye, I thought about what Nellie had said—"her mother's daughter." For the first time in my life, I had a blood relative, someone who was a part of me. Even her smell felt familiar to me. I would pass some of myself on to Courtney, characteristics I would recognize as she grew. With her in my arms, the presence of my own birth mother felt like a phantom limb. What part of her did I carry? Where was she now? Was she living in a run-down apartment somewhere with fifty-two cats? Or was she someone I might want to know? If only I knew the answers to those questions, I thought. Shaking off the thought, I turned my attention back to my daughter. Courtney and I would be enough for one another. I just knew it.

I wasn't the only one enchanted by Courtney. In the first days after we came home, Hank could not hold her enough. His face lit up at the sight of her, he wrote pages of poetry for her, and he bragged to everyone about his exquisite new baby girl. In our excitement, we even forgot to argue with each other. Jack and Louella adored her as much as we did, and the barriers between us fell away in the presence of my daughter. They cuddled and sweet-talked her endlessly.

Aunt Rosetta called one day and said, "Your father says the baby never cries."

I laughed and said, "Everyone says she's the happiest baby they've ever seen."

For once I wasn't upset that Rosetta had referred to Jack as my father. His love for Courtney reminded me that I still felt affection for him, difficult and vexed though it was.

COURTNEY'S PEDIATRICIAN, Dr. Burns, was an older man with a jolly, Santa Claus–like demeanor. Whenever I brought Courtney in for an exam, he raved about her progress. She was smarter and quicker than the rest of the babies he saw. She laughed as easily and heartily as she cried, and she was almost always peaceful. My only worry was how difficult it was to calm her when she was upset. She startled quickly and at inexplicable things: a door closing, a car horn outside. It sometimes seemed as if she had just woken from a nightmare, and she cried so hard that I found myself exhausted and frustrated, believing I should know how to soothe her.

"Be firm," Doctor Burns counseled. "She will only cry for a little while. She has to learn to stay in bed."

But I usually gave in, holding her for hours on end or letting her sleep in bed with me.

AT FIRST HANK and I moved cautiously around one another, intent on avoiding the terrible battles we'd had before Courtney's birth. But the truce didn't last long. Within months of Courtney's homecoming, we were fighting again, usually about money, but also about my concerns with his lifestyle. With a small child around, I became more protective of my space, less willing to have strangers around, and more worried about the dangerous choices he seemed to make.

One day a check arrived in the mail from the New American Mental Health Center.

"Look at this," Hank said, waving the check for twenty-five hundred dollars. "Our financial troubles are over."

I was suspicious. "Why would they send you all that money?"

"I applied for a grant. I'm going to open a center for people on bad LSD trips."

Later that day, I imagined an LSD center in our house, people hallucinating around my baby daughter. The allure of that way of life vanished, replaced by a desire to shelter Courtney.

That night I lay beside Hank, listening to him breathe and feeling paralyzed. *Maybe he'll die,* I thought, trying to feel there was an end in sight. I relaxed. In the sleepless nights that followed, I began to embellish the thought, imagining scenarios where the police came to the door in their blue uniforms and asked me to sit down. Hank's death was quick and painless, they said. It became a routine to lie there, imagining Hank dying, as I grew calmer and fell asleep.

ONE UNUSUALLY WARM summer day, right after Courtney turned one, we dressed her in a little blue and pink swimsuit and took her to a friend's pool in San Mateo. The three of us played with bath toys and Hank was cautious and tender as he held her in the water. She squealed with laughter when he showed her how to blow bubbles. I could see how much he cared for her, and I wondered how I could think of taking her from him. That idea came easier at night than in the light of day.

Late that summer, Judy returned from Europe and we met for lunch at the Far East Café, our favorite Chinese place. The minute I saw her, I felt unburdened in a way I hadn't since high school. Judy always reconnected me with the parts of myself I liked best: my curiosity, my humor and optimism. We began our conversation with laughter and catching up, barely pausing between sentences. But we got serious when I told her what it was like to live with Hank.

"You have to get out of that marriage," Judy said. "Don't you remember when Sister Bernadine told us that when we choose a husband, we are choosing a life? Is this the life you want?"

"I didn't choose him!" I insisted, even though I knew no one had forced me to marry Hank. I felt like the whole relationship had been out of my control from the very beginning.

"Sorry, that's not how it works," Judy snapped. "What happened to the spunky friend I used to have? You chose him by shutting your eyes and letting your life happen. Wake up, Linda!"

Judy spoke the truth I already knew myself. I could just hear it better from her.

"I want a divorce," I said to him that night.

He protested, but I was unyielding. "Stop it, Hank. You won't change my mind."

"Don't try it," he said, "because if you do, you'll never see Courtney again."

It was his eyes that scared me the most—hot embers of pure rage. He stomped out of the house, and I locked the door behind him, even though I knew it wouldn't keep him out. Courtney was crying. I rushed upstairs and held her tightly. "I'll protect you," I whispered, as I heard from the bedroom window the sound of Hank driving away.

After that night, Hank began to stay away for days at a time, and I never asked where he was. A few weeks later, he let me know he had a girlfriend and then it was over, fast and unexpected, as if we both lost steam at the same moment and the fight just fizzled. I served him with divorce papers, and the long war of our two years together ended in court with barely a whimper. Hank didn't get violent; he didn't even shout. He packed his things, agreed to pay fifty dollars a month in child support, and left the house.

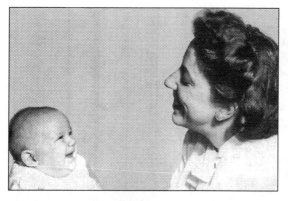

Linda, age eighteen
months, with
adoptive mom,
Louella

Jack, Louella, Linda, in the family Christmas photo, 1946

Louella, ever elegant, in
her first fur stole, 1949

A worried Linda at the communion rail, about to make First Communion, 1951

Linda's best friend, Judy Carroll, in her high school graduation photo, 1961. Twenty years later, Linda would take her name.

Linda and her first-born daughter, on Courtney's first birthday, July 9, 1965

Nicole and Courtney, singing a Christmas carol, 1968

Frank, Linda, Courtney, Nicole, Jaimee, picnic at the park, Eugene, Oregon, Summer 1971

Courtney, Nicole, Joshua, and Jaimee, in Marcola, Oregon, 1972

Courtney, age seven,
on Halloween, 1971

Courtney and Jaimee,
coloring together, 1972

Courtney and Jaimee on their way to school, 1972

Hippie mom Linda with Jaimee in New Zealand, 1976

Baby Elki, two days before he died, 1974

Courtney in front of her brand new whare, 1976

Tim with his and Linda's Malamute, Sylva, Orcas Island, 1992

Linda and Frances, at Nicole's birthday party, 1997

Paula Fox, New Mexico, late 1940s

Paula and Jaimee, visiting in Santa Barbara, 2000

Nicole, Jaimee, Tobias, and Daniel, on vacation on the Oregon Coast, 1999

CHAPTER 17

After Hank left, my life grew calm and steady. Beth had quit college, broken up with Tony, and moved in with me again. We slipped back easily into our old rapport, and she loved caring for Courtney alongside me.

I had found a part-time job at the University of California Medical Center, working as a clerk in the orthopedic ward, answering phones and greeting visitors. I was immersed in the drama, the stories, the people. I remembered what Miss Madison had said before I graduated high school: "Work with people, make them laugh."

Hank had Courtney one night a week and every other weekend. One day she came home with psychedelic magic marker drawings covering her arms and legs. And I was horror-struck by her nightmares after the visits with him. She woke up screaming, "No, Daddy, no!" It was virtually impossible to soothe her afterward. The more I tried, the more she would stiffen, arching her back and resisting as though my touch were painful.

I called my lawyer to see if I could stop Hank from seeing her. "I have to be honest," he said. "I'd be concerned about my daughter visiting him, too. He doesn't seem to know a lot about appropriate behavior." But in 1966, in the most liberal city in the country, there was little a court could do about my concerns, he told me. "I don't even think we can get him to pay his child support—that's how loose the system has gotten."

Then Hank found a new girlfriend. Kind and sad-eyed Ginny Robinson had been orphaned very young and had a large trust fund. For the first time, child support payments arrived on time. I was less fearful now when Courtney went to stay with him, knowing Ginny would be there too.

On the Friday night of a weekend when Courtney was gone, I went to a party with Beth, the first one I had been to since Hank left.

"Who is that?" I whispered, directing her gaze to a man in a dark suit across the room.

The man I stared at had straight black hair and a square jaw. He was short, freckled, not particularly handsome, yet there was something compelling about the way he stood loosening his tie, talking confidently to a small group of people.

"Oh, that's Michael Cohen. He's a resident psychiatrist at San Francisco General."

"Is he with someone?"

"From what I hear, he goes out with lots of women, but I've never seen him with anyone."

From across the room, I stared at him until he caught my eye. Neither of us broke the gaze for several seconds. At home in bed that night, I was startled at the sheer eroticism of my thoughts about a man I had not even spoken to. His magnetism had aroused me, and my body felt a sensation I hadn't experienced since I was thirteen with Mickey.

The morning after the party, I lay in bed thinking about what to do with my free weekend. My thoughts turned back to Michael Cohen and the sprinkle of freckles across his perfect Roman nose.

As if on cue, the phone rang.

"Hello." The slightest pause ensued, a split-second that made my heart skip. "This is Michael Cohen. I saw you at the party last night and I'd like to take you out. Are you free today?"

I couldn't believe it was him.

"I remember you," I said, trying to sound casual. "What do you have in mind?"

A few hours later, Michael drove up in a sleek 1966 Pontiac Grand Prix. It had bucket seats, a leather interior, and every bit of chrome shone with polish. A current ran between us as we exchanged greetings and walked to his car.

"I don't even like cars," I confessed, "but this is something."

"I think so too," he said. "That's why I named her Ethel."

As we laughed, I realized his naming the car made me like it—and him—even more.

Michael was just as smooth as Ethel. He was dressed in well-pressed slacks, his shoes shone with polish, and his hair was perfectly cut. The way he carried himself exuded confidence.

"Shall we go to Golden Gate Park?" he asked. "I like the tea garden best."

The Japanese tea garden was one of my favorite places, and I nodded as we exchanged eager smiles.

As we sped through the streets, the Supremes sang "Baby Love," and we joined in the chorus, laughing at our off-key singing. I felt drunk with excitement and surprised by the strength of these new sensations. I was not used to feeling anything but numb and tense around a man.

We walked toward the big greenhouse that housed the exhibitions, and Michael reached for my hand. Inside we found display tables filled with tiny, perfectly shaped replicas of the big trees outside—pines, rhododendrons, blossoming cherries—some only three inches tall.

"Have you seen bonsai before?" Michael asked.

"No, I haven't," I said. "How do they keep these trees so small? They look stunted."

"Not stunted," he corrected. "They're carefully pruned, and it takes great skill to make a tree like one of these. Look at this," he said, pointing to a camellia in bright pink bloom.

"How do you know so much about this?" I asked as we made our way through the exhibit. I liked him even more for knowing about a subject so foreign to me.

"As a kid, I spent summers with my grandfather. Bonsai was his passion."

I had an image of an old man carefully sculpting the roots and branches of a tree, his grandson looking on. So much nurturing attention to detail must go into each tree. It revealed something about this man I hardly knew—his attentiveness, his confidence and skill—that attracted me. *He knows what he's doing,* I thought as he guided me toward the tea garden.

We spent the rest of the day walking through his neighborhood in Noe Valley. When evening came, he offered to make me dinner at his apartment. In the doorway, he kissed me, and I returned the kiss with a hunger that astounded me. He took off his shirt, and I saw his arms were covered with freckles too. I wanted to kiss each one. His touch, at once gentle and certain, brought my body to life. I kept my eyes closed as we moved to his bedroom and made love, letting each sensation flood over me, wanting to feel each one as fully as possible. When it came to sex, the refrain in my head had always been: "When will this be over?" Now it was: "I hope this never stops."

Later that night, I wandered around his apartment, surprised at its starkness. No pictures hung on the walls, and the dreary mustard-colored curtains cut out the daylight.

"Anybody could live here. Your place doesn't tell me anything about you."

"I'm only here for a short time. In six months, I return to New York."

I looked at him in disbelief. All the empty years, the loss of Mickey, the disastrous pregnancy with Randy, the fear and trouble with Hank, came rushing in.

"Don't look so upset," he said. I thought he sounded annoyed. "Let's make what we have count."

I forced myself to return to our earlier conversation.

"Those trees. I can't believe how ancient they were," I said. "Hundreds of years old, some of them. Can you imagine what life must've been like back then? I can't. Even fifty years ago seems beyond imagining."

His eyes crinkled as he laughed. "I love the way you say what you think," he said. "Free association is just a part of your conversation, isn't it?"

I grinned at him, appreciating that he liked the conversational style that had agitated Louella so much. I was content to sit and watch him make au gratin potatoes, to talk about bonsai, and I didn't let myself think about him leaving.

We couldn't have been more different. If I was diffuse, with no solid core, he was all sharp contours, rules, and form. He knew exactly who he was, where he came from, and where he was going. Once a week, he called to set a date to see me, and I made sure I was available on the day he chose. Although I knew not to call him or ask for anything more, I felt safe in his company.

But I felt more than that—I was in love. I stopped wrestling with my guilt about leaving the Church and my fear about being punished for "sins" like sex. Bodies were made to feel desire, I realized, and for the first time, I reveled in physical pleasure.

I took care of Courtney, went to work, and did laundry, but my feet barely touched the ground. The troubles of the world seemed far away. I seldom glanced at a newspaper or listened to the radio. I stopped calling my friends and worrying about the future. I was entirely wrapped up in Michael, and little else mattered besides my daughter.

Sensing my distraction, Courtney began to demand more attention. The babysitter lived across the street and Courtney had always liked to go to her. But now when I dropped my daughter off to go to work, she clung to me, winding her little arms around my legs. Her screams of outrage followed me out the door. At two, she was already perfecting the dark, glowering look I began to recognize as a declaration of war.

I was living in the middle of two worlds, each with its own center of gravity. Both worlds were compelling, intense, and gratifying, but they didn't overlap in any way. Every time I introduced Courtney into a conversation, Michael changed the subject. Stories about her that made my friends smile left him indifferent.

"Sorry, Linda, I'm not interested in kids," he would sometimes say.

When Michael came to pick me up one afternoon, Courtney arrived at the door before me. She liked the sound of the doorbell. I caught up to her and opened the door.

Now he would see how beautiful and precocious she was. "This is Courtney," I said, lifting her into my arms.

In the doorway Michael looked at my daughter, but he didn't smile or say hello. He looked at his watch impatiently. I had a sudden urge to slam the door shut. Here I was, organizing my whole life around his schedule, and he would hardly acknowledge her presence.

Courtney was no friendlier. Ignoring Michael, she tugged on me.

"I don't like this dress," she said. "I want the bunny dress." She loved to change clothes; if I let her, she would do it all day long.

She began to feel heavy, and I set her back on the ground. She stomped her feet and raised her arms in the air. "Carry, carry," she whined. As she yanked on my skirt, I grew tense, afraid she would start to yell and I wouldn't be able to stop her. My maternal inadequacy would be on full display.

"Up, up," she demanded. More insistent, she began to punch my thigh with her little fist.

From the other side of the threshold, Michael glanced at his watch again with a sigh.

On the verge of panic, I had another urge, this time to bolt out the door with Michael and leave Courtney behind. I was hostage to both of them in this crazy push and pull.

Then, for no apparent reason, Courtney stopped whining. She walked into the kitchen where Beth was cooking and asked her to play. I could walk out the door with Michael without feeling I had abandoned her. We got into the car, the tension between us palpable.

"That kid of yours has a real look in her eye," he said.

I said nothing. The years I had spent listening to Louella and Jack argue, feeling uneasy even when I was not the subject of their quarrel, and my endless fights with Hank had left me wary of conflict. Yet Michael's coldness toward my daughter cast a pall. As we entered his apartment, its bareness reminded me of all he withheld about himself.

He reached for me. *I should leave*, I thought. But instead I withdrew into my dream world as we made love, going through the motions.

"Where the hell did you go?" he said when it was over. I was surprised and gladdened that he noticed. Desire for him returned, ignited by his mix of remoteness and attentive focus on me.

Michael would laugh affectionately at what he called my "insatiable curiosity." I told him all about the patients on my ward at the hospital: the man who never slept, the little girl who was learning to walk again. When he revealed that one of his rotations took place at a sex clinic, I was mesmerized by the juicy stories he told.

"What do you want to hear about now?" he would ask, smiling roguishly.

"Everything."

"Well, my first patient said he could only have sex with his shoes on."

"You're making that up."

"No, it's true," Michael insisted. "If his shoes fall off, he loses his erection. It's called a fetish," he explained. "In order to get turned on, a certain object has to be present. I've even read about balloon fetishes."

"Balloons! How could a balloon be sexy?"

"Well, the guy I read about loved the smell, the squeak, the feeling of that thin layer against his body, and most of all, the excitement that it might burst. Some people like to pop it, and some like it unpopped."

We laughed, but went on to discuss what made people need balloons and shoes to feel sexual. I wondered what could be done to help them.

"You're so interested in all this, Linda. Why don't you go back to school and study psychology?"

"School never worked for me."

"Maybe you never had a reason to make it work. There were four women in my class at medical school. You'd be so good at what I do. You don't want to be a ward clerk for the rest of your life, do you?"

His question surprised me. For a moment I believed him: I could aspire to something more than making ends meet. I could have a career, even do what he did.

Then I remembered he was leaving. With a pang, I traced the

freckles on his arms. How would I live through the loss? Who would I be without him?

WHEN I WAS SHOPPING one Saturday, I spotted a woman sitting by a huge cardboard box with a sign. I told myself I had better not look inside, but I couldn't resist, and within a few minutes, I was returning home with a bag of groceries and a brown and white collie/shepherd puppy.

The puppy was adorable, and Courtney immediately fell in love with him. She carried him all over the house in her arms, wrapping and unwrapping him in blankets.

The two of them played together on the thick-carpeted landing of the stairwell. That's where they were, squealing happily, when I went out to the kitchen one day to make lunch. Suddenly, there was a sharp scream from the dog. I rushed in to find him lying at the bottom of the stairs, yelping with pain. I turned to Courtney, and her expression startled me more than the dog's cries. She was smiling at me and raising her arms. "Hug," she said.

"Honey, the puppy is hurt," I said, gingerly picking up the dog.

"Hug! Hug Courtney," she insisted, as though she couldn't hear the creature's cries. Luckily, Beth was at home and stayed with her while I rushed the puppy to the vet. He had broken his hind leg, which the vet put in a cast.

"Puppy hurt," Courtney announced when I returned home.

Again I was surprised by her lack of feeling. She had always loved cuddling and playing with dogs, and I couldn't shake the awful sense that something about her reaction was off. I thought of the nightmares she had and how it seemed impossible to comfort her. She had not grown out of it, in spite of what the pediatrician said, and deep down, I worried that something was happening with Courtney that I didn't understand.

Yet there were so many extraordinary things about her. She wasn't like other babies, who only liked their mothers. Courtney reached her arms out to strangers as trustingly as she did to me. I took this openness as a sign of how well adjusted she was. She would never do anything to hurt anyone, I knew. Maybe she had a scientific mind, expressing an innocent, if detached, sense of inquiry. That must be why she didn't seem upset in the face of the dog's pain. Anyway, she was too young for a pet. We would give the puppy away.

That afternoon, Louella came to show off her new car, and we went for a ride. As we drove along in her gold Chrysler, the Bayshore Freeway offered a panoramic view of San Francisco, but Courtney looked up at the sky.

"Mommy, Mommy," she called, pointing out the window.

"Yes, honey. Tell me what you see."

"The dogs, the dogs," she said, growing excited.

I saw only cumulus clouds.

"Look, Mommy," she said. "Look up at the angels. They are my friends."

I saw no angels, but her fierce expression told me not to doubt their presence.

"Mommy, Mommy," she said once again.

"Yes, Courtney, love."

"Look, look. There it is."

"There what is?"

"It's Courtney in the sky."

The joy she radiated was so powerful, I could feel it fill my own core. Love for her overpowered me. I sat back and closed my eyes.

THAT NIGHT I tried in vain to interest Michael in Courtney's clouds, but he remained aloof and disinterested. He said very little, as though to underscore the end of our time together. He was going back to New York in a few days.

Throughout the meal, I kept noticing things about him I hadn't seen before: his boring clothes, his crooked upper teeth, his loud chewing. I couldn't figure out what had driven me crazy with longing. I thought again of the bonsai trees that first day. Now they seemed to reveal a whole other side of Michael—his controlling nature, his desire to keep everything perfectly managed. Who would want to confine a tree, keep it so small?

After dinner, he dropped me at an empty house. Courtney was at Hank's. Beth was out. I lay down on the bedspread, tracing its tulip pattern with my fingers, feeling empty. My time with Michael had been so extraordinary that for it to fizzle out seemed worse than a dramatic breakup. Yet I was also relieved he was leaving. I knew I could never get involved with anyone again unless he would learn to love my child.

I called Judy. When she heard my voice, her own turned frosty.

"What's wrong?" I asked.

"I can't believe you called me. After all we've been through together, when you finally find a man who isn't crazy, you dump me."

"Judy, I didn't dump you."

"Call it what you want, you disappeared for months. I thought we agreed the worst thing a woman could do is leave her girlfriends when she gets involved with a man."

I apologized and hung up, feeling awful. I called my old friend from high school, Hannah.

She was on her way to the Fillmore Auditorium to see the Jefferson Airplane and suggested I join her. "You've been out of it," she told me. "This concert is what's happening; it's called 'Rock for Peace.' " I decided to go.

As we neared the concert hall, groups of barefoot people danced in the streets with buttons on their clothes, beads around their necks, wearing every sort of hat: bowlers, Uncle Sam toppers, colorful Guatemalan knit caps. Men dressed like women, in flowing robes, with flowers tucked behind one ear. Women dressed like men, in dungarees and black military boots. Some carried Bibles, others statues of the laughing Buddha. Glass hookah pipes filled with marijuana were passed freely. Smiles and peace symbols were ubiquitous. Above this carnival, the voice of Grace Slick floated like a mystic cloud, amid the flashing colored lights.

Come on people, now
Smile on your brother
Everybody get together
Try to love one another right now.

The bands worked the crowd into an almost Pentecostal fervor. People flailed about in ecstatic states and spoke in the tongues of rock-and-roll.

Yet against the light of a revolution based on love, the television coverage told a darker story. Young teenagers were flocking to the Haight and taking LSD like it was candy. Many found the experience enlightening, but someone I knew drove off a cliff, and others ended up in psychiatric wards. Boys I had gone to school with were dying in Vietnam or fleeing to Canada to avoid the draft. Face-to-face with photos of napalm-burned children, flower power faltered.

By the spring of 1966, I changed from believing we were entering an era of peace and love to thinking the world was coming to an end. For the first time, I read every newspaper I could. Every day, the reports were more terrifying: the escalation of the war, rumors of defoliating chemicals destroying the Vietnam jungle, race riots in Chicago. I was increasingly afraid about the future.

My relationship with Michael had served as some kind of anchor, and without him I felt truly alone. That absence, combined with the apocalyptic feeling in the air, gave me a sense of hopelessness. I wanted to grab up my baby and run to a safe place. But I could not imagine where I would find it.

udy had never been good with children. "I don't get them," she confessed to me once when Courtney was clambering around on my lap. For a while, I let her get away with not spending time with Courtney, and we'd meet for coffee at her place or at a café. But after Michael's refusal to interact with Courtney, Judy's attitude started to bother me. "Judy, you two are the people I love most in this world," I said to her one day on the phone. "Just *try* with her, for my sake." After some coaxing, she agreed to watch Courtney one afternoon while I worked. I was elated. Finally, I thought, all the parts of my life will come together.

But it did not start well. When we arrived at Judy's place, Courtney hung back. I had to dangle a toy-filled duffel bag before her eyes. She trudged inside and I showered the living-room floor with toys. "No toys," she said, and climbed up on me where I sat.

Judy sat next to us and gave me the latest on her wedding plans. In two months she was to marry Ben, a law student she had met at one of Hank's salons.

"Babies and weddings. God, we've become so conventional," I said, gathering my things to leave.

"No!" Courtney said, clinging to me. "I won't stay here."

"Look at all your special things I brought. Judy will play with you," I said, trying to disentangle myself from her grasp.

"Nope!" she said, and then looked right at us both. "I don't like Judy."

Judy gave me an "I told you so" look.

"But Mommy has to go to work," I answered, hating the conciliatory tone in my voice. Courtney screamed and hit me as I put her down. I held her close, begging her to stop, but she only kicked harder. The only thing I knew to do when this happened was lie down on a bed with her, holding her until she grew calmer. I looked up and saw shock on Judy's face.

"Two-year-olds always have temper tantrums," I said, not sounding convinced myself. Then, almost in an instant, the crying stopped. Courtney demanded I let her down. She looked from Judy to me, and then, almost as though she were an adult weighing her situation, the tears were gone. She walked toward Judy with her favorite alphabet book. "Read to Courtney?" she asked, and Judy quickly complied. I left them on the couch, reading. Courtney's face was blotchy from crying, but she seemed calm, and Judy looked relieved. *It's going to be fine*, I thought, closing the door behind me.

At work, I was asked to deliver a chart to the nurse's station next to the new baby ward. On an impulse, I walked across the hall and watched the newborns behind the glass. I was fascinated by how tiny, helpless, and yet complete they seemed. Over twenty years before, I had been born in this same hospital, and my "real mother" had stayed in a room somewhere nearby. Now I was Courtney's "real mother."

For a moment, I felt the ghostly presence of the mysterious woman named *Paula*, the woman who gave birth to me, as if she were standing near me, looking in on the newborns. Could she give me insight into my brilliant, complex child?

I had always believed there was something magical about the relationship between a birth mother and her child, that it would be a panacea for any difficulties. But thinking back to Courtney's tantrum that morning, I felt like I was failing. Louella knew how to manage my behavior and soothe me when I was young, while I couldn't control my real daughter or figure out how to calm her down. Shared blood doesn't mean guarantees, I thought, recalling my friends' difficulties with their mothers. Still, I suddenly ached for Paula so much that I turned, half expecting to see her in the flesh. But the hallway was empty.

WHEN I RETURNED to Judy's hours later, I saw Courtney huddled in the far corner of the sofa with her arms folded across her chest, an angry expression on her face. I turned back to Judy for an explanation, but she looked just as glum.

"What's the matter with you two?" I asked.

Courtney rushed over. I picked her up. When I tried to set her down, she clung to me. Judy stood in the doorway.

"Linda, I don't think I'm made for kids. I mean, it wouldn't matter whose baby she was. I just don't have what it takes."

"Judy, come on. Other people can't believe how clever she is. And she's part of me."

"She was into everything. She ignored whatever I said," Judy complained.

"Your house isn't set up for a two-year-old," I said. As I glanced around, I noticed her house looked wrecked: the cat's litter box was upside down, and the entire contents of the kitchen seemed to be strewn across the floor. Still, I was angry at Judy. Courtney was the best thing to happen to me, even if she was headstrong. Judy should have tried harder.

But then, as I looked over at Judy, I saw she was quietly crying. "What is it, sweetie?" I asked, putting Courtney down and sitting on the couch with Judy. She rarely cried, and the sight of her tears softened me.

"Everything, just everything! I hate how much trouble I have liking your daughter, but I hate it even more that you are such a wimp with her. That's just the beginning. I don't think Ben wants to get married," she said, staring out the window as she spoke. "It's this damn war, my mother's drinking—everything just seems so messed up."

We leaned close, our knees touching, and talked. Courtney, miraculously, sat on the floor, playing quietly with a toy. Later, as we were leaving, I thought to myself that we had successfully fulfilled—for a little while, at least—my biggest wish: for the three of us to be together.

I WAS LEAVING work one day when a garbage truck pulled up. In the back, a man stood astride a heap of trash. A double take proved he looked like a Greek statue, tall and muscular with chiseled features. He caught me staring and flashed a wonderful, deep smile. We smiled at each other for a moment before I turned away. Later I told Judy about seeing the man, whom we dubbed the "Garbage Adonis."

A month later, I was delivering juice to patients on the orthopedic ward, when my favorite nurse grabbed my arm. "One new patient has come in," she said. "And he's got a very cute friend."

The two men had been riding on a motorcycle when a car turned into them, she told me. Now, one lay in the ward with a broken pelvis and leg, while his friend, unhurt by the accident, sat beside him. I pushed the cart into their room. The patient lay with his leg in a cast, and his friend fed him ice chips from a paper cup. I was curious about this man who had spent the better part of a day by his friend's side.

"How about some juice?" I asked.

"Sure," he said, turning around to answer me. I saw a handsome, well-dressed man in a button-down shirt and tan slacks. As he smiled, a dimple appeared in his cheek. I realized with surprise it was the same man I had seen on the garbage truck.

We smiled at each other nervously as I handed him cranberry juice.

"Are you, by any chance, a garbage man?" I asked.

"Yeah, this hospital is on my route. I think I saw you a few weeks ago."

"I thought you looked familiar."

"My name's Frank."

Each night I looked forward to seeing him. He was outgoing and attractive, and would entertain me with funny stories over the juice cart.

One night he offered to walk me to the bus after work.

"What's your job like?" I asked as we walked outside.

"It's not something I want to do forever. But it's a good physical workout, and I find amazing stuff all the time."

"Like what?"

"Antiques, a Persian rug—I even found a diamond ring once. And the money is nice."

"Garbage men have always had a sort of mystery to them," I smiled.

"Well, in the olden days, they used horse-drawn carriages and collected garbage in burlap sacks. They salvaged all kinds of things and sold them to be reused."

"That sounds like the Diggers," I said.

"The Diggers? Who are they?"

"Oh, they're a group in Haight-Ashbury. They take unused food and spread it around to feed the people. They say money is wicked, that we shouldn't waste things."

"I've never been to the Haight. I always wondered what it was like."

"It's like a carnival. People dress any way they want," I said. "When I see men in suits now, they look so uptight I think they should go to jail."

He laughed. "Maybe we could go there together. The Haight, I mean."

"Sure," I agreed.

Long past the bus stop now, we kept walking. He told me how much he wanted a better education: he was taking night classes, although his job began at 3 a.m. Like me, he had been raised a Catholic, and had become disillusioned with the dogmatism, but he, too, still believed in some of the ideals of the Church. He talked about wanting to find a different path from the one his parents had followed. I knew exactly what he meant. Soon we had walked four miles across the city.

When we arrived at my house, I couldn't get the key to work. Frustrated, I jiggled it in the lock. Frank took the key from my hand and effortlessly unlocked the door. As it swung open, I felt a rush of tears. I was so tired of shouldering my own burdens, taking care of everything myself, being uncertain all the time. I longed to lean on someone who could manage it all better than I could. I swallowed hard, pulling myself together, and said good-night. But I was delighted when he called the next day to ask me to dinner.

Once he came over, we forgot about going out again, because we both got wrapped up in playing with Courtney. She liked him right away, climbing into his arms, sitting on his lap, showing him her favorite toys. Watching the two of them play, I was thrilled. I'd found a man who appreciated Courtney. After that day, we quickly became a trio.

My parents were dismayed that I was dating a garbage man. When

I told Louella, she was silent for a moment, then said, "We were just thinking you were growing up, dating that nice Jewish doctor, and now here you are springing this on us."

"I'm not springing anything on you. Michael Cohen didn't care at all about Courtney, and you haven't met Frank. How can you judge him?"

Reluctantly, she invited the two of us over for dinner. She and Jack were both frosty at first, scrutinizing what Frank said, how he carried himself. But as we sat around the table, I could see them warming to him. He was ambitious, polite, attractive, and even a Catholic. Courtney was clearly enchanted by him. And he was making a big effort to draw them out. By the end of dinner, Louella was laughing openly with him, and Jack was showing him his prized bottle of hundred-year-old brandy. I knew they were impressed.

The next morning Louella called me, sounding excited.

"This is a man you should keep," she said. "Believe me, I know a thing or two. We would stop worrying about you and Courtney if you settled down with a man like him."

As much as I wanted Louella to like him, by the time we hung up, I felt trapped. I'd known Frank less than a month and here was Louella, trying to marry me off. Still, it was easy to be with him, and we had fun together. I felt so normal going places with him and Courtney, because we looked like a perfect, happy family. Most of all, with Frank, I was no longer afraid of the world's craziness. I just wished that Judy liked him more.

"Are you still seeing that dustman?" she asked, smirking.

We were sitting in our favorite booth at the Far East Café.

"Don't be horrible!" I said. "You hardly know him. Besides, he's not just a garbage man. He's been going to night school, even if it means he doesn't sleep."

"Well," she said, "he's a lot better than Hank. If it's what you want, what can I say?"

"True—what can you say?" I said, heatedly.

"I'm sorry," she said, softening. "It's your life, and I know Frank is good to you. Besides, who am I to talk about choosing men?"

"I still can't believe Ben cancelled the wedding," I said, touching her hand.

"It was so humiliating to have to call everyone when it was a week away. But now he says we can set another date—he just got scared."

Judy paused and looked up at me. I noticed how chic she looked in her black V-neck pullover and tight beige capris. She was the most beautiful woman I had ever seen.

Ben had to be crazy, I told her.

Beth left for a job in Washington, D.C., and Frank moved in. He cooked and helped me fix up the house. As the eldest of five children, he was comfortable with responsibility, and made caring for Courtney seem easy. The three of us spent Saturdays in the Haight, where people dressed like biblical characters, handed out free food, wine, and peace buttons. Sundays we visited Jack and Louella or else Frank's large family, who accepted Courtney as though she were their own.

Frank's father, his namesake, was a tall, skinny man with knobby fingers and warm, mischievous eyes. He had grown up in Puerto Rico and came to America when he was a teenager. A lifetime of fighting racism and years of hard labor at the garbage company had worn down his body, but his spirit was strong, and family loyalty meant everything to him. I could see where Frank got his charm: his father was chivalrous, and often winked at me. He was full of corny phrases, like "I was sorry I had no shoes until I met a man who had no feet," which made me like him even more.

Late in that summer of 1966, Frank surprised me with two tickets to see the Beatles. We drove to Candlestick Park. The wind and fog that night were typical of San Francisco weather, and the amphitheater was packed. As usual, Frank brought everything to make the concert comfortable: soft seats, colorful wool blankets, and a magical-looking bottle.

"What's this?" I asked as he pulled it from his pack.

"Wait a second and you'll see," he said, as he unwrapped two crystal glasses. He uncorked the bottle and filled the glasses.

"Part of tasting something wonderful begins with how it looks," he said. The glass glistened with an amber liquid.

"It's beautiful," I said.

"It's called Armagnac. It's a brandy named after the part of France it comes from. Cup your hand around the glass and let it warm up. Then sniff."

It smelled like plums. We drank. The Beatles appeared onstage and the crowd shrieked. People smiled at each other as though we were all part of the same club, none of us knowing that this concert would be their final one.

Just before leaving the stage, John Lennon plucked a few notes on his guitar to a new song called "In My Life." I'd never heard anything so beautiful, except maybe Bach's Brandenburg Concertos. We sipped Armagnac and nestled under the blanket.

Frank put his arm around me and whispered in my ear, "What would you think about getting married?"

I smiled with pleasure at his words. I'd found the right man to settle down with. Although we had only known one another for a few months, we loved each other—why would we need more than that?

"I'd love it," I said, leaning back into his arms.

The following day I was invited to a family lunch at Frank's parents' house. I arrived to find the cramped living room filled with people, balloons and crepe paper taped to the stucco walls. As I stared in confusion at the scene, Frank's father came up and shyly pinned a white gardenia on my sweater. Then it dawned on me: this gathering was a surprise wedding shower. Instead of feeling overcome with joy, I felt dizzy and a little sick. I asked if I could sit down. Misreading my queasiness as overwhelmed delight, Frank's father led me to a chair. He stood proudly next to me as I looked around at the faces smiling at me.

Is this a terrible mistake? I wondered, filled with panic. Despite my obsession with Mickey, my ectopic pregnancy, my marriage and divorce, and my affair with Michael Cohen, Frank was my first real boyfriend. With him, I felt as if I were fourteen again, not like an adult woman. It was exciting and easy to be together, and we both needed life rafts, to stay afloat, to be carried to someplace new. The idea of getting married suddenly seemed all wrong.

Just then Frank's father shook me out of my thoughts, putting his hand on my shoulder. "How are you holding up?" he asked.

I surprised myself by answering honestly. "Sometimes I don't feel I belong anywhere."

"I know just how you feel," he said, and I knew he meant it. He held out his hand and I grasped it.

WE CHOSE THE Lady Chapel at St. Dominic's for the wedding. During the service, Courtney sat with Judy in the front row. In the middle of the ceremony, she left her seat and ran to where we stood, taking our vows. She stretched out her arms to Frank, demanding to be held. The guests laughed, delighted by her antics. He picked her up and held her for the rest of the ceremony.

After a honeymoon in Mexico City, I returned home two weeks pregnant, frightened of going through childbirth again but thrilled at the idea of having a child with Frank. I found a doctor I trusted who taught me about Lamaze methods, encouraging me to see birth as a natural, healthy process. In August, I gave birth to another daughter. Frank was the perfect labor coach; he never left my side. I was conscious throughout the delivery, and watched my second daughter's birth in a huge mirror in the delivery room. Nicole was born with a tuft of long hair sticking straight up from her head. She was gorgeous, with Frank's dark skin and huge, curious brown eyes.

Right away I noticed how different this new baby was from Courtney, who was now three. When Nicole woke, she would lie in her crib cooing and amusing herself. Sometimes I didn't even know she was awake. When I went in, she would look at me and smile, exuding happiness. Courtney woke up wanting contact immediately; sometimes she was glad to see me, but other times she was panicky and alarmed. With the birth of Nicole, I was aware of Courtney's harder start in life, and felt more protective of her than ever.

FRANK AND I enrolled in school part-time, and I took classes in psychology and comparative religion. Three afternoons a week, we brought Courtney and Nicole to the babysitter's house across the street.

Mrs. Antonelli was a large, friendly woman whose house was filled with children, the smell of garlic cooking, and statues of the Blessed Virgin. Courtney had been going there for three years, and we both loved "Mrs. A.," as everyone called her.

One afternoon when I came to pick up the girls, Mrs. Antonelli asked if she could speak with me alone. I took Courtney and Nicole across the street to Frank and returned to sit on a couch in her living room. She sat down next to me.

"I think you should know that Courtney comes here with lots of coins, and passes them out to the other children. It makes me very uncomfortable."

"I can't imagine why she would do that."

"She says they all hate her," Mrs. Antonelli said, "but if she gives them money they become her friends."

When I got home, I went to the big jar where Frank put his loose change. It was almost empty.

I asked Courtney about it and she started crying, hard.

"I didn't take any money," she said.

She was becoming hysterical, and Frank came in and picked her up. Through her tears, she insisted Mrs. Antonelli was lying. I didn't know what to do. I knew the babysitter was telling the truth, and this situation scared me, like the experience with the puppy. That she would steal money every morning was upsetting enough. But why would she think the other children hated her? That bothered me the most.

Kids can be mean to each other, I thought. Maybe they were ganging up on Courtney. After we put the children to bed that night, Frank suggested we find a more structured child-care program.

A friend of mine recommended a woman on the other side of town, a former kindergarten teacher named Sherry. For the first few months, Courtney went happily, but soon she began to complain, saying she didn't want to go. Every morning, she refused to get up or threw tantrums, but she would never explain what was wrong. Then one afternoon, while preparing to visit Jack and Louella at their summer home, I went into Courtney's room to pack and found she had taken scissors to her hair. I knew this was something kids did, cutting bangs and giving themselves haircuts. But she had cut her hair to the scalp. Her head looked bald on part of one side. In a reasonable voice that belied my anger, I asked her what had happened. "I didn't do it," she replied, the scissors in her hand and her golden hair all over the floor.

Her lie brought my fury to the surface. "You *did* do it, Courtney. Why?" I demanded, shaking her.

"It's because of that mean woman you leave me with," Courtney sobbed. "Don't leave me there, Mommy."

"But honey, you've got playmates there," I said, my arms around her now.

"No, I don't." She began to cry even harder. "Sherry hates me, and everyone is mean to me."

I couldn't bear to see her so upset. I sat down with her on the bed, comforting her.

"What does she do that's mean?" I asked.

"She locks me in a closet," Courtney choked out.

I was horrified. If it was true, it was child abuse, although that term wasn't used much in those days. If it wasn't true, then Courtney's vivid imagination was turning into a serious problem. I had no way of knowing if she was lying, but I knew people did horrible things to kids. I decided to believe her.

SOON AFTER, I started a day-care center in our house and hired someone to come in part-time, when I was at school. The rest of the time I was home. Courtney finally seemed settled. She loved playing "teacher" with the other children and made up games, plays, and puppet shows the whole day.

"I can't believe how happy you are with all those kids in the house," Louella said on the phone one day. "It would send me to the madhouse."

"It's so easy," I said. "I love taking care of them. Every single day something new happens with them."

It wasn't just being a mother that I loved. I looked forward to school for the first time, and was particularly intrigued by the Russian philosopher G. I. Gurdjieff, who I had learned about in my psychology class.

I told Frank, "He believes we are all sleepwalking, and that inner work is the only way to wake up. I want to go to one of the study groups."

"I just saw a notice for a meeting at City College," he said.

We decided to try it. We liked the philosophy, the teacher, and the rigorous meditation exercises we were asked to do, so we joined the group.

Then, when Nicole was a year old, our teacher made a somber announcement: before his death the psychic Edgar Cayce had predicted that a massive earthquake would destroy San Francisco, and one of his protégés was certain it was going to occur the following month. Fortunately, there was a secure place for all of us to stay until the danger passed.

While the Gurdjieff philosophy focused on self-development, it also stressed the centrality of the spiritual leader who would guide his practitioners on this journey. It didn't occur to us to question this hierarchy, nor did we realize we were just transferring our old Catholicism onto a new belief system. We were convinced that we had found a unique, true path. So when we heard about the impending earthquake, we immediately made plans to leave the city. I called Louella to tell her where we would be.

"You know we're in this group," I said, a bit hesitantly.

"You and Frank are always in groups. What's this one about?"

"Transformation. Leaving consensus reality."

"Nonsense," she said. "The only reality I care about is being able to pay my bills, stay healthy, and spend time with your daughters."

So limited, so uptight, so Republican, I thought. Yet she and Jack were incredibly supportive these days. They loved Frank and were terrific grandparents for the girls. I didn't want them swept away in the apocalypse.

"Look, Edgar Cayce has never been wrong before, and his protégé predicted an earthquake is about to hit San Francisco. There will be hundreds of people where we're headed. Why don't you come with us? You could stay in a hotel."

"Honey, I'm too old to give a damn about this kind of thing."

"But you don't understand," I cried, "mainstream society is ignorant of the higher truths to be found through psychic power."

Needless to say, she wasn't convinced. We left the following week in a giant caravan of brightly painted buses and Volkswagen vans for a camp in the Sierra Nevada. There we slept in tents and ate vegetables and brown rice, awaiting news of the catastrophe. We cooked, cleaned, chopped wood, cleared trails, cared for children, meditated, chanted, and attended long, tedious meetings. Frank and I barely had time to look at one another. After two weeks, the leader announced we were all safe, and we packed up for home.

"I don't think I'm a very worthy person," I admitted as we drove back to the city.

"Me neither," Frank said. "I'm so glad to be out of there."

"I have to say, a lot of those people were more uptight than the people I grew up with."

"I know—so many rules. But I thought you liked it. You were working hard right alongside everyone else."

"No, I felt crazy being there. I thought you were the perfect commune person."

"Not me! I hated the food."

"So did I," I answered, sighing with relief.

We spotted a truck stop, pulled in, and ordered pork chops and mashed potatoes for the whole family.

Back home again, we decided the study group was no longer for us. I stopped the day-care center in my home, and found a preschool that Courtney and Nicole loved. With my new free time, I took classes in philosophy and poetry, and continued to read up on every new form of psychology and spirituality I heard of.

The tower of books that was growing by my bedside made me think of Judy. We hadn't seen each other in three months. A few days later, one gray day in late November, Louella offered to take the girls for the afternoon, and I drove to Chinatown to meet my friend. I parked in front of the cathedral of Old St. Mary's. I walked past the grocer selling ginger and bamboo shoots and squawking chickens hanging by their legs, across the narrow street to the doorway of the Far East.

Through the plate glass window, I saw Judy waiting for me in the lobby. As usual, she was absorbed in a book. The girl who had cracked gum a mile a minute, wearing a coat with a fake leopard collar, was now a woman with silken hair pulled back into a fashionable twist. She wore sheer black nylons and a white-collared black dress that she had purchased in France. Only her left foot in its stiletto heel, which she tapped up and down, betrayed any sign of her tremendous energy. Suddenly she looked up, and there was that marvelous dimpled grin.

We both laughed, delighted to see each other.

"Is the curtained booth available?" I asked a somber-looking Asian waiter, who ushered us to the cubicle.

"Tell me everything," Judy said. "God—two kids now. I can't believe it."

"There isn't much news. It's all very ordinary," I said. "You tell first."

"Well, I love living with Kate and Ben. The three of us are a perfect fit. I think Ben and I will finally get married. I'm afraid to even say it, but I think he means it this time. Aside from that—I miss you so much."

"I miss you too. Nobody takes your place."

She lit another cigarette and we stared at one another. I marveled at the pleasure I felt, being with her. It didn't matter what we fought over—the friendship felt invincible. Together, we had learned about loving, tormenting, hating, making up, and loving again.

"I'm feeling so guilty about my relationship with Courtney," she said. "I want to spend more time with her. I promise I'll make it work next time."

"Courtney has been in Montessori half-time for months, and her teacher says she's one of the most imaginative, gifted children she's ever known. Judy, I know you two will discover each other one day."

"I'm going to learn to love her at least half as much as you do. And Nicole too. That's a promise," Judy said.

"How could we let so much time pass without seeing one another?" I asked.

"We have to promise to do this at least once a month," she said. "How's your truth search going?" she asked, using our familiar phrase.

"Right now I'm finding the most meaning in being a mother. That and Carl Jung."

She smiled. "I think I'll find it in community justice. I feel like I was born for social work."

The meal came to an end too soon, and we walked out the door with our arms around each other.

Out on the street, she gave me a quick hug and began to walk away.

"Wait," I said. "I'll drive you home. That way you don't have to take the bus, and we can talk more."

"I have to get home and study. The bus will be faster."

I couldn't bear to leave her.

"Come on, Judy. We can cruise Chestnut Street for old time's sake."

"Sweetie, I've got to catch my bus. Our time's up," she said, kissing my cheek.

CHAPTER 19

The following weekend, some friends invited Frank, the girls, and me to their country cabin. The weekend was filled with good food, wine, conversations, and long walks. On our last night, I had a dream about Judy. She was shaking me hard.

"You have to wake up," she said. "I need you right now."

"What do you want? I'm trying to sleep."

"Open your eyes," Judy insisted in the dream. I did, and she looked straight at me. "It's time for me to go. You'll understand later."

I heard myself reply, as though from a great distance. "No. Don't leave!"

"Listen. My mother's drunk. My father's in jail. Ben is hurt. Kate is out of town. You're the only one. The key is under the flowerpot. Get my diary. There's a blue dress I just got back from the cleaners. Use it to bury me in. You have to do this for me."

We argued for a minute, and then the dream shifted. Our bodies were flying through the air together, until I watched Judy leave hers, a spirit moving into a pulsating light so bright it swallowed her. "Don't go," I cried, but I knew she was gone. For an instant, I felt as if the entire universe was at peace. There was order and meaning in everything. I stood outside of time as I had always known it, in a space of perfect calm.

Then I heard a thump as her body hit concrete.

I woke up. Lights were on. Frank and our friends stood over me. I was pale and shivering.

"You had a nightmare," Frank said. "You were screaming."

"I had a dream that Judy died. Only it seemed real."

"No, no," my friend Natalie said. "It was only a dream. Go back to sleep, it's only five a.m."

It seemed pointless to argue. I lay down again, but could not sleep. My mind was reeling. Frank was restless too. We got up, packed, and left for home right after breakfast. As we drove down the mountain, I rubbed my hand along the inside of the windshield.

"What are you doing that for?" Frank asked.

"I'm thinking," I said, "about what it would feel like to be thrown through the glass." I found myself rubbing the back of my neck, kneading and kneading until Frank asked me to stop.

SOON AFTER WE got home, the phone rang.

"Linda," the voice said. "This is Sandy Sampson, a friend of Judy's. I have something horrible to tell you."

"Judy's dead," I said immediately. "She died in a car accident."

I heard the woman gasp. "Oh, my God. Who told you?"

"I dreamt it early this morning."

Sandy told me the details. Ben's father had had a heart attack the night before. Shortly before 5 a.m., Judy and Ben were driving to the hospital to see him, when a drunk drove through a red light on Guerrero Street and hit their car. Judy crashed through the windshield, cutting her jugular vein, and landed on the pavement. She bled to death before the ambulance arrived. Ben had suffered only minor injuries, but was in deep shock.

I found Kate's friend's number in L.A. and called her. I went to Judy's house and got the key under the flowerpot. Inside, I found her diary in a desk drawer and put it in my purse. I went upstairs and opened the bedroom closet. There was the blue dress, still in its plastic, fresh from the dry cleaner.

After Judy's death, everyone in her life was shell-shocked. Her mother was never without a glass of whiskey. Ben remained in the hospital, too emotionally torn up to return home. Kate, home from Southern California, spent her days sprawled on a sofa, staring into space. I was left to handle the details. I sent a death notice to the newspaper and made arrangements for the service. Kate helped me choose a quote for Judy's headstone—"That which is essential is invisible to the eye"—from her favorite book, *The Little Prince*.

I waited for the tears to come, but they didn't. This was different from the usual way I managed trauma, going numb to avoid the pain. I never felt loss or stopped sensing Judy's presence. It wasn't something I could explain logically, but I knew I had followed Judy into the place of her death, and I had brought something back with me, indescribable but unquestionably real.

We had devoured the poems of Rilke and Wordsworth as teenagers, as though our hearts understood what our minds could not grasp. Now the meanings were true. No longer able to talk to Judy, I didn't know who I could share them with.

I WENT TO visit Louella a few weeks after the funeral.

"You're handling her death much better than I expected," she said, her arm on my shoulder.

"I dreamt Judy died. I dreamt of her accident at the exact time it happened. I know it sounds nuts but—"

"Don't do that!" Louella interrupted.

"I knew I shouldn't have told you," I sighed.

"Don't belittle your experience—that's what I meant to say," she said. "Dreams like yours do happen. We just don't understand why."

I was taken aback. She looked at me expectantly, and I told her every detail of the dream.

"I'm not a bit surprised," she said. "The two of you were like twins. Are you frightened?"

"No, but I don't feel like I'm fully back in this world. The strangest thing is, I haven't shed a tear."

"If we could see the world as God sees it, we wouldn't be afraid," Louella said. "For that brief moment, you were able to see the big picture. Maybe you don't cry because she's still with you."

I don't know the half of her, I thought, smiling in wonder at Louella.

DRIVING HOME, I felt strangely elated. Judy wasn't dead—she was just somewhere else. I would always feel her presence around me. Later that night, though, I became frightened by my dream. I could no longer ignore the presence of that "other world"; it was real to me now beyond doubt. The certainty of that realization was awesome and terrifying. How would I live now, always aware of this other dimension? I lay wide awake for hours, thinking it all through, before falling sleep.

The next morning, I woke up more refreshed than I'd felt in ages. For the first time since Judy's death, I felt able to live fully in this world, in the present moment, instead of searching for something I couldn't see. It was as if someone holding on to my heels had finally let go.

CHAPTER 20

The place called the real world, where I lived most of the time, was not as easy to negotiate as it once had been. The social optimism that had lit up the sixties seemed to be on the verge of collapse. By 1968, tour buses drove down Haight Street to see the hippies, who were getting harder to spot. The summer of love had passed, and flower children were leaving the city in droves. Hell's Angels and drug addicts were taking their place. The war in Vietnam was escalating. So were the protests.

The day after Nixon was elected president, students at San Francisco State College held a massive strike. Five hundred students stormed the administration building and demanded a change in college policies. An agreement was reached to enroll more minority students and add Black Studies to the curriculum, which Frank and I both supported. But the changes brought bad news for us when we received a letter saying that the quota for Caucasian students had been reached. We would not be admitted.

———

MEANWHILE, COURTNEY GREW from a toddler into a little girl, and became adamant about not wanting to see Hank. She came home from their visits looking pale and exhausted. Frank and I were afraid for her safety.

I went back to my lawyer.

"I know things haven't changed much in the court system," I told him, "but I have to do something."

"Is he still writing all over her?" he asked.

"Yes, and her nightmares are even worse now."

"I can't do anything without a court order—and that will be almost impossible to get," he said, shaking his head sympathetically.

"Well, I have to try. She can't protect herself at four years old. Tell me what I need to do."

He told me that he couldn't do a thing unless several people were willing to testify against Hank. I called his ex-wife, who initially refused to be involved. But to my surprise, she called back a week later and said that, because the situation concerned a child, she was willing to come forward. Other people who had known him, past friends and teachers, all offered the same initial resistance, then agreed to testify after realizing that my daughter was involved.

I contacted Hank's mother and told her what was going on.

"Oh, honey, I'm so sorry it's come to this," she said. "He's been through so much already. You don't know how horrible his father was to him." She began to cry. "I should have protected him more. I was so young—I didn't know what to do. And now I blame myself for Hank's troubles."

She took a deep breath. "I believe he's got a lot of good in him. But I know you have to do what you think is right, for Courtney's sake."

Enough people volunteered to testify that our lawyer thought we had a chance to require his visits to be supervised. On the first day I entered the courtroom, holding Frank's hand. Hank walked in through a different door, and I caught his eye. As we looked at each other, sadness washed over me. I knew he loved Courtney, truly and deeply. And I also believed that he was dangerous, and that I needed to protect her. I looked away and squeezed Frank's hand tightly.

The hearing lasted several days, with testimony about Hank's behavior and activities. In the end, the judge put a stop to overnight visits at Hank's. Now he could visit Courtney only at our house or his mother's.

BUT WE DECIDED that the court victory was not enough. We wanted more distance from Hank, and both Frank and I were ready for an adventure. We decided to move to Oregon, where we stood a better chance at getting back into school.

In November 1969, we filled a van with our possessions and drove to Jack and Louella's to say good-bye. As exciting as it was to go, it was hard to leave my parents, especially Louella. Since I had married Frank, we had developed an easy, affectionate way of being together, with our shared focus on Courtney and Nicole. As for Jack, since the day Kennedy died, we had moved slowly toward a cautious peace. We never talked about what he had done to me, but I could appreciate the parts of him that had helped enrich my life. The hardest part of leaving was separating Louella and Jack from the girls. The time they spent with Courtney and Nicole was the highlight of their lives, and they would miss each other terribly.

As we pulled out of the driveway, I looked back to see Louella watching us from her window. She seemed so shrunken and sad. I was surprised at the heaviness I felt, watching her figure get smaller and smaller as we drove away.

WE HAD A long drive through a snowstorm—the first one the girls had ever seen. They were enchanted, and when we reached Eugene, they tumbled out of the van, shouting, "We're home!" and playing in the snow. After the bustle of the big city, the quiet streets were relaxing, and everyone we met seemed to be an artist, a professor, or a student. We rented a ranch-style house, enrolled Courtney and Nicole in a Montessori school, and Frank began work on his teaching degree at the university. Meanwhile, I was pregnant again, and spent my days playing with my daughters, cooking elaborate meals, and getting to know Eugene.

Our life seemed easy and carefree. Frank and I never fought; when things got tense, we buried any uncertainties and conflicts. And so much else was going on, with two daughters and another child on the way, that there was always an excuse for not exploring our feelings in any deeper way. Besides, neither of us had the skill to do it.

I was increasingly distracted by Jack's failing health. When we visited San Francisco for the holidays, he looked shriveled and complained about being tired. His face lit up, though, every time Courtney or Nicole entered the room. A month later, Louella called to tell me he had been diagnosed with multiple melanoma. She sounded angry when she reminded me of all the times he wouldn't wear a shirt when he worked outdoors at our summer home. Then her voice broke.

"Honey, we're going to lose him. They don't think there's anything they can do."

At first I didn't understand. How could we lose him? Then I thought of his gaunt face the last time I had visited.

I loved how he treated my girls: they teased each other sweetly, and he loved giving them maraschino cherries from his private bar. He sat through endless games of Go Fish and Chutes & Ladders. Still, I was careful never to leave them alone with him, and I would hurry them away from his hugs.

A few weeks after Louella's call, I flew to San Francisco, knowing it would be to say good-bye. Louella had told me that he had changed dramatically in just a few months, but nothing prepared me for the tiny, shrunken man lying on the white hospital sheets, woozy with morphine. The moment he saw me, he began to cry and shake in his bed, as if afraid. As I sat beside him, he calmed down. I took his hand and told him how much his granddaughters loved him.

His eyes grew bright, and he shifted his gaze away. "I need a priest," he muttered. "Find a priest!" he said again, this time louder.

His body shook, and I let his hand go. In the hallway, I asked a nurse to call the chaplain. I returned to wish him a final good-bye, but he stared at me blankly.

I felt depressed when I returned to Eugene, and spent days moping around the house, talking to Louella for hours about Jack's condition. One afternoon, to lift my spirits, I took my daughters shopping. In the children's department at Meier and Frank, I picked out a pretty spring dress for each of them. Courtney's was green with tiny yellow tulips, and Nicole's was pink with blue lilacs. I was feeling fiercely proud of them as we left the store with our shopping bags. Out of nowhere, a woman popped up in front of us. Tall and ungainly, she reeked of cheap perfume.

"My God, that's a beautiful child," she said, pointing at two-year-old Nicole.

I glanced quickly at Courtney. At first she looked expectant, but receiving no compliment from the woman, she squirmed and moved away from us. I said pointedly to the woman, "Yes, I have two beautiful girls."

The woman's appraising eye passed over Courtney, and she said, "Well, she certainly is a *big* girl."

Enraged, I wanted to shout at this woman, but my attention shifted quickly to Courtney, who was visibly upset. I looked at my eldest daughter as objectively as I could. She was just as beautiful as her sister. Her features were smooth, her eyes framed by long dark lashes, and her laughter was infectious. Every day she chose a different-colored ribbon for her golden brown pigtails. Today it was green, which matched the color of her lovely, curious eyes. She was a charming mixture of costume jewelry and gumboots, tomboy and princess.

I whisked the girls away from the woman. We went to lunch, where I told Courtney to order anything she liked. But she wasn't interested. She glared at Nicole and me, not speaking. I believed that any bad mood of hers was a direct reflection of my parenting, and I felt desperate to appease her. But nothing seemed to work. She slouched farther down in the booth and refused to eat her food. Then I asked her if she wanted another dress. To my relief, her mood brightened. After lunch, she skipped happily back to the store, Nicole and I following closely behind.

CHAPTER 21

One month later, in March 1970, Jack died. Though I had said good-bye to him at the hospital, my body shook all day on hearing the news. I wanted to be there to help Louella, but I was due to deliver anytime.

And, the next day, our family's focus on death was diverted by new life. I gave birth to my third daughter, whom we named Jaimee, French for "I love." She was beautiful, with fair hair and blue eyes. The stressful circumstances of Jack's death made us cherish her glowing newborn presence even more.

"This feels as close to a miracle as anything I can think of," Louella said. She promised to come meet the baby as soon as she could. It made me happy to hear her making plans for the future. The day before, it had seemed as if her life was over too.

In the hospital, I often thought of how much Jack would have loved to see little Jaimee's first days. But I wasn't able to cry for him the way I felt I should.

Once home, I was quickly distracted by my daughters. Jaimee had large watchful eyes and woke up every morning smiling. One of our friends said that holding her for an hour was better than months of therapy. Nicole delighted in every flower and creature she discovered. Courtney, vital and dramatic, was full of exciting stories about first grade at the local public school. Most recently, she would regale us with tales of her new classmate, a Swedish girl.

Ingrid, Courtney reported, had joined her class in the middle of the year. A large child with a poor grasp of English, she wore unusual and colorful handmade dresses. Courtney, who loved fashion, would describe the clothes in precise detail. After school each day, she would tell Nicole and me the latest; for instance, how Ingrid had invited Courtney to share her extravagant lunches. They ate together on a red tablecloth provided by Ingrid's mother, overflowing with cheeses, breads, and sweets.

After a few weeks, however, Ingrid turned nasty. She tormented Courtney until my daughter cried at the thought of having to go to school. The sweet friendship had become the cause for nightmares. When I told Courtney I was going to see her teacher, she appeared relieved.

That afternoon, after the children had left the classroom, I met with Courtney's teacher. As I explained the situation with Ingrid, the teacher seemed perplexed.

"I'm sorry to tell you this," she said. "We did study Sweden briefly, but there is no such girl in our class."

At first I was astounded, then embarrassed, and finally, afraid. Once again, Courtney had made up a story about being singled out for persecution, and she believed her story was true. Similiar incidents—her nightmares, her irrational fears, her aloneness—arranged themselves like glass pieces in a kaleidoscope. In the pattern emerging before my eyes, I had my first recognition that I might not be able to hold my child tightly enough to protect her.

WE SEARCHED FOR someone who could help us with Court-ney, and found a Viennese-trained child psychiatrist. I was certain that, with her credentials, she would give us the key to fix whatever was wrong.

"Why do I have to go and see the doctor, Mommy?" Courtney asked.

"Because sometimes you think people don't like you when they do. She'll understand what happened with Ingrid, and help you make better friends."

Courtney nodded. At six, she was a guarded child, and I was glad for her trust.

Dr. Driscol saw Courtney four times before sending us a letter, which said that Courtney believed I preferred the company of Frank and her sisters to her. The report suggested I devote more time to Courtney. I was shocked by the assessment, which ignored my main worries and validated Courtney's most irrational beliefs.

Fortunately, Courtney didn't want to go back to her. So we switched to a child psychologist who saw Courtney several times, and then asked Frank and me to come to her office.

"I'd like to hear your concerns before I tell you mine," she said.

"First of all," I said, "the nightmares. She wakes up suddenly, shrieking, and for a moment she doesn't even seem aware I'm sitting on the bed. She looks terrified, but is never able to tell me what she's so afraid of."

"Yes," Dr. Saunders said, jotting something down in her notebook. "Go on."

I told her that Courtney's teachers had described her as exception-ally creative, but isolated. Although her sisters loved her company and followed her everywhere, she was never invited to play at another child's house, and no one ever came to ours.

"And she says she sees angels," I added.

Dr. Saunders stopped writing and looked up. "How often does she say that?"

"A lot," I said. "Perhaps she does see them, because she stays calm for days afterward."

Dr. Saunders put down her pen and looked at me firmly, this time with clear disdain. "I can assure you she does not see angels," she began. "The child needs extracurricular activities to help her make friends and to stop worrying so much about feeling alone in her family."

"What do you mean?"

She told me that if Courtney felt more secure, she wouldn't hate school or have terrible nightmares. "We have to look at the mother if something is wrong with the child," she said, looking at me intently.

My face burned. The first doctor had been right: Courtney's troubles were my fault.

"Perhaps Courtney should join a Brownie troop," she suggested. "Scouting might do wonders for her."

I dragged Courtney, who hated the idea, to our first Brownie meeting a few weeks later, in the brightly lit basement of the local school. We filed in and sat on metal folding chairs. As Courtney clung to me, I glanced around the room at the sea of children. Could this gaggle of little girls in brown uniforms cure Courtney's nightmares, or reassure her that she was loved? I had my doubts, but hoped for the best.

I held Courtney's hand and whispered, "Wait and see. This could be a good thing."

After opening the meeting, the Brownie leader suggested the girls draw pictures. Courtney was always engrossed when she had a crayon in hand, and she happily joined in. The pictures she drew were unique: fairy-tale figures with expressive faces, bloody battles with body parts piled high or limbless people dripping blood from sword-fights, dancers in glamorous outfits, movie stars and queens with jeweled crowns.

She drew one of her more startling pictures, with wounded bodies in pools of blood and birdlike elves hovering in trees. When the girls finished, the troop leader announced a contest. Each girl would hold up her artwork, and the one receiving the loudest applause would win. Courtney gave me a desperate look, and I knew we were headed for disaster.

"Do you want to go?" I asked.

"Please, Mommy."

Her face relaxed as I took her hand and led her out.

Frank and I decided to stop seeing therapists for a while. Courtney was unusually bright, we decided, and smart children were difficult to raise. She would be fine as long she knew she was loved by a secure family.

Yet a distance between Frank and me had begun to grow. Sometimes I would look at him and wonder what we ever had in common. I began to daydream about Mickey Malloy, fantasizing about the perfect life we would have had if we'd stayed together.

But Frank and I refused to acknowledge our problems. Instead, we focused even more attention on our family. We surrounded our children with folk music, art, and the antiwar, antiracist politics we believed in. We read books on parenting and education, and one day Frank showed me an article about adopting multiracial children.

"Maybe we should consider adopting a boy," I said.

"It would make our family complete," Frank agreed.

Adopting a child seemed like a perfect way to give something back to the world by doing what we loved—raising a family. I also felt like it was my duty, since I had been adopted. And, beneath all these good reasons, both Frank and I secretly hoped that this child would be a shared vision, something to reinvigorate our faltering marriage. We completed the application process, and were told it would be a two-year wait to receive our child.

That summer, we took the children to Skinner's Butte, one of Eugene's oldest parks. As we settled in for our picnic, I glanced over at a man who was sitting on a blanket nearby. With his deep tan and blond hair, he had the look of a surfer.

"Hello," I called over, smiling.

"I'm admiring what a beautiful family you have," he called back.

As if on cue, Frank began to take pictures of the girls and me.

After a few minutes, the man came over and asked, "Would you like me to take a photo of all of you?"

"Yes, thanks," Frank said, handing him the camera and joining me.

The photograph, still in an album, shows the sun catching Frank's wire-rimmed spectacles. He is wearing a denim shirt, one arm around me and holding Jaimee with the other. Wearing a cotton top from India and faded blue jeans, I lean into him, my long hair pinned in a blue kerchief. My smile looks strained. Three-and-a-half-year-old Nicole, bare-chested, grins, and I have a hand on her little shoulder. Courtney, six, is laughing in a blue bikini swimsuit and pigtails; she leans between the two of us, her hand holding Nicole's.

Later that day, as we strolled through the small zoo located in the park, we came upon a large brown bear in a tiny cage. He paced constantly. His concrete platform was too small for exercise, and there was nothing for him to play with. We watched, saddened by his distress. "Do something, Mommy," Courtney begged. That night, we wrote an outraged letter to the editor of the local newspaper.

Courtney asked, "Will they help the bear be happy, Mama?"

"We'll see," I told her. "Sometimes people listen."

The next week, our letter was published in the *Eugene Register Guard,* and a few days later, the city council announced they were transferring the bear to a zoo where he would have lots of trees and other bears to live with.

Courtney was elated; she carried the article around with her for days. Watching her response reminded me of what an enigma she remained to me. Ever since she was two and watched the puppy scream without awareness of his pain, I noticed that often she didn't understand when people were in distress, nor did she feel sorry when she caused it, like when she teased or hurt her sisters or me. But other times, as with the caged bear, it was as if she took the creature's misery into herself, unable to rest until it was alleviated.

But if we had won a small victory with Courtney's bear, Frank and I were slowly losing our battle to keep our marriage together. We had begun fighting, at first over small things, but soon about our larger differences. He was angry about how much time I spent with my friends. I used to love his willingness to take charge, and the security he offered, but it was beginning to feel stifling. Though we would sleep together every night, our bodies would not touch, as if an invisible line divided the bed.

We were in the middle of a nasty argument one day when the phone rang. It was the social worker from the adoption agency we had applied to six months earlier.

"I have wonderful news," she said. "We have a child much earlier than we thought—a three-year-old boy from Tennessee."

"Oh . . . umm," I stammered. "We were thinking it would be good to have longer to get ready. Didn't you say two years?"

"Yes, but this just came up. He has been with a foster mother since he was born. She is in her seventies and has just had a stroke," she said.

I motioned to Frank to come over and wrote down what was happening on a nearby pad of paper.

He shook his head no, and I agreed; this was not the time for us to bring another child into our family.

"We just aren't ready," I said.

"But you are the perfect fit for him," she said. "He'll have to go into the foster care system if you don't take him now. And he is such a sweet boy, I'd hate for that to happen."

"But aren't there any other families who could take him?" I asked.

"There's nowhere else for him to go," she said.

A month later, a social worker brought a handsome, quiet boy, not yet three, to our house. Our new son, Joshua, had Norwegian, African American, and Cherokee bloodlines. He was beautiful and had a gentle air. As we clamored around him, Joshua spoke little, just watched everyone with his huge green eyes. The girls took to him immediately, and they quickly became a foursome, tromping around the house.

LOUELLA CAME TO visit us at the end of summer. When she opened her neatly packed suitcase, I peeked in at the contents: clothes, gifts for the children, two bottles of Chivas Regal, a package of vitamins, and a copy of *Let's Eat Right to Keep Fit*.

"Oh, dear. I didn't want you to see," she said.

"I can understand why," I said. "That's a lot of liquor."

"Oh, no. It's not the Scotch. It's the other stuff. I'm afraid Morton Henry is going to find out I'm taking those pills."

"That's ridiculous," I said, shaking my head.

"It certainly isn't. Doctor would be furious if he knew I was taking vitamins. He says they're just like snake oil."

"Why do you still go to him anyway? You shouldn't be afraid to tell your doctor you're trying something new."

"He's known us our whole lives. I can't change doctors at this age. I'd be too embarrassed." She turned away.

The children were playing in the living room and she offered to read them a story. They clambered up around her: Courtney sat on one side, Nicole on the other, Jaimee curled up in her lap, and Joshua watching her from a nearby beanbag chair. As usual, she delighted in them and was quick to express affection, rearrange a hair ribbon, or retie a shoelace. She smiled so much when she was with them that I barely recognized her. They were her real grandchildren, I realized. The line between adoptive and blood relatives had somehow been erased.

As she was packing to leave several days later, she poured herself a small glass of Scotch. "It helps my nerves on those damn planes," she said. "Besides, you don't know how alone I am without him."

"I know it's hard," I said. "But you always complained that Jack would never go anywhere. Now you can see the entire world; you just need to find people to travel with."

She shrugged, and I tried to ignore how frail she seemed.

SHE TOOK MY suggestion, and by fall, she'd signed up for a cruise to the exotic ports of Asia with two friends of hers. I was impressed by her chutzpah—she was determined to see the world, she said. I left the kids with Frank for a weekend to help her shop for travel clothes. But when I arrived in San Francisco, I was taken aback: she looked even more gaunt than I'd remembered. I noticed her hands were shaking. Worried, I pleaded with her to see a different doctor.

"I've lived a long life, and you have to stop telling me what to do. I've never interfered in your life, although I could have said plenty about the decisions you made," she replied tartly. She was right about that.

Two months later, on the day she was to set sail, I went to see her off in San Francisco. I took a cab from the airport to her place on Taylor Street. The wind was fierce in the city that January morning in 1972, and my cotton voile dress from India was no protection against the cold, even with the thick Mexican sweater I wore over it. Shivering, I jumped out of the cab, my long hair blowing into my face, and pressed on the bell to her home. When she didn't answer her doorbell, I found the manager. He unlocked the door and we found her lying slumped on the floor, barely breathing.

I called an ambulance. When it arrived, I climbed in and sat next to her as it shrieked its way through the city streets toward the hospital. The contrast between us would have been startling to a stranger: me in a skimpy hippie dress, my loose hair down my back, she in impeccable blue tweed, her hair still perfectly coiffed.

I knew she was dying. I reached to hold her small cold hand in mine as I whispered in her ear. "No matter how hard it's been between us, you've always been there for me. You've never stopped trying to make it work. I want you to know how much I love you."

Her eyes fluttered a little, some color came back into her face, and her arm began to warm. Faintly, she squeezed my hand. A few minutes later, she died.

The next day, I went to the Williams Funeral Home. A stiff-looking man in a brown suit sat with me as I chose a mahogany casket, assuring me that it had a soft mattress and wouldn't corrode. I ordered rolls of pale pink satin sheets for her to lie on and asked if the casket was top of the line.

"An elegant choice," he said. "She will be comfortable there."

As bizarre as the conversation was, a part of me took comfort in the fact that the casket wouldn't rust, and that Louella would have been pleased by the color of the sheets.

"Do you mind if I ask your age?" the mortician asked.

"I'm twenty-seven. Why do you ask?" I answered.

"I remember your father died just over a year ago," he said. "How tragic for you."

I could feel a sob rising in my chest, but I pushed it down. I had to move ahead, not look back.

I bit my lip and asked about the bill.

The morning of the wake, I went back to the mortuary, feeling the need to see Louella in private. A man let me in. I walked up to the open casket with its mounds of satin and saw her body, which looked like a mannequin. I touched her face. It was cold and stiff.

She was gone. Once I knew she was not trapped inside her corpse, I felt relief. I would no longer have to think of her every day, wondering who she would talk to, imagining her loneliness, thinking of her shrunken figure in the window the day we left for Oregon.

I remembered that interlude of triumph when Jack gave her the fur coat with hundred-dollar bills filling the pockets. For that one moment, everything had seemed right in our family. Tears came to my eyes, and I blinked them away. I was glad she did not know how my marriage with Frank was crumbling, and that I spent more of my nights worrying about Courtney than I did sleeping in peace.

About fifty people came to her service, including Sugar Spinoza, her husband, Woody, and Uncle Harry. Even the Willards showed up. Florence cried and Dr. Willard coughed into his handkerchief, and then quickly wiped his eyes.

After the funeral, we went to Louella's house. Passing through her walk-in closet on the way to the bathroom, I found myself standing among her clothes, crying. I kept smelling her silk suits and blouses, and it was as though she was in the room with me.

Our life together had begun with such estrangement. Little felt natural between us when I was growing up, and we both struggled to understand each other. For years, I had assumed my being adopted was to blame. But now, being a mother myself, I had experienced firsthand the feelings of incompetence that come with the territory. I appreciated anew how Louella must have felt with a daughter who seemed so completely unlike her, how difficult it must have been for her. But she never stopped trying to understand me and make our relationship work.

I stood there for several minutes, touching the fabrics and textures she loved, missing her with every bone in my body. Then I splashed cold water on my face and returned to the living room.

That night, I gave many of Louella's things to people who had loved her: fur coats, jewels, even her car. It felt good to give them away, because I knew she would have wanted it. She was unflinchingly generous, always.

When everyone else had left, Kate and I sat down for a glass of wine.

"Do you think you'll look for your birth mother now?" she surprised me by asking.

"Never," I answered with certainty. "It took Louella and me almost twenty-eight years to make our peace. Another mother is the last thing I want in my life."

CHAPTER 22

When Louella died, I was given a sizeable inheritance. My first feeling, when I was informed, was sadness. For me it represented Jack and Louella's unlived life—the adventures they never had, their denial of little pleasures—and their endless worrying about finances. I remembered Jack's daily ritual of reading the stock quotes at the table, his brow furrowed. Having grown up with little money and lived through the Depression, they were always afraid their wealth would vanish.

But my deeper feeling was guilt. It didn't feel rightfully mine, in the same way I never felt like I belonged to Jack and Louella. So I mostly tried not to think about the inheritance. I gave a lot of it away to charities and to their friends and relatives. The biggest purchase I made was a home in Marcola, a town fifteen miles east of Eugene. The white Colonial house looked out over the Mohawk River, and had a swimming pool edged in Mexican tile.

But on the day before we moved in, I walked around the empty house and suddenly burst into tears. The place felt like an empty shell. It reminded me of how my marriage felt—beautiful on the out-side, but lifeless within.

Frank and I decided to see a marriage therapist, a man our age named William, who had hazel eyes and a full ginger-colored beard.

"What brings you to counseling?" he asked, looking at Frank.

Frank looked over at me. "I want her to appreciate me more. She's so distracted by the kids, the classes she's taking at school, her friends. I'm last on her list."

"When do you think this started?" William asked.

"It began a few years ago, about a year after we were married. First her best friend, Judy, died, then both her parents, all within three years. Those deaths have changed her."

William said to me, "Losing both of your parents and your best friend is a lot to deal with. I can't imagine the amount of grief you must feel."

I nodded, but mechanically, willing the words not to sink in. I did everything I could to avoid thinking about all the deaths in my life. Some nights, I'd wake in a panic, sure that I'd lost something, or that something was wrong, trying to make sense of my fear. I'd dart out of bed and look in on the kids, and then wander the house before going back to sleep. But to face my grief would mean to examine who I was without the people I'd lost. And I had no idea.

"It has been hard," I said to William, "but I don't think that has anything to do with this marriage falling apart."

Frank just shook his head. The rest of the session was full of bitter recriminations, and we both felt exhausted and resentful. We drove home in silence.

That night, I was making dinner. The pasta sauce started to burn, and Frank came rushing in. He whisked the pot off the stove.

"Listen, if something's burning, you hold the pan under cool wa-ter, and the burn taste disappears."

"That's it, exactly!" I whirled on him and shouted. "You can't even let me cook dinner. You always have to be in charge—it makes me crazy."

"I can remember a time when you liked my help," he said angrily.

"Well, I don't now. I can hardly breathe around you."

"I can't take much more of this," he sighed. "I'm sleeping in the living room."

"Maybe you should sleep somewhere else permanently."

"Yes, maybe I should!"

That night, he stomped off with a pillow to sleep on the couch. The next day, he left to spend a few weeks in town. We barely looked at each other as he got in the car.

"Daddy's going away to see a friend," we told the kids. "He'll be back soon."

Though it had become increasingly painful to live together, I felt a sense of panic after he left. The thought of raising my kids alone terrified me. To make the situation even more complicated, I received an official letter about finalizing Joshua's adoption. Here I was, in a troubled marriage, with a daughter who occupied much of my attention and two other little girls to care for—and now I was making Joshua a permanent part of this complicated life. He was an easy little boy to love, but he needed security and stability, and my life was falling apart.

At William's urging, I went two nights a week to his therapy group without Frank. One evening, two new members joined our session. I was pleasantly surprised when I recognized one as the handsome surfer who had photographed our family months earlier. We smiled at one another across the room.

"Hi, I'm Mark," he told the group. He explained that he was joining because his marriage had broken up, and he wanted to understand why.

"The same thing is happening to me," I said to him after the session as we were collecting our coats.

He looked at me with surprise. "You seemed the ideal family that day in the park."

"We got good at looking that way," I said with a wry smile. "Only the picture wasn't real."

We ended up standing there for a long time, talking about our marriages.

"I still don't know what went wrong," he admitted. "One moment we were in love, traveling across Europe, and the next minute we were fighting all the time."

"Yeah—once the fighting starts, it's like the dam bursts, isn't it? You can't have a conversation without arguing."

"Exactly," he said, nodding. "I found myself turning into someone I don't even recognize."

After we parted, I kept thinking about how open he seemed, how he didn't judge me the way Frank did.

The next week, we stayed after the session again.

"I appreciate your talking to me about this," he said. "My friends and I don't talk a lot about this sort of thing."

"I know what you mean," I said. "I can talk with my girlfriends some, but it's hard to understand something if you're not going through it yourself."

He smiled. Then he hesitated, as if he wanted to say something.

"What?" I asked.

"Well, I heard you say you were interested in having more adventures. Some friends and I are going to float down the Salmon River in Idaho in two weeks. There's an extra spot in the boat."

"Thanks for the invitation, but I'm frightened of the outdoors," I admitted. "Once it gets dark, I imagine hungry bears and biting vipers waiting just for me."

He laughed. "Well, I'm an Outward Bound instructor—I'll take care of you. Besides, you talked in group about wanting to learn more about yourself. This is the best way I know."

I was intrigued. Maybe it was time to conquer some of my fears. I said I'd think about it. Then, as I was leaving, I turned back to him and said, "You know I'm still married."

"Hey—me too. I'm just looking for a friend."

A few days later, Frank came by to visit the kids. I told him about the river trip with Mark.

"Who is this man?" he asked, with more irritation than jealousy.

"He's just a friend, going through similar problems. There's nothing between us," I said.

"Well, do what you need to do. Maybe you can figure out what you want on the trip," Frank said, and agreed to stay with the children.

I had never been away from my children for so long, and as the day of departure neared, my anxiety grew. The morning of the trip, I called Beth. She had just moved to Eugene, and I talked to her about everything. "I'm worried about leaving them. I think I'll have to cancel."

"You'll never be free if you think like that," she said.

"Sometimes I wonder what we're all trying to get free *of*," I answered.

"Free from whatever held our parents in check. Free from being dead while we're alive. If you don't go, you may miss a once-in-a-lifetime chance."

AND SO THAT day I found myself in a Volkswagen van, headed for Idaho. As we drove across Oregon, John Denver sang on the tape player, and Mark and his friends told humorous, thrilling stories about wilderness trips they'd taken. I felt lighter than I had in years.

The first night, Mark showed me how to set up a tent, and he pitched his alongside mine. In the morning, I woke to the smells of bacon, pancakes, and coffee. After breakfast, we climbed into the rubber rafts and drifted downriver. The rapids were terrifying and exhilarating; after we navigated each one, we let out great whoops of joy and relief. In the afternoon, we were floating serenely along when Mark grabbed my arm. "Look up there," he said quietly, pointing to a tree branch above us. Perched on it was a golden eagle.

We spent three serene days floating on the river. On the fourth day, we came upon an overturned kayak on the river's edge. Its occupant was alive, but badly hurt. After administering first aid, Mark volunteered to go find help. He showed us a place to carry the hurt kayaker and wait for an emergency team. As he began climbing out of the canyon, he suddenly spun around.

"My God, there's a den of rattlers up here," he shouted, and swiftly changed direction. As he disappeared over the crest, his friends talked about what a hero he was.

In the evening, a helicopter arrived to rescue the hurt man and drop Mark back to rejoin us, as we cheered. He is truly an adventurer, I told myself. I'm lucky to have him for a friend.

BY THE TIME I got back to Marcola, Frank was packing his things.

"I can't go through with this," he told me. "I can't be here and have you go off with someone else, and then do the same thing myself. It's over."

I was troubled at our family breaking apart, but I knew he was right. Together, we gathered the children and explained that he was moving out. They watched, tearful, as he packed his Volvo.

"Don't worry," we said, trying to soothe them. "We're both still here for you."

That night, I let all four children sleep with me. As I lay awake, my elation about my new freedom slowly turned to fear. I was alone in the world with four kids. They were devastated, and I didn't know how I could comfort them. And what would I do with my life now?

My marriage with Frank had given me a sense of structure that had now collapsed. I had loved my courses at the University of Oregon, but my most recent classes—biology and semantics—were disasters. I couldn't understand what the teachers were saying, and I kept failing tests. It was like high school all over again.

In those first weeks after Frank left, each night brought a primal kind of fear. I put the kids to sleep and crept into my bed. *I'm protected*, I would say to myself. *Nothing can get me here*. But I didn't believe it.

One night I was roused from sleep, certain I'd heard a sound. A rustling of trees? Footsteps? I had trouble breathing, as if a cement block were sitting on my chest. My heart pounded. Maybe this was the way people felt when they were dying. I didn't know how to help myself. So I called 911.

"I just heard someone trying to get in the front door," I said, telling myself it wasn't a lie. The operator kept me on the line until a patrol car reached the house. The instant I saw the flashing red lights, my breathing returned to normal. I threw on a bathrobe and ran to the door. I barely noticed what the officer looked like, but was reassured by his uniform and badge. I made coffee as he walked around the house and looked for footprints. The sound I had heard was probably a raccoon, he assured me, but he promised to "keep an eye on me."

I woke up feeling embarrassed and childish.

But the next night, my dreams were worse than ever, with ghosts dressed in St. Elizabeth's hospital gowns. They whistled around the room, shrieked, flew at me with batlike wings. It was only when I let my kids sleep with me that the ghosts stayed away.

My kids needed comfort even more than I did. My bright little Nicole grew stoic and quiet, and I could tell how much she missed her father. Joshua, who had recently begun to emerge from his shell, retreated back into himself. Only two-year-old Jaimee continued to be bubbly, and I held her a lot, hoping her good cheer would rub off on me.

Courtney's troubles with sleep only increased when Frank moved out. Once I turned her light out, she turned it back on or read under the blankets with a flashlight. Many nights I found her getting food in the kitchen, or watching television at midnight, or going into one of her siblings' rooms to climb into bed with them. As a result, she was exhausted and irritable all day. She slammed doors and cast fiery glances at her siblings and me.

One morning I went to wake her. "We have to get to school," I said. "You're going to be late."

"I can't, I just can't," she muttered, burying herself deeper under the covers.

"Maybe if you didn't roam the house all night, you could get up in the mornings. Now, get up!"

"Mommy, it is not my fault! I try to sleep, and I just can't. I'm too tired."

I stood in the doorway, studying the outline of her slight eight-year-old body. She was so worn-out and distraught—I wanted to climb in beside her and hold on tight. I felt desperate to make her life better. I thought about all the counselors I had taken her to see. I had been told that I was too sweet, too cold, overly rigid, overly loose. No response to her was ever right.

And so I backed away, from her bedroom and from the fight it would take to get her up.

I buckled the kids into the car and drove them to Montessori. When I returned, I glanced at the photographs hanging in the hall. One showed Courtney not even a year old, with me next to her. She was dressed in pink pajamas, holding a baby doll in a pink dress, and I was beaming at her.

Another picture showed Courtney with a look of pure concentration as she colored in her coloring book, her chestnut hair cascading over her shoulders. Jaimee sat next to her, her hair full of Courtney's barrettes. I thought of the elaborate tea party Courtney had recently created for her siblings, the way she poured make-believe tea and patted their mouths with a pretend napkin. So much love ran between them.

I tiptoed to Courtney's room. She was sleeping peacefully. I felt the familiar urge: *I have to find a way to help her. There must be a way to focus that energy.* Then I thought that ever since she was five, she had begged me to buy her a piano. Now she was eight and we had a house big enough for one.

I woke her and told her my idea.

"Oh yes, yes, that's just what I want." She clapped her hands.

We drove to a music store in Eugene, where we spotted a used walnut Baldwin upright.

"This one!" she said, placing her hand on its smooth side.

The day the piano arrived, all of us watched as two men carried it into the house. As soon as they set it down, Courtney began to bang on the keys.

"It's very loud," I said.

"It sounds good to me," she answered.

"Courtney, you're pounding on it."

"This is how I like it."

After one week of ceaseless banging, I called Beth to vent my frustration.

"Well, maybe she hears something you don't," she said. "Remember how our parents hated rock and roll."

I found someone up the road to teach her: a nervous, retired schoolteacher with a tight perm. Courtney hated her on sight, refused to go back, and pounded harder. The piano sat in the center of the house, and I asked her to limit her playing to an hour a day.

"It's my piano," she answered and went on banging.

I issued an ultimatum. Either she took lessons and learned to play the instrument properly, or else she would have to give it up.

"You hate me!" she cried.

For days, we were at war. She tormented her sisters and refused to take a shower. She left dirty dishes, clothes, and books strewn throughout the house. I covered the piano with a sheet and said she couldn't touch it until she took lessons. She carved letters and strange shapes into the wood. Desperate, I called Goodwill Industries. This time, only I watched as a couple of men took the piano away.

Later, I remembered how I had felt when Jack and Louella took my dog away. I had believed "real parents" would never do such a thing. Now I was a real parent doing the same—maybe worse. I felt compassion for them, but I remembered my feelings of betrayal, and knew I had failed Courtney.

Guilt was filling my life—over Courtney's alarming behavior, my impending divorce, and my inability to give my adopted son the attention he needed.

"I have to find something to pull me out of this," I said to my therapy group the next day. "My life isn't working. My kids are unhappy, and I've lost touch with who I am. I need to make a new start, somehow."

CHAPTER 23

A few days later, Mark came over with a bag of organic oranges and a dog-eared copy of *The Whole Earth Catalogue*. Though we were still calling each other "friend," our friendship was evolving into something more. Mark represented everything I didn't get from Frank: while Frank had increasingly wanted middle-class stability, Mark wanted adventure. He had dropped out of college because his father wouldn't support his decision to be an art major, and now he made money doing odd jobs as a carpenter and teaching outdoor courses. In his spare time, he read books on nature and spirituality. He said to me once, "I don't want to do things because someone tells me to. I want to find my own way." He loved making things himself, and was always engaged in ten different projects at once. We often took hikes in the woods with the kids, and he taught us the names of trees and birds. I admired his combination of practicality and restless dreaming.

That day, we pored over *The Whole Earth Catalogue*, reading articles on how to build a house, plant a garden, raise pigs and goats, and educate children. The last item was most exciting to me—I'd been reading about free schools lately, thinking about Courtney's problems. I brought out A. S. Neill's *Summerhill School, A New View of Childhood* and read Mark a quote I had underlined:

> The function of the child is to live his own life—not the life that his anxious parents think he should live, nor a life according to the purpose of the educator who thinks he knows best. All this interference and guidance on the part of adults only produces a generation of robots.

"I wish someone had told that to my parents," Mark said. "I hated school. I ran home from kindergarten every day. Every night my father beat me for it, but the next day the same thing would happen."

I nodded. " 'Try harder, you can do better.' If I hear those words again, I'll scream. If only I'd gone to a school like the one in *Summerhill*. I'd love to send my kids to a school like that."

Each page in *The Whole Earth Catalogue* spoke of a new kind of life, one we both had dreamed about. Then Mark read me one of the classifieds in the back:

> We are two friends in Nelson, the creative center of New Zealand, who are keen to see to it that our children receive the sort of education envisioned by people like A. S. Neill, founder of Summerhill. We seek like-minded people to join us in building a free school for children in the most beautiful country in the world. If you share our philosophy and believe in community life, please write or call.
> —Rebecca Sawyer and Tim Barraud

"I don't even know where New Zealand is," I admitted.

"I've been reading about it for years," he said. "It's near Australia. One end of the country is covered in snow and glaciers. The other end is warm enough to grow oranges."

"It sounds magical," I said, intrigued.

"The Maoris call it *Aotearoa,* the land of long white clouds," he said. "People say it's one of the last unspoiled places."

Later, I found New Zealand on a globe, and ran my finger over the two islands. Everyone I knew, it seemed, was leaving America, hoping to find a better life abroad. I began to imagine a new adventure: a shared life in a valley with orange trees, sheep, grassy meadows, and a Summerhill school for the children.

By the end of the month, Mark was spending most nights with me. This must be love, I thought, and I viewed him as a hero who could rescue me from my shipwrecked life. With him, I felt a new sense of purpose, like my life was headed in the right direction.

It didn't occur to me that I had felt the same with Frank and even Hank. No matter how much I talked back, spouted self-knowledge, and read books about women's liberation, I lived in a Sleeping Beauty fantasy, waiting for the right prince to wake me with his kiss. The fact that Mark and I had met in a therapy group for people in failing relationships was not something I allowed myself to acknowledge.

IN SEPTEMBER, COURTNEY started at the local school near our house. She had outgrown her Montessori school, which was only for students below third grade. I was anxious about sending her to public school, but hoped it would help her make friends. But she hated it from the first day.

I urged her to keep an open mind. "It's hard to start over, Courtney. But give it your best shot, okay?"

Every day her protests grew stronger. No one would talk to her, she said.

When I went to talk with her teacher, she told me Courtney was provocative, and would say the very things she knew would make her classmates turn against her.

"They're so mean to me, Mommy. Everybody hates me. Don't make me go back."

After some searching, I found her a private school in Eugene, which emphasized outdoor experience and espoused some of the *Summerhill* school's beliefs. For the first time since she was in Montessori, she went to school every day without a fight. One day, her teacher stopped me as I was picking her up.

"You have a wonderful daughter," she said. "She's smart and funny, and her artistic ability is over the moon. She doesn't miss a thing."

"I know just what you mean," I said, elated to hear a teacher praise my daughter.

There were so many ways Courtney reminded me of myself as a kid. She was never without a book. She was insatiably curious about the world around her, and she loved to make up imaginative stories. She was scattered, and found it hard to concentrate on one thing at a time, making school as hard for her as it had been for me. And she was very funny, tossing off witty comments without a second thought. But she was also different from me in ways I couldn't understand—and no one I spoke with, no teacher, doctor, or therapist, could help me make sense of her difficulties.

I had relied on my friends to get me through hard times: they were like my family, and Kate and Beth were still a regular part of my life. Courtney, on the other hand, alienated her classmates. She lived in her imagination in an all-consuming way, unable or unwilling to tell the difference between reality and fantasy. And while I had always had a temper, I had learned early how to control it. My daughter's rages, by contrast, were out of control, terrifying, and utterly irrational, as though she had no internal compass that let her know when she had gone too far.

What scared me most, though, was her constant preoccupation with death.

One afternoon, she walked by me to the freezer to get a Fudgsicle. She had just had one—her mouth was ringed with chocolate—and I stopped her. "No, Courtney, not until after supper," I said. She ignored me and opened the freezer door, pulling one out.

"I said you can't have it," I said. "Give it to me."

She shrugged her shoulders and started eating the Fudgsicle. I grabbed it from her and threw it in the trash.

"Didn't you hear me say no?" I asked.

She began to wail, crumpling onto the floor. Then she looked up at me, her face streaked with tears. "You hate me," she spat out. "You wish I was dead."

"Courtney, that's an awful thing to say!" I bent down and put my arm around her.

"Don't touch me!" she screamed. "I wish I was *DEAD!* I want to *DIE! I HATE YOU!*"

"Stop saying that!" I said, shaking her until she quieted down. Then she ran off to her room, slamming the door.

"PLEASE, TELL ME something, *anything* I can do," I said to William later that week.

"Linda, you've taken her to a series of psychiatrists, psychologists, and counselors. Your pediatrician even tested her for diabetes and epilepsy. What else is there to do? You haven't gotten one clear diagnosis."

"I don't believe she can't be helped," I said. "Maybe her troubles are spiritual."

"What do you mean?"

"When I was studying Asian philosophy, I read about 'old souls,' people born with great promise, but with many obstacles to overcome," I said. "She has her own kind of wisdom. In some ways she knows more than her years." I knew it sounded grandiose, but it felt possible.

"Well, even if you're right, there isn't much you can do to help her," William pointed out. "She'll have to find her own way. If you want to make a difference now, then look into Nicole's eyes. She's terrified of something, and I suspect it is her sister. Nicole is one child you can help."

That knocked the wind out of me. I'd never thought of Nicole as troubled. She seemed such a happy child, social, energetic, full of enthusiasm. But what William said was undeniably true: lately, Nicole was quieter, and seemed tense whenever Courtney was around. I realized all the time I devoted to Courtney made me less aware of my other kids, less focused on their needs. Courtney's behavior was not just self-destructive—it was harmful to her siblings, too. I was furious at myself for not seeing all of this before. And, deep down, I was furious at Courtney as well.

When I walked in the door that evening, Nicole ran up to me in tears. Courtney sat on the couch, her face impassive.

"Mommy, Courtney says I'm not your real daughter."

"What?"

"She says you adopted me because you felt sorry for me. She said I was born retarded. Is it true, Mommy? Am I really a *mongoloid*?"

Nicole's story made all my pent-up anger rise to the surface. I was fed up with the constant battles with Courtney. Her blaming me because she couldn't make friends at school. Her insistence that if I said no, it meant I hated her. Her awful moods and ferocious rages. Her sabotage of my time and energy. And now, the cruelty of the story she had told Nicole.

"Courtney, how dare you? Don't you ever talk to your sister like that again. I've had it with you. You are way out of line."

Courtney's eyes shone with wrath. But she spoke with an unnerving coolness. "You will pay for that, Mother," she said.

As she walked away, I realized that I was afraid of her. I had no idea where she would stop.

Later that night, I was reading a bedtime story to the younger children when I smelled smoke. I dropped *Alexander and the Wind-up Mouse* and ran upstairs. The smoke was coming from Courtney's room. I rushed to her door, but it was locked.

"Courtney!" I said. "You have to open this door."

"Why should I?" she yelled.

"Something's burning, that's why. You either let me in, or I'll break down the door."

"Why do you hate me?"

"Courtney, I am going to count to three, and if the door isn't open by then, I'm going to break it down."

The door swung open. On the floor, I saw my old prayer book, the St. Joseph Daily Missal, ripped apart. Smoke was rising from one of Louella's antique Royal Doulton serving bowls, where charred pages from the missal lay alongside torn bits of Holy Cards I had saved. The cards had messages scrawled on the back from Judy and Sister Caroline. They were among my most precious objects, and Courtney had loved playing with them.

"I can't believe you would do this!" I shrieked.

"Believe what you see," she said defiantly, her arms crossed.

I tossed the burnt bits into the toilet. As I flushed away the last emblems of my life as a Catholic schoolgirl, I saw clearly that my beautiful, clever eight-year-old daughter was also the glowering spirit who stood before me. Her two sides were indivisible.

I also saw something else, with a rising sense of dread. Though I'd had to deal with Courtney's anger before, I had never been its direct target. Now, in Courtney's unapologetic smirk, I saw a whole new set of battles beginning. Instead of being her sole advocate, she was beginning to see me as her main antagonist.

IN THE FALL, Frank and I finalized our divorce. He had stayed very involved with the kids' lives, taking them all out for ice cream, movies, and weekend visits. But when we saw each other, we ended up blaming each other for the failure of the marriage.

My relationship with Mark, meanwhile, kept growing.

"What I love about being with you, Linda," he said one day, putting his long arm around me, "is that we're both chasing the same dream." I agreed with him. We seemed like travelers about to begin an exciting journey together. We just had to find the right path.

One night, I asked Mark, "Do you ever think about living somewhere else?"

"All the time," he said.

"America gets more dangerous every year," I said. "I want my kids to live in a place that feels safe."

"Well, I think we could find that in New Zealand." We sat in silence for a minute.

"I have money," I said. "We could do this, if we wanted to."

"We'd find a spot just as beautiful as the places we saw in Idaho, only safer," he said, smiling at me. "I could build a wonderful house and help you raise the kids in clean air."

We sat for a long time, talking it over. We could buy a farm, and the kids would grow up in a healthier, happier place. A new start was just what we all needed, especially Courtney. By the end of the evening, we decided to visit the country, to see if living there was feasible.

I wrote to Rebecca and Tim, who had placed the appealing ad in *The Whole Earth Catalogue,* and asked if we might visit them in Nelson. Rebecca wrote back swiftly, saying that Tim and his wife were overseas, but we should stay with her. Impressed at her warm hospitality, we booked our trip. Frank agreed to care for the children for two weeks while Mark and I were gone. It was my first journey overseas.

AS OUR PLANE descended into Auckland, I gazed out the window with amazement. The land was a shade of green different from any I had ever seen: deeper, richer, more lush. Everything I saw confirmed my sense that this was the right place for us.

There was little to fear here: no reports of police brutality, few criminal acts, not even rattlesnakes to worry about. The newspapers seemed to be filled with only good news. We visited the glaciated peaks of the South Island, drove over rolling farmland dotted with sheep, and swam at long, sandy beaches. But it was Nelson, a sunny town on the northern tip of the South Island, that won our hearts. Nelson was filled with young people of many cultures searching to find new meaning in life. They formed co-ops, and artisans thrived, selling their pottery, jewelry, and paintings. A local bookstore owner opened his bookstore on Friday nights to discussion groups. Here the locals debated hotly, inviting the mayor and other local dignitaries to participate. "Alternative" was the word on everyone's lips. All the people we met were interested in counteracting whatever seemed life-denying and corrupt.

There we met Rebecca, whose easy warmth drew us to her. She brought us to the Chez Elco, a wonderful little restaurant filled with local art and rows of homemade pastries.

"Most people eat with their families here," she explained when I asked why there were so few restaurants in town. "Kiwis believe in strong family ties, and in doing things ourselves."

"That's what's drawing us here," I said. "I hate the values my kids are learning in America."

There was only one catch: to become residents of New Zealand, we would need to get married. "It's just a formality," Mark pointed out. I nodded at him, but I felt uneasy. As we sat in the immigration office before leaving for the States, going over the forms with an official, I kept looking over at Mark. *This will never last,* I thought. We were a pair of adventurers, not true partners. In a flash, I saw another marriage, another divorce. I shuddered.

Mark touched my arm. "What's wrong?" he asked.

I pushed the uneasiness away. This was my chance to live in a new place, in a new way. I no longer had a family to keep me in the States. And Mark and I loved each other; we would find a way to make it work. *It's just nerves,* I told myself.

"Never mind," I said, grabbing Mark's hand. "I got scared for a moment, that's all."

BACK IN OREGON, the Watergate scandal unfolded on the news as we packed up boxes. The scandal made us even more confident about leaving. "This country is bankrupt," Mark said with disgust.

We figured my money would last about five years, enough time for us to develop a self-sustaining life on a farm. Our plan was to travel to Nelson and stay in the local campground while we looked for property. The campground was near the beach, and the children could play there all day.

Frank was upset about the kids moving to another country, and we had several tense talks. But he admitted that it was a great opportunity for them. "And remember, you can visit whenever you want," I told him. It didn't occur to me that taking the children from Frank could harm them. Somehow I'd grown up discounting the importance of fathers. I had mostly tried to avoid Jack, and Louella had been my main parent. And my fantasies about my "real" parents were mostly about my mother.

The excitement of a journey to the other side of the world temporarily countered the apprehension the kids felt about leaving their father behind. We got books from the library on New Zealand, and they all chattered excitedly about their new home.

All, that is, except Courtney.

"Sounds dumb to me," she kept repeating, "dumb dumb dumb."

Since I had taken William's advice and focused more attention on my other children, Courtney's fury had only grown. She heaped open scorn on Mark, and she defied us at every turn. Sometimes she slept all day and was up all night. Other times she didn't sleep at all. She called the trip "torture." She would say, "You hate me—that's why you're making me leave here." No amount of convincing would change the angry expression on her face.

I kept hoping that when Courtney saw New Zealand, her attitude would be transformed. But as the day of our move drew closer, she only seemed angrier and more defiant.

"I don't know what to do," I said to Beth one day. "The idea of living in a campground, with Courtney acting this way, is unbearable."

Beth took a deep breath. "Well, I've been thinking. Why doesn't Courtney stay with me, just until you find a house?"

I was initially resistant. The last thing I wanted was to split up our family more—the whole point of going to New Zealand was for all of us to start over, together. But the more I talked to Beth about it, the better the idea sounded. Courtney loved Beth, she had known her all her life, and if she stayed she could continue to get counseling from William. We would fly her out as soon as we got settled, in just a matter of months.

So I agreed to leave Courtney behind in Oregon.

"I've been saved," Courtney shouted on hearing the news. Her elation seemed to confirm that it was the right thing to do.

Not until she and I were packing up her things, a few days before we left, did she raise any objection.

"Why are you leaving me behind?" she asked abruptly.

"Honey, I thought you wanted this. Do you want to be cooped up in a tiny tent with all of us? This seemed better for you."

"I remind you of my father. That's why you find me so repulsive."

I froze, stunned by this new allegation.

"Courtney, there's not one thing repulsive about you."

She turned away from me, then, with a hardened face and dry eyes. Now I felt like the most wretched mother on earth. No matter how perfect New Zealand would be, I was leaving behind my distressed nine-year-old. What made me feel worse was that I was looking forward to the time away from her.

Nothing I had done for Courtney had made any difference: all the therapists, private schools, and special attention had been dead ends. Standing there in her half-packed bedroom, I told myself that our new life in New Zealand would make up for everything, once she rejoined us.

A FEW DAYS before we left, Mark and I got married by the Mohawk River in Springfield, Oregon. It was a stunningly bright day, and the sun gleamed on the river. The kids played with armfuls of goldenrod that ran along the river's edge. Only Courtney hung back, standing by Beth and sulking as Mark and I exchanged vows. Still, I felt an overwhelming sense of hope. *Maybe I've found the right life*, I thought, rubbing my stomach.

I had just learned, the day before, that I was pregnant with Mark's child.

CHAPTER 24

I n the high summer of December 1973, Mark, Nicole, Jaimee,
Joshua, and I arrived in Nelson, where we moved into the campground. We met people in the community kitchen at the campground and quickly felt welcomed by our new friend, Rebecca.

Rebecca was the kind of fiery person I liked best. She had a nurturing nature, but if one of her beloved causes—apartheid, the plight
of the Maoris, discrimination against women—was challenged, her
warm commiseration transformed into an articulate, scorching re-
buttal. She loved bringing people together, and introduced us to her
closest circle. Cal, her partner, was an American. Once a student in a
Jesuit seminary, he had lived alone in the Himalayas for a year, studied with a Hawaiian kahuna, and spoke fluent French and Spanish.
He loved to stir up trouble with relentless questions and canny obser-
vations until Rebecca would interject in a no-nonsense tone, "Cal!"
He would apologize then, saying with a smile, "My mother always
told me I went too far."

Tim was a veterinarian who thought of himself as a rational man of
science. Yet I soon found he had other sides: he saw life as a quest for

spiritual truth, and was the first person I met who loved dogs as much as I did. His understated humor revealed itself best around a table of friends, where his dry asides would crack everyone up. His wife, Mary, was beautiful and vivacious, brimming with pleasure over fragrant Indian spices or wildflowers, and she was never more comfortable than when entertaining a room full of kids. She hated confrontation: at its first sign she would exclaim, "Oh dear, oh dear." Yet she had a wicked teasing streak, and delivered her arrows of sarcasm with warm familiarity.

Mark and I weren't interested in communal living, but in a genuine sharing of our lives with others who had the same values. We were amazed to have found such a group so quickly. We had picnics by the Maitai River, canned berries and peaches together, and tramped through the hills with our kids. On Sundays, all of the families shared big meals and talked about ways to teach our children spirituality without churches. By January, we had found a temporary house, white clapboard with a big front porch and hollyhocks growing up the side.

Driving to a nearby town could become an instant adventure, waiting for a farmer to cross the road with large herds of sheep. Shopping for groceries involved going to a vegetable stand, a fruit market, a butcher, and a bakery. Nicole and Jaimee loved being in New Zealand, where the green hills, unpaved roads, and secret hideaways seemed straight out of their children's books. Joshua seemed to enjoy it too, although he was more reserved.

Beneath my joy at finding a community that I loved ran a steady current of guilt about Courtney. When I talked with her on the phone she was unresponsive, answering my questions with monosyllabic retorts. And in the space of just two months, Beth's letters shifted from reassuring to concerned to frantic.

One day, I received a letter that described a phone call from the manager of an adult bookstore, who had discovered Courtney reading pornographic magazines.

Immediately, I phoned.

"God, Linda, things are bad here," Beth said. "I've loved her since she was a baby, but I don't understand who she has become. I was just asked to find her another school."

I groaned inwardly and thanked her for all she had done. The next day I wired Courtney a plane ticket to New Zealand, and braced myself for what would come next.

When she arrived at the Nelson airport a few days later, my worst fears were realized. Courtney made no eye contact, and her expression was knotted and hard. She didn't look like a nine-year-old, and her expressive green eyes seemed empty of everything but resentment. It was as if two years had passed, not two months.

I gave her a hug. "How was your flight?"

"Please spare me your questions," she said. "How do you think it was?"

We drove silently to the house, her body tense with fury. My mind anticipated the familiar cycle again: panic at her pain and rage, then a desperate search for possible solutions. By the time we got home, I had decided to enroll her in the only therapy available, offered by the local hospital.

When I brought her to intake the next day, a counselor met with me privately. "She's obviously a child with difficulties. She should attend our day program here on the grounds."

With some reluctance, I agreed. In the months that followed, the staff offered no diagnosis, except to say that she had a "difficult temperament." By then, Courtney's sleep disorder had become extreme. She was awake for days at a time, and then she would hibernate. Unable to attend school, she spent much of her time walking around like a zombie, either from lack of sleep or from the tranquilizers the doctors had prescribed for insomnia.

"Please send me back to America," she begged. But there was nowhere better for her. And so, once again, Courtney became the center of my life. She lodged accusations against me. I hated her, she would say. I wanted her to be unhappy. When I wasn't trying to appease her, I was resentful and frustrated. I always felt relief when I could steal away to Rebecca's kitchen or go for a walk in the hills.

MARK, MEANWHILE, WAS enthusiastic about building his dream farm. He read about fruit trees and raising sheep, and found work with local carpenters, tearing down and restoring houses in the area. He'd save old windowpanes and solid planes of wood to use in building our home. "We'll have a recycled house," he said one day with a proud grin, showing me a beautiful old door he had salvaged.

And he was unabashedly excited about his first child. He built a wooden crib for the coming baby, and leaned close to my belly each day, listening for any tiny sounds the baby made. Though I was preoccupied by my worries about Courtney, I was as thrilled as he was about the baby's impending arrival.

In march 1974, I gave birth to a baby boy, Elki Michael. He had blue eyes that seemed to dance with delight. Right away, we noticed how alert he was: he loved looking at faces, and would gaze at us for hours, grasping our fingers with his tiny hand.

Jaimee had spent the last few months pushing around a baby doll named Blueie in a toy buggy, practicing, she said, for when her real baby came. When Elki was born, she had no doubt he was all hers. Nicole and Joshua couldn't hold him enough. Only Courtney didn't share our joy: she said he looked mean.

But for once, a powerful presence in our household outweighed Courtney's. The kids were fascinated by everything about the new baby—his sweet smell, his little fingernails and toenails, his happy burbling. And Mark and I felt connected by our infant son. It seemed like all the fantasies we had dreamed up in Oregon about a whole new life had come true, embodied in this exquisite new creation.

"We're the luckiest people alive," I said, kissing the baby's head.

ONE AFTERNOON, I took the baby to the doctor for his three-month checkup. As Dr. Davies listened to the baby's heart, an expression of alarm passed over his face, and I could feel my own heart skip a beat.

"What's wrong?" I asked him.

"I thought I heard a murmur, but it's probably nothing. Let me recheck it." As he listened again, the same look crossed his face.

"You're scaring me," I said. My hands trembled as I reached for Elki.

"I want you to take him to the hospital right away."

I leaned forward in my chair and my legs felt like jelly. "Please tell me what's happening."

He opened a drawer in his desk and pulled out a bottle of brandy. He took out a glass and poured me a drink. "Just have a drop of this."

I couldn't believe a doctor was giving me a drink. I took it and sipped from it, one arm cradling tightly around my son.

"I'm not sure what's wrong," he admitted. "Maybe the doctors at the hospital will know more."

I swiftly gathered our things and rushed to the hospital.

In the children's ward, the nurses made a bed for me beside his crib. Nothing about him seemed that different. He was his usual wide-eyed, gurgling self, and the nurses said he seemed fine. I called Mark, and told him the doctors would be doing some tests on Elki—"nothing to worry about," I said, echoing the nurse who checked his vitals. We'd be home in the morning, I assured him. I laid Elki next to me in my bed, and nursed and cooed to him all night. When the curtain opened the next morning, a nurse scolded me for keeping him in my bed. "It's against the rules," she said disapprovingly. Then she told me it was time to get him ready for tests.

When I woke him to change his diapers, he began to cough. Quickly, his face turned a chalky blue. He started to choke, and I screamed for the nurse.

"My God," she said as she took him from my arms. She rushed from the room, calling, "I need help, now!"

I stood in the hallway, listening as his feeble cry grew distant. Time seemed to stand still. All I could hear, faintly, was my own heart pounding. Then the nurse was standing in front of me again.

"Oh, my dear," she said, her face frozen in shock.

The doctor found me then, looking grim. "Elki," she said, putting her arm on my shoulder gently, "suffered a transposition of the great arteries. It's a congenital heart defect, where the positions of the pulmonary artery and the aorta are reversed. I'm so sorry. There was nothing we could do."

I called Mark, who arrived in what seemed like seconds. I remember only that we held one another in silence for a long time.

BACK HOME, MY life seemed like a strange dream. Our friends filled the house, cooking, watching the kids, trying to comfort us. Mark and I moved about in a daze. I felt afraid to touch down in reality, afraid of what I would have to feel. I ached for Judy's presence. She would have said the one thing that could have helped.

The doctor gave me pills to sleep, but the first night I didn't want to take them. I just lay in bed, thinking about never seeing my son again. Then I thought that wherever Elki was, Judy was there with him. When we were girls, we believed that if we could catch the exact instant when we dropped into our dreams, we would walk with the spirits of the dead and know the secrets of the universe. I thought of my dream of Judy, how I had traveled with her for a moment before she landed on the pavement, her body broken, her spirit free. Falling into sleep, I felt myself suspended for just an instant, like a roller coaster hesitating at the top before it plunges down. In that split second, I imagined I could feel Elki's presence.

I woke up somewhere in the darkest hours of the night, and for a moment, I wondered why he had not cried out for a feeding. Then I remembered he was dead. I hurtled out of bed and looked in on my other children, to make sure they were still breathing. Then I stood by Elki's empty crib. I could still smell his sweet, powdery scent. For a long time, I stayed there, weeping. Finally, I took one of the pills the doctor had prescribed.

A few days later, Elki was buried in a quiet, sad service. Afterward, Mark and I gathered up our traumatized children and packed them into the car. Not knowing exactly where we were headed, we drove along the South Island's west coast toward Queenstown. It had been raining all day—"the sky's crying," Nicole said—and we all stared blankly out the car windows. But slowly, the sun began to peek through the clouds, tiny golden rays beaming onto the green fields.

"Look," Jaimee pointed.

In the distance, a huge rainbow arced across the sky. Then Joshua tugged at my sleeve. "There's another one," he whispered.

"Elki's saying good-bye," Mark said.

IN THE DAYS that followed, my breasts swelled with milk. I kept hearing Elki's cry as they rushed him to surgery. I wept constantly, wondering what would have happened if I had taken him to the doctor a month earlier, searching for clues that I had missed. It was too terrifying to accept that my baby could seem healthy one minute and dead the very next.

I wasn't the only one filled with guilt over Elki's death. Nicole crept up to me one morning in the kitchen, looking distraught. "Mama," she said quietly, "it's my fault. I was holding Elki the night before he died, because you and Mark were fighting in the other room, and he started crying. I got mad and thought, 'I wish he'd never been born.' I made him die with my thought."

"Darling girl," I said, pulling her close, and telling her what I couldn't tell myself, "nobody's to blame. He died because his heart didn't work right."

Jaimee walked around the house clutching her blue-eyed baby doll. "Mommy, I miss our baby," she said one afternoon.

"Me too," I said, and hugged her and Blueie.

Courtney was subdued. Some of it, I knew, was the medicine her psychiatrist had given her, which left her listless and zoned-out. She spent a lot of time in her room, drawing and reading. I was relieved that she wasn't asking for much—I had so little to give.

Joshua withdrew again, hanging out in the shadows. I knew he needed more attention, but I felt flattened by my grief. I could hardly get out of bed each day.

At first Mark and I held each other a lot, clinging to our shared bereavement. But soon, we both retreated into our private sadness. He threw himself even more into his projects. Every day he would leave early to work with friends on old houses, and come home exhausted. We would barely talk as we ate dinner and went to sleep.

ABOUT SIX WEEKS after Elki's death, I dreamt I was confined in an iron lung. When I woke, I could barely breathe. My chest and stomach felt empty and sore. Even brushing my teeth hurt. All the deaths crashed over me at once, like an immense tidal wave: Judy, Jack, Louella, and now my baby boy. I felt as if I were drowning.

For months I felt immobilized. Sometimes I cried, other times I stared at the walls, and for days on end I slept until noon. When I did get up, I walked around rubbing my stomach, as though Elki had been torn right out of my flesh.

Though he didn't know how to comfort me, Mark took over, feeding the kids and getting Courtney to her program and the others to school. "Mommy's just tired," he'd say when one of them would ask where I was. "She's resting right now."

ONE NIGHT I dreamt about the Taj Majal. I stood close enough to see the agate and jasper stones inlaid in white marble.

I told Mark about my dream. "Maybe we should go to India," I said. "Something is calling me there."

He stared at me incredulously. "Linda, nothing's going to bring Elki back. We've got to move on from where we are."

I knew my idea sounded crazy, but I kept longing to see the white marble dome. Fantasizing about traveling there got me out of bed every morning. Though I still felt empty inside, I began picking up the pieces of my old routine—cooking, cleaning, and spending time with the kids.

One afternoon, I ran into Tim as I walked to the local store. He stepped off his bicycle to walk beside me.

"I've been thinking of you so much these past months," he said, his gray-blue eyes full of empathy. "Honestly, tell me how you are."

I didn't know where to start. Instead of talking about Elki, I found myself telling him about the powerful dream I'd had. "I'm obsessed with the idea of going there," I said.

"There's such a different attitude about death and life in the East. There is a recognition that one is part of the other," he said, quietly. "I can understand why your soul is pulled in such a direction."

I looked at him, and thought, *Judy would have said something just like that.*

I realized that my dream was not literal. It was telling me I had to connect my private grief to something larger. I remembered that sense of peace I had felt the first night, thinking of Elki's and Judy's spirits together in another world. For the first time since Elki's death, I felt calm.

"Thank you," I said, grateful for Tim's presence. "That was just what I needed to hear."

We walked the rest of the way to town in contemplative, companionable silence.

CHAPTER 25

The kids all struggled with Elki's death. But Nicole and Jaimee knew how to cheer each other up, checking out piles of library books or playing dress-up from a trunk of fancy gowns and costume jewelry. Courtney would sometimes join them, directing them in plays or making up games. Only Joshua kept to himself. He bit his fingernails to the quick. Seeing how distraught he was, I promised myself I would work harder at making him feel cared for, but I failed at it over and over again.

One day Mark was telling our neighbor his concerns about Joshua. She mentioned that one of her friends from church had several adopted multiracial boys. "You know, I bet they'd love to meet Joshua," our neighbor said.

Mark told me about the idea that evening. We looked over at Joshua, who was curled up on the corner of the sofa, watching the other kids play. We had never imagined how it felt to be a multiracial boy in a white family. It might do him good to have other boys to play with—especially boys who were multiracial too.

Later that night, Mark talked to Joshua. "Listen," he said, "there's a family with lots of little boys on a big farm. Would you like to go and visit them?"

"You mean just me, all by myself?" he said, scratching his cheek with two fingers.

"Yes, just you, Joshua," Mark said.

"Do they go to church?"

Joshua was always asking us if we would take him to church. He talked about men and women dressed in glorious purple robes, clapping and swaying as they sang Gospel music. It was his happiest memory from the three years before he came to us.

"The whole family goes," Mark told him.

"Then that sounds like fun." He smiled a guarded little smile.

Our neighbor called her friends, the Mitchells. They invited him to come on a Saturday. Helen Mitchell was a tall white woman with homemade dresses and brown hair in a bun. She seemed friendly and efficient, and welcomed Joshua into her home with a wide smile. "He'll be just fine," she assured me when I dropped him off. And indeed, all Joshua's shyness seemed to disappear as he scampered off with two of the other boys.

When I picked him up later on, he said he loved playing with the other boys, and the Mitchells were fun. All week, he talked about his visit, and kept asking me when he could go back. I called Helen, who said, "He can come anytime he likes. We love having Joshua. Maybe he could come for a real visit, maybe even a week or two. He fits right in here."

After talking it over with Mark, I agreed to let Joshua spend a week with them. It seemed like a good idea for everyone. I felt relief at having found a place where Joshua felt so comfortable, and guilt that it was not his own home. On the day of his visit, Joshua grew more animated, clearly thrilled to be going back to the Mitchells.

Joshua's visit passed without any word from the Mitchells. Mid-week I called, and Helen assured me everything was fine. Then, on

Sunday morning, I was about to leave to pick Joshua up when Helen called.

"He doesn't want to go back to you," she said.

Her matter-of-fact tone caught me off guard. "But we're on our way to get him," I stammered.

"I have to be honest with you. He says he doesn't feel at home with you. We're more of a family than he's ever known."

Her words stung. I sensed that what she was saying was true. At the same time, I was furious. "What are you saying? I'm not going to just give you my child!"

"Well, we think you'll do what's best for him," she said evenly. "We know you lost a baby and have an older, unmanageable child. Here he has brothers who are also mixed race, he loves our big farm, and we have so much to give him. Why don't you talk to him?"

I heard the phone handed to him.

"Momma Linda, Helen says I can stay here. I don't want to go back there." He began to cry.

"Honey, I won't make you do anything. Let's just think about this." He handed the phone back to Helen, and we said we would speak again later in the week.

I remembered my ambivalence when the final papers came for his adoption, my fears about not having enough to give him. Now, with Elki's death, I had even less to give.

The next morning, I spoke with a social worker in Nelson who knew the Mitchells. "This is a family who has everything to offer him," she said, "while you have so little." With a heavy sigh, I agreed with her, and called the Mitchells to say he could try it for a month.

LATER THAT DAY, Nicole and Jaimee strode into the kitchen together, wearing worried expressions.

"We want to know about Joshua," Nicole said.

"Yes, we do," said Jaimee, her hand on her hip.

I told them what had happened.

"He's my brother! He doesn't belong there!" Nicole shouted.

Jaimee started crying, and I felt my own tears welling up.

"None of us wants to lose Joshua," I said. "But the truth is, he feels more at home with the Mitchells. If that's the family he is meant to be with, we have to accept that. Let's just give him a little time there."

They both nodded, forlornly.

I BEGAN TO wonder if our purpose in adopting Joshua had been to bring him to this family. I remembered daydreaming about being readopted when I felt I didn't fit in with the Risis. The idea that Joshua had found a better home was easier to bear than acknowledging I was losing another child, this time by my own doing. I assuaged my guilt by talking to the social worker, who gave me glowing reports of how easily Joshua fit in with the Mitchells. At the end of the month, she came to our house to talk with Mark and me.

"Well," she said, "he seems to have found a real home there. He never bites his nails, and he's very talkative. He's coming out of his shell. I think the Mitchells are right: he is where he belongs. They'd like to keep him permanently, and I would recommend that."

Mark and I looked at each other and he nodded in agreement. Mark wasn't bonded with Joshua at all; he had little interest in him. The irony of the situation slapped me in the face: here I was, an adopted child, giving up my adopted child to another family. Though I told myself that this was the best thing for Joshua, I knew that this was a monumental failure on my part. But I had no fight left in me to make it any other way.

Resignedly, I agreed to let the Mitchells adopt Joshua, with the stipulation that we would still be able to visit him. "Of course you can," Helen said when I told her my decision. "We know how important you all are to him. We'd never stop you from seeing him."

I packed up Joshua's clothes and toys, and brought them over to the Mitchells. Helen showed me where he was playing in the backyard with his brothers. I was filled with contradictory feelings: happy that he seemed so content, angry at myself for letting this sweet child go, relieved there might be a happy outcome for this situation. I said good-bye quickly and got into my car. As I drove home, all my emotions resolved into one thought: this was the wrong choice. But I kept driving.

THE CRAZINESS OF my life began to feel normal, each day just a breath away from a major drama. With Joshua gone, my worries shifted back to my oldest daughter. The medication the doctors were giving her had made her bleary-eyed and lethargic for months. And I hated that at ten she wasn't getting a solid education.

Our family doctor suggested I talk with Beverly, a retired teacher in our community.

Beverly was a tiny woman, with gray braids piled on her head and blue eyes shining out from wire frames. She was known for her ability to help the most difficult children on the South Island, kids everyone else had given up on. I decided to pay her a visit.

Beverly greeted me warmly and made me a cup of tea. Sitting in her snug cottage, full of old-fashioned furniture and local folk art, we began talking about Courtney. She said she understood the challenges Courtney presented. "But those who present us with difficulties have much to offer," she said, smiling. "Our greatest heroes and heroines were challenged." She held little faith that therapy or most educational systems could nurture these personalities. "It takes a certain kind of care," she continued, "to bring out what they have to of-fer." I nodded. Perhaps she could give Courtney that kind of care, I thought.

The next day, I brought Courtney to Beverly's, and they had a brief conversation about Courtney's favorite books. Beverly asked polite, firm questions, and Courtney gave cautious answers. As I watched them interact, I noticed something promising: Beverly was not at all intimidated by Courtney's sullen temperament and abrupt re-sponses. Instead, she seemed composed, in control of the situation. I was impressed.

Beverly said, "I think we can work together. What do you think, Courtney?" Courtney slowly nodded. Beverly's no-nonsense manner had clearly made Courtney respect her as well. For the first time in years, I felt hopeful about my daughter.

BEVERLY SAID SHE would like Courtney to stay with her dur-ing the week, and with us on weekends. "It's the only way to make a real difference," she urged. I agreed, but felt another pang: our family seemed to be shrinking day by day.

The night before Courtney left, we went out to dinner at the Rutherford, the fanciest hotel in Nelson. Everyone dressed up, and even Courtney was enthusiastic. The restaurant, with its linen table-cloths and carved-ice swan, made a thrilling contrast with our coun-try kitchen. But it was the change in Courtney that got our attention. She took charge of the whole evening, as if on center stage. She was charming and funny, and ordered with certainty as the rest of us looked on, spellbound. We couldn't believe this was the same girl we lived with. I was reminded of what a captivating child she had been. At the end of the evening, the maître d' set the bill down in front of her and said, "It's clear who the star is in this family." I had a moment of searing hope: *Maybe she doesn't have to leave us*, I thought. *Maybe she's getting better on her own.*

But by morning, she was sullen and unresponsive. When I tried to talk to her, she just glared at me. "I can't wait to get out of here," she snapped when Mark asked her how she was doing. She wouldn't hug me good-bye, just darted into the car and locked the door.

When Courtney left, the house got very quiet. We were all faced, in that silence, with all the absences, all the changes that had swept through our lives. The girls comforted each other by playing quietly. Mark continued to be absorbed in his projects for the farm we still hadn't found. After Elki's death, he and I had lost touch. Though we lived in the same house, and still talked about the same dream, something vital between us had turned off. He increasingly felt burdened by all he had taken on by marrying me: moving to a new country, being a stepfather, losing his child. He was growing disillusioned with the life we'd made together.

As for me, I was still grieving for Elki, and now Courtney and Joshua were gone, too. At least I could still see Joshua. The girls and I were missing him a lot. So I called Helen to arrange a visit.

"Oh, he is doing so well," Helen said. "It would just upset him to see you."

"He was a part of our family for three years," I protested. "I can't believe he doesn't miss us."

"Do you think it's in his best interest to get attached to you again when he is fitting so perfectly into our family? He'll just get confused, Linda. Don't make this more difficult."

Without quite knowing what I was doing, I agreed with her. But when I hung up the phone, I crumpled to the ground, sobbing. Joshua had slipped from my grasp. Elki was dead. Courtney was gone. It seemed I could not escape loss: first my birth mother, then Judy and my adoptive parents, now three of my children. *How have*

I made such a mess of things? I wondered, burying my face in my hands.

OUR FAMILY DESPERATELY needed some good news. Then, as if by magic, it appeared. Mark found a farm for sale in a river valley just outside Nelson. There were sixty-seven acres of mixed terrain, including gently sloping paddocks, steep hillsides, and a creek. It was perfect—everything we had dreamed of. We bought it the day we went to see it, and moved into the dark old farmhouse a few weeks later.

On this beautiful homestead, our family slowly came back to life. The girls fell in love with the land, and spent weeks exploring the hills. Mark planted thousands of trees, set up an irrigation system, and fenced the paddocks. Though we continued to argue, his mood had infinitely improved, and he had a hundred projects he was working on all at once.

One day he came home with Tim, announcing that they'd found a hundred Romney sheep, and he was beaming; he'd been looking forward to raising sheep for years. A few days later, the sheep arrived, along with Blackie, a retired, sharp-eyed dog.

When Jaimee got home from school and saw the sheep, she got a very serious look on her face. She went inside and changed into her old Tinkerbell costume. Then she ran outside to the sheep, bestowing "magic dust" on the new baby lambs with her wand. When I asked her what she was doing, she called out, "I'm helping them be blessed."

I began to emerge from my paralyzing depression with the help of my children, the beauty of my surroundings, and my community of friends. Rebecca and Cal were a central force in pulling me out of myself. I spent entire days walking in the valley and cooking beautiful dinners with them. Tim took me into the country with him for a long day of veterinary work, during which he would pull down bulls with ropes to tend their hooves, or spay farm cats on kitchen tables. He and I took meditation classes together, and I listened with fascination to stories of his world travels.

As soon as we bought the property, Mark had started building us a house using the recycled materials he had been collecting. It came together fast, and one evening he walked me around, showing me the progress he had made. Looking at the house, I realized that our old dream was materializing. And yet, as we stood there, I remembered the feeling I'd had in the immigration office two years before—that we didn't belong together. When the adventure was over, I wondered, what would be left of our relationship?

Yet I tried, valiantly, to put those feelings aside once more. I had just discovered I was pregnant again. Part of me was terrified at what might happen. I simply could not bear another loss. But another part of me clung to this new life growing inside me with a new tenacity.

The following October I gave birth to another son, Tobias. Blond and blue-eyed, he looked much like Elki, and we all treated him with extra care, as if he were fragile and frail. He was perfectly healthy, but we were terrified that he might die. Nicole and Jaimee would come running into the room when he cried, asking if he was sick. At night, I would stand over his crib as he slept, touching him to make sure he was still breathing.

When I told Cal about my worries, he said, "You're going to screw that kid up. You need to get over your fear."

I knew he was right. So when Toby was four months old, I made myself bring him to a neighbor's house for a couple hours a week. The first time I dropped him off, I sat on her porch the entire time he was there. It was excruciating to let him out of my sight. I just knew the woman would come rushing out, telling me something awful had happened. But I slowly grew to trust that the baby was going to be just fine.

Tobias laughed easily and had a friendly, inquisitive nature. He would sit in the backseat of our Morris Minor, observing the world intently, as though it were a fascinating and slightly amusing sight. He was always making discoveries, and we loved watching his earnest smile light up his face.

One night I woke to find him crying. I went in and cradled him in my arms, but he continued to whimper. I bundled him up and took him outside. In the night air, he quickly grew calm. I showed him the cows, and he smiled at the sound of their mooing. When we returned to the house, we were both sleepy and content. The next night, we went out again. It became a ritual, looking at the sky and walking together in the hills by moonlight. Each night, I was reminded of how much I loved this place. Finally, I had found a real home.

AT FIRST, COURTNEY seemed to thrive at Beverly's. She read *Alice in Wonderland* and *Treasure Island*, and helped Beverly plant a vegetable garden. When she came back on weekends, she was friendly and cooperative for the first time in years. We often went to films together, and her incisive comments reminded me how much Courtney knew about things I paid little attention to. It took three months before the conversation I prayed would not happen occurred.

"Everything started out fine," Beverly told us, "but I can't help her. She will have to leave."

"But things were going so well!" I said, feeling panicked.

Beverly looked apologetic. "I have been getting terrible headaches these last few weeks, and I know it's the stress of living with Courtney. She's broken my antique furniture, and screams at me if I get her up before noon. I've seen it all, but she's just too much for me."

I imagined Courtney would be upset when I went to pick her up. But she was livid.

"She's evil," Courtney hissed. "This whole place is backward."

I didn't want to return her to the hospital, where they would sedate her. Instead, I enrolled her at the local girls' school as a boarder. That school lasted another three months. When she was asked to leave, I called Frank in Oregon. He suggested she return and live with him.

"Maybe she needs to be an only child for a while," he said. "I can give her a lot of time and attention."

"I just want to get out of here," Courtney said when I told her about my conversation with Frank. Two weeks later, Rebecca and I took her to the little Nelson airport. We sat around the pot-bellied stove, watching the runway, and I asked Courtney if there was anything she needed. I didn't even know what I meant. She stared at me for a moment and said, "Ta-ta, Mother," as the stewardess came to accompany her on the flight to America.

Relief, sorrow, and regret crashed like waves over me after she left. I missed her every day. But in the weeks that followed I felt lighter, as though someone had lifted a heavy load off my back.

MARY AND I spent hours playing with our children, making jam and homemade dresses for the girls. On the winter solstice, our families got together to blow out candles and then light them again with a wish for the coming year. We made up blessings for new babies and marriages, and read one another our favorite poems. Our circle of friends grew to include musicians, weavers, architects, and tuna fishermen, and community life flourished. Nicole and Jaimee starred in plays and learned to sing and play the piano. Frank sent good reports of Courtney's life in America. It seemed almost too good to be true. It was.

After six months, I got the phone call I'd known would come. "I can't do it," Frank said. "She has to come back to you, Linda, I can't control her." I didn't even ask him to explain: I understood.

I went to pick her up at the airport, determined not to make her my central focus again.

"Courtney, we're out of options," I said to her as we drank hot chocolate in the airport restaurant. "There is nowhere else to send you. You'll have to keep living with us, and we'll try homeschooling."

For a moment she looked angry, and then she softened. "Mommy, I'm sorry," she said. I hugged my daughter and was surprised to feel her return my embrace. I felt a new determination to help her make her life work. She was so big-hearted, I thought, so beautiful when her face lost its hard edge. I took her to the market to buy the first of the season's strawberries, her favorite, then brought her back to the farm. Her sisters were ecstatic to see her, and they all ran to the paddock to play.

Mark, who had accepted a part-time teaching job at the local junior high school, got home at the same time as us and greeted Courtney with an enthusiastic hug.

"Have you ever heard of a *whare*?" he asked us both.

"Isn't it a separate structure, outside the house?"

"That's it. My sixth graders who have one say they love having a separate space."

Courtney was twelve now, the same age as his sixth graders. If she could have privacy, maybe she would start drawing and reading again.

"I was thinking of putting it where the chicken shed is," Mark said. "It's only ten feet from the house, right next to the little creek, and it's so beautiful there."

"Right, Mark. Like I'm going to let my daughter live in a chicken coop."

"I didn't say we'd use the shed. I'll build a new structure there."

Courtney loved the idea too.

"I'll make it so beautiful, you'll think it's a palace!" he promised her.

Mark built Courtney's *whare* out of beautiful redwood. It was fully insulated, with oak floors, a Dutch door, octagonal windows, and a railed porch. Inside, Mark built shelves and a closet. When he was finished, we bought her a new double bed.

With great ceremony, we brought Courtney out to see her new space. Her envious little sisters pleaded to be allowed inside, but we emphasized that the new room was just for her. Courtney invited her sisters to sit on her bed as she unpacked her things. She handed them scarves and bracelets with characteristic generosity, and invited them to stay with her that night. Then the three of them disappeared for the day, climbing to a hilltop where they could see the ocean. *Maybe we needed all of the trouble to happen*, I thought, *to get us here.*

In just a few weeks it was Christmas Eve, and we were exchanging gifts with our friends and drinking homemade apple wine. Courtney asked for some, and we gave her a small glass. When we weren't looking, she managed to sneak more in her eggnog glass. After a while, I noticed she was slurring her words and swaying unsteadily. I pulled her aside. "Courtney, have you been drinking?" I demanded.

Her breath reeked of wine. "No," she said, wobbling. She looked green.

I made her lie down in my bed, and gave her some water. Then I said good-bye to my friends and joined her. She was hiccupping and her face was hot. Soon she started throwing up. I lay awake most of the night with her as she threw up. We fell asleep around dawn, both of us worn out.

When I woke up a few hours later, Courtney was gone. Alarm coursed through me, remembering how sick she'd been. I ran through the house, looking for her. She wasn't in the house or her *whare*. I ran into the fields, still in my nightgown, calling her name. I couldn't find her anywhere on the farm.

After an hour of frantic searching, I found Courtney sitting in a neighbor's grassy field. "What are you doing here, sweetie?" I asked, angry and reassured all at once. "Didn't you hear me calling you?"

Then I saw her arms. She had been cutting them with sharp sticks, and there were trails of blood all up and down them.

THE LOCAL HOSPITAL blamed me for taking her off her medication. I agreed to put her back on it. But this time she just got angrier. For the next few months, she spent her time sulking around the house and causing trouble.

"Will you sweep the floor?" Mark asked.

"Sure," she said. In addition to sweeping, we soon found, she had pulled the plug on the freezer. A full season's produce was spoiled.

"Please vacuum the living room," I asked.

"Sure," she said. She turned on the vacuum cleaner and plunged the hose into the fireplace to suck up hot coals.

"I hate this farm," she said disdainfully. "Who would want to live here?"

FINALLY I CALLED William, our old family therapist.

"I was worried about what would happen when puberty hit," he said.

"God, I don't know what to do," I said. "I'm so afraid for her. Isn't there anyone who can help her?"

William found a program in Portland, Oregon, which assessed kids with behavioral problems by focusing on chemical imbalances. "Someone has to help figure out what's wrong," he pointed out. "And the doctors there are top-notch."

I hated the idea of sending my twelve-year-old to a treatment center far away, but at this point, there wasn't any choice. We had exhausted all possible options in New Zealand, and I feared that keeping her with us was the worst idea of all. If she had an illness—and many people who came in contact with her seemed to think she did—she needed care that only professionals could provide. William offered to fly to New Zealand to bring Courtney back to the States. After thinking it over, I agreed.

Courtney's leave-taking was quiet. "I'm sure glad to get out of here," was the last thing she said before boarding the plane.

BOTH MARK AND I secretly hoped that our baby boy would restore our closeness, but our delight in Tobias failed to reconnect us. While our kids and community were fulfilling for me, Mark spent all his time on the farm. We had sheep, chickens, turkeys, a pig named Rosie, bees, and a large garden. Nicole, Jaimee, and I loved caring for the animals, and we rescued bummer lambs whose mothers had died and fed them from bottles. But I was hopeless at manual labor and worse when the work required skill, like helping Mark with building or fitting doors and windows.

Mark didn't understand why I needed to devote so much energy to other people—"all you do is *talk*," he spat at me one night during an argument—while he had to keep up the endless work. He grew frustrated by its backbreaking repetitiveness, and by the lack of profit we made on it. "I'm in my midthirties, and what do I have to show for all the work I've done?" he said to me one night. "And I miss the Northwest. I don't belong here."

I was so torn. I did belong here: our friends had become like family, and Nicole and Jaimee were thriving. I loved the sea, the alpine lakes and green pastures, and the fascinating people I was always meeting. Returning to America meant leaving Elki buried in a cemetery and Joshua with another family. Even though I couldn't see either of them, there was some small comfort to be living near to where they were.

But in my heart I knew we would have to leave. Courtney kept running away from the treatment center and ending up at William's house, and he couldn't take care of a troubled thirteen-year-old on his own. One of the doctors said she had signs of autism. That sounded wrong to me, but I still had no idea what the problem was. Her caseworker called to tell me Courtney was out of control. "We had to tape her legs together after she kicked in a window," he told me. "Another time, she smashed a wall repeatedly until we stopped her." I was horrified. He felt she had to be in a secure center until she could learn to control her impulses, and I knew I needed to be near her.

Soon after, on an early February morning Norm, the local shepherd, stopped by for a beer. From the porch, he surveyed our gorse-covered hills.

"Reckon it's burning time," he said to Mark. "It's the only way you'll get rid of that damn weed if you want new grass to grow. To-day's a good day to burn."

Mark wasted little time. In the late afternoon, he went out and set fire to the gorse. The temperature was cooler, but a wind arose and blew the fire into great flames that leaped up the hillside. The fire jumped to our neighbor's property, destroying his trees, and soon threatening his house.

When we saw what was happening, we made frantic phone calls to nearby friends, who rushed to our aid. The hills were soon filled with men trying to douse the fire with buckets of water, but it raged out of control. Every time Mark ran down for more water, he looked more desperate. "It's going to burn down their house!" he shouted at me on one run, his face black with smoke. Then suddenly the wind changed, and the fire burned itself out without destroying any homes.

When it was over, we all stood silently, surveying the charred hills. Our fire had left a long scar of scorched trees across the valley. All our neighbors were furious with us. The fire had damaged valuable property, and it confirmed their suspicions that we were just amateurs. "Don't you know, you never burn the gorse alone? You should always have help!" one of our neighbors said angrily to Mark the day after the fire.

But the fire had done deeper damage. It had destroyed, once and for all, our long-cherished fantasy. As we stood in the smoky air, staring at the blackened valley, we knew that the old dream of ours had burned out. It was time to go home.

A few days later, Nicole was making the batter for a cake when I entered the kitchen. She was trying to earn another merit badge. She looked startled when she saw my expression. The shadow that came over her face told me she had guessed what I was about to say.

"No," she said. "No!"

"Sweetheart, we can't stay on this farm. We can't make a living here. Besides, Courtney is there all on her own."

She shook her head violently, her long black hair flying. "Courtney can come back here," she shouted. "This is my home and you can't make me leave."

"We have to, Nicole. Mark wants to go back to school."

She began to cry. "Why can't he just leave, then?" she asked between sobs. "He's not even my father. Why do we have to go?"

I put my arm around her. She wriggled out of my grasp and walked out, leaving the bowl of batter on the counter. I heard the screen door shut and knew she had gone into the hills to find comfort. I sat alone, looking out the window at the land we all loved. I couldn't believe we had to leave it behind.

CHAPTER 26

In May 1978, we left New Zealand for Corvallis, Oregon, a college town where Mark could get his teaching certificate. During the plane ride, I watched Nicole silently staring out the window. I held Tobias and Jaimee close.

When we arrived in Corvallis, we moved into a downtown motel. The alley nearby smelled like urine and garbage, and at night, we could hear the clanking of homeless people's shopping carts. Nicole was sullen, and Jaimee kept asking when we were going home. Even Tobias, usually an exuberant child, was grouchy. We spent each day looking for a temporary house, as we had when we had first arrived in Nelson, but now our mood was somber instead of elated.

Soon I began to feel flulike symptoms: I was tired, nauseous, and my head hurt all the time. When I didn't get better, I found a doctor in the phone book.

After examining me, she said, "I think you're pregnant."

"I can't be!" I exclaimed. "My husband got a vasectomy right before we left New Zealand."

"Well, the urinalysis test you just took suggests otherwise."

I shook my head in disbelief. "When I was eighteen, I was told I might never have children. Now I can't seem to stop! I must have been pregnant when my husband had the operation."

"Well, you have produced quite a flock," she said, looking at my chart. "Apparently that one ovary and fallopian tube refused to give up."

The pregnancy couldn't have been more ironic. I had finally shed my distaste for birth control, a remnant of my Catholic upbringing, and urged Mark to get a vasectomy, and here I was, pregnant again. This seemed too much, even for a Catholic. And the timing couldn't have been worse. Mark and I were barely hanging on.

I should have felt terrified, but instead I was thrilled. This baby seemed a sign of hope amidst the most difficult of circumstances.

"What did the doctor say?" Mark asked when I returned.

"I can't believe I'm saying this, but—I'm pregnant."

For a moment he stared at me, and then he started to laugh.

"Well, I'll be damned," he said. "Something about it makes me feel glad. It's a good sign."

We sat the kids down to announce the news.

Mark said, "We have something to tell you."

Nicole and Jaimee looked at each other and then at me.

"Mom, are you pregnant again?" Nicole asked.

Tobias, nearly three, just mimicked his sisters. "Not *again*," he said.

MY PREGNANCY DIDN'T stop Mark and me from fighting. We mainly argued about how to use the money from the sale of the farm. I wanted to buy a house and invest the rest, and he wanted to build a house. After long late-night fights, I gave in. House building seemed to be all Mark could talk about, and I felt this was our last chance to make a life together. With the new baby coming, I tried to convince myself that this new venture would succeed.

Mark took us to a piece of land he thought was perfect. It was a gray day and the field was bare.

"Let's walk all around this plot," Mark said. "I'll show you exactly what I plan to do, where all the rooms will go."

I swallowed my fears and tried to see it through Mark's eyes.

"It'll be a solar house: I've read all about heat transfer theory and hydronic collection. The house will stay warm in the winter."

He talked excitedly. I felt a sense of dread. The kids clung to me, looking anxious.

I ENROLLED NICOLE and Jaimee in the local elementary school, which they hated. Their long hair and homemade dresses, so appropriate for New Zealand, did not fit in among the fast-talking, mall-rat Corvallis kids who wore mood rings and collected pet rocks.

Courtney's problems loomed larger than ever. She had run away from the treatment center several times and was involved in what the social worker called "a new culture" of dropouts living on the streets and doing hard drugs. By the time we got back to Corvallis, she had assaulted staff and peers at the group home, and a nurse had found her pulling out clumps of her own hair. She was now in the juvenile system and was accumulating a record with the police.

Most weekends I drove with the girls to Salem to visit her in Hillcrest Youth Correctional Facility. Jaimee and Nicole were always excited to go, though their pleasure was tinged with fear. They saw their big sister as glamorous, but with sharp claws and teeth. I felt overwhelming guilt whenever I saw her, forced once again to confront the fact that I had not protected her—not from Hank, from drugs, or from an unstable home life, and certainly not from her own inner demons.

In the visitors' room at Hillcrest, all the girls chain-smoked.

"Isn't that against the law?" eight-year-old Jaimee asked.

Courtney smoked, too, waving the cigarette around like a movie starlet from a different age. She spoke mainly to her sisters, and impressed them with monologues on popular culture, descriptions of her recent exploits, sexual and illicit, and various musings on style. She often stopped in midsentence and moved to a different subject.

"The Ramones haven't done a thing since—anyway, Nicole, you've got to stop letting Linda buy your clothes. You're almost twelve! What's that bra made of anyway—papier-mâché? Where are my cigarettes?"

Inevitably, she would lose interest in the girls and look away, aloof and condescending. I would step into the breach, then, and ask banal questions.

"Do you need anything? How about some new shoes? Is the food okay?"

When she responded at all, it was to ask for money or to make some denigrating comment about my hair or clothes. Yet sometimes a change would occur, often at the visit's end. She would fasten her eyes on one of us and ask softly, "Do you love me?"

I always looked for ways to reassure her. Before one visit, I made her a book of all her baby photos, but she threw it aside dismissively when I gave it to her, rolling her eyes. A few months later, she mentioned that it had been stolen and asked if I could make her another. That afternoon, I found a bunch of negatives and rushed them to the photo store for prints, so that it would be ready by the next week's visit. When I gave the new book to her, she looked at me as if I were delusional.

"That's what I need, Mother," she said scornfully. "More memories of my golden childhood." I never saw either album again.

On the ride home, the girls would always talk rapturously about Courtney, unless she had belittled them into silence. At the wheel, I would try to calm myself, afraid that my heartbeat was so loud and hard that the girls would hear it.

ONE AFTERNOON, I was on the phone long-distance to Rebecca when Mark came in from a ten-hour workday.

"Who are you talking to?" he asked.

Hearing the accusation in his voice, I ended the call. "Rebecca," I said.

"I can't believe you're making an international call when I'm breaking my back to make money," he said angrily.

His tone made me livid. "Well, I can't believe you made me leave New Zealand. We're no better off here than we were there—but here we don't even have friends."

"Well, maybe if you worked with me instead of talking on the phone all the time, we could make a home here," he snapped.

"You don't know how to do anything besides work!" I shouted. "You never spend time with us. You're too busy chasing your dream."

"I'm doing this for us. Don't you see that?"

"But I don't even think you like 'us' anymore. You certainly don't seem to like me," I said, more quietly now.

"I don't," he admitted.

"Well, I don't know how to fix this," I sighed. He stared out the window at the half-finished house, then stalked out. Within minutes, I heard him hammering away again.

I decided it was time to return to school. I needed only one statistics class to earn a bachelor's degree in psychology. I had always dreaded this course, and the first week of class confirmed my worst fears. Nothing the teacher said made sense to me. While everyone else in the class was making insightful comments, I failed to understand the most basic concepts. "Univariate data," "decision trees," "Bayesian analysis"—it was worse than Latin or Spanish at Dominican. All my old feelings about school came rushing back. In the evenings, as I looked over the textbook and my halfhearted class notes, I tried to convince myself that I could succeed, but the next class would sink my hopes again.

After getting my second exam back, marked with a gigantic D, I hired a tutor. Frederick was a tall, bespectacled man with a serious air, who met me twice a week in the student union. He brought with him a bag of pennies, and, instead of explaining statistics in abstract language, as my professor did, he used the pennies to show me the principles in action. I immediately grasped the concepts. Frederick told me that I had a different style of learning, and that our educational system does a poor job with students who are experiential learners, as I was. "It's not your fault, Linda," he said, earnestly.

For the first time, I had an explanation to account for my failures at school. More important, I was improving in class. I soon found myself participating in class discussions and feeling confident about the material.

I passed the class with a respectable grade and enrolled in the master's program in counseling at Oregon State. I loved my classes, every one of them. For the first time I got straight A's and followed everything the professors said. My curiosity about the inner workings of the human mind and heart, and my enthusiasm for interpersonal relationships, what Louella dubbed the "busybody" in me, actually made me successful. I reveled in the feeling.

MIDWAY THROUGH MY first semester, I gave birth to my son, Daniel. Mark and I put aside our troubles in the presence of our perfect new child.

"Look at him. He's a Botticelli baby," I said, staring with admiration.

"He's wonderful," Mark agreed.

Just then, Nicole burst into the hospital room.

"What are you doing here, sweetie?" I asked, alarmed. We had left the kids with the sitter.

"I had to come," she said, smiling. The minute she heard Daniel was born, she had snuck out of the sitter's house and had run the two miles to the hospital.

She climbed onto the bed to inspect him.

"Mom, I can't believe our new baby," she said. "He looks just like a chimpanzee!"

Mark left to pick up Jaimee and Tobias so they could meet our Botticelli monkey. I looked around at their smiling faces. In that moment, we all seemed united—a glowing, happy family. But under that picture was another, with three children missing and a crumbling marriage. By the time I returned home from the hospital, Mark and I were fighting again.

After ten more unhappy months, we agreed to separate. He was offered a temporary job in Wyoming, and we decided to take that time to reevaluate whether we wanted to try again. But we both knew that the relationship was over.

When he left, the new house was still unfinished. It was uncarpeted, with nails jutting out of the floor; some of the insulation hung out of the walls; and the yard was a clutter of clay and weeds. The temporary kitchen door was so thin that slight winds blew it open. But the kids and I moved in anyway.

IN 1980, I finished my master's program, and began working as a counselor. I loved my work. Every patient I saw helped me understand the human condition a bit more.

I marveled that I made money doing what I loved. But though I felt stable and successful during the days, my nights were plagued with insomnia and bad dreams.

The nightmares always started the same way. I would step into

Disney's Haunted Mansion, and then run down one of the sinister hallways with gliding chairs chasing me. Sometimes the chairs had hateful human faces. Often they would morph into the ghosts of babies at St. Elizabeth's, slipping in through the walls, or a prowling wolf that entered the house through the temporary kitchen door. In every dream, my biggest dread was that the demons would find my children. I was never able to protect them. Every night, I would wake up sweating and terrified.

One night, I awoke to find my three-year-old, Daniel, standing next to me, looking scared. "Mommy, you were screaming," he said. I hugged him close and realized I had to make my nightmares stop.

Two weeks later I sat in an old house on Hancock Street in Portland, with beautiful photographs on the walls, Persian rugs on the floors, and classical music playing on the radio, waiting for a therapist I'd heard about from a professor in my counseling program. I remembered that moment on the beach in San Francisco so many years before, after I had peeked at my therapist's notes; I had been hurt, but I had also glimpsed some important truths about my life. Yet I had bottled up all those feelings and turned away, too scared to look at them. Now I had become a therapist, helping others to move past their fears and look closely at those very truths. The irony seemed glaring.

Still, when a short blonde woman introduced herself and invited me into her room, I followed with great reluctance. Eyeing her suspiciously, I wondered what she could possibly offer me.

"What brought you here?" Clare asked.

I told her about my recurring nightmares. As I talked, I realized that they were the same dreams I'd had for years.

"Maybe you're secure enough to let yourself feel the fears you've always carried," she suggested.

I thought about what she was saying. Slowly, an insight dawned. Though I had lived on the other side of the world, and had learned a lot about how people worked, the same hollow center I had as a child had never gone away.

"What did you fill that emptiness with?" she asked me.

"Fantasies," I said. "I'd imagine the same story about being rescued, found, set free by love." I was too embarrassed to say that my current fantasies had returned to Mickey Malloy. In the same way I had dreamed of my "real" mother whenever Jack and Louella hadn't understood me, I thought about my "real" lover Mickey whenever relationships failed in my life.

Clare asked about my family, and I froze. "My parents have been dead for years, and I've already dealt with it," I said.

"Just say a little about them," Clare asked patiently.

"I'm not here to talk about them," I replied stubbornly. "I just want to figure out how to stop the nightmares."

"If the nightmares are the same as when you were a child, then it's the child who is still afraid. That's who we have to work with," she continued. "But we don't have to do this—nobody has to look at these things. You have to make the choice, Linda. There is no rule that says you can't live a good life without facing your deepest fears."

I decided I would rather be anywhere on earth but in this room. I could not remember feeling so much discomfort. I tried desperately to look unaffected by her questions, but I could feel my face twitching and a lump rising in my throat. I knew there wasn't a choice.

For two years, I drove the 110 miles to Portland weekly, sometimes twice a week. I usually felt like I was going for a root canal.

IN ONE SESSION, I was telling Clare about my first day of school.

"Did your mother always introduce you as her adopted daughter?" she asked.

"Yes—that was how she was told to do it."

"How did that make you feel?" she asked.

"Humiliated, like I had a scarlet branding."

"What strikes me is how different adoption was then," Clare said. "Nowadays, adoption is celebrated; it's very different compared to 1944. Back then, it was a sign of failure: a man or woman who didn't produce their own child was lacking something essential. And something was certainly wrong with a child who was given away."

"That's so true," I said. "It was used as an excuse for all my foibles. And it must have reinforced the feelings of inadequacy my parents already had. There was so much silence in my family—we never talked about any of this."

Clare nodded. "Because it was never talked about, you filled in the blanks with your imagination. You knew you didn't fit, and you began to yearn for your real mother. She would understand you—she would be like the imaginary lover who makes all things better."

"Oh God, Clare," I said, sitting up straighter. "I can't believe how obvious this is. As I grew older, I transferred the yearning from her to the make-believe man who would fix it all."

"You could only love an imaginary man, Linda," Clare said, leaning forward.

"Still—I loved my friends, and I've kept the same ones all my life. My kids aren't perfect and I love them."

"But intimacy is different," said Clare. "That's where all our deepest wounds emerge."

Jack's face came suddenly to mind. Talking to Clare about him, I realized his abuse had primed me for a sexual relationship by the time I met Mickey. And after Mickey left my life, I let myself be swept into relationships, hardly aware of what it meant to "choose," never expecting to feel truly respected and understood, to connect emotionally with a lover as I had with my friends.

I had gone into therapy thinking Mark and Frank were to blame for the disintegration of our marriages. As I finally talked about Jack,

I began to see how my rage at his behavior was often just under the surface of my interactions with my husbands. Understanding my part in the breakups helped me to find common ground with both of them. Though Mark and I had divorced in 1980, we found a counselor to help us end the marriage less acrimoniously, and, over the next few years, learned to work together to raise our children.

I was breaking out of my patterns of wishful thinking, hoping that my "real" mother or a fantasy lover would come along to save me. I understood that only I could save myself.

Judy had always tried to teach me that. I decided that I would change my last name to hers, Carroll. She was the first person I ever felt at home with, and my other last names, the Risis' and my exhusbands', had never felt right. Taking her name was a way of honoring our friendship and the strong person she always saw inside me.

IT WAS AN exhausting time. I was never off duty: I was either working, parenting, driving to Portland to see Clare or to Salem to see Courtney. Though the nightmares had finally stopped, I only got about four or five hours of sleep a night. The kids were finally settling into life in Corvallis: they all had teachers they liked and met good friends. Cal, now a high school teacher in Nelson, kept me up to date with Joshua's progress. He was a star basketball player and popular student, he told me.

Though I was glad to hear about Joshua's successes, I worried about my other children. Raising four kids alone was a daily struggle, and we all needed an adult community to help support us. So in 1981 I joined the Unitarian Fellowship with my children. The Fellowship welcomed discussions about philosophy and politics, and the people who attended reminded me of my friends in New Zealand.

It was there that I met Hazel.

Hazel had recently moved to Corvallis at sixty-five. She had gotten a divorce after fifty years of marriage, and her youngest daughter, Lucy, had been killed by a drunk driver. Hazel had bright blue eyes, and her warmth and laughter reminded me of Nellie. We connected instantly, falling into a conversation about my girls, who were playing with some of the other kids. I loved her humor, her youthful, girlish laugh, and her stories of her years as an actress. Before long, we were spending afternoons together, taking walks with the kids and having long talks. Our conversations were raw and honest, ranging from family traumas to spiritual wonderings.

Part grandmother, part best friend, Hazel loved children and spent countless hours with the kids and me. I opened up to her about my difficulties as a single mother and my failed marriages. She told me about the death of her daughter, and the depression she'd faced afterward. We both needed a good friend, and were glad to have found each other. Hazel became a part of our family, eating dinner with us and picking up the kids from sports practice. She told me how glad she was to "feel of use" again, and the children loved having a grandmother figure in their lives.

One spring day, Hazel stopped by for a visit. We sat on the lone piece of furniture in the living room, a sofa. She opened her purse and pulled out an unsealed envelope.

"Now forget about arguing," she said, "because I have made up my mind." She pressed the envelope into my hand. "It's the check I received from the insurance company—the death check—after my daughter was killed. It would be impossible for me to spend it. What would I buy with it?" She glanced around. "Take it and finish the house. Hire a contractor to seal the floors, the banisters. Get somebody in here to paint. Buy a bunk bed for the boys. My only request is, don't refuse me."

I took a big breath and started to do just that. "To begin with—"

"Please, Linda. It's blood money. I can't hold on to it."

"I can only accept it if you'll let me repay you when I can."

"I don't need money. You'll pay it back in your own way, but to others, not me. You are giving me a gift by accepting it: I can imagine I am helping the grandchildren I will never have from my daughter."

Her generosity left me breathless. I reached over and hugged her tight.

With Hazel's money, I had the house finished and bought appliances and furniture. The children and I planted a garden in the backyard and hung pictures on the walls. Jaimee brought home a tiny white poodle named George. I found an orange cat on the freeway, whom we named Rowsers. Slowly, our home came together.

One night, I had a dream that I was being chased down the streets of Corvallis by something I couldn't see—a demon spirit. After dashing up and down alleys and back roads, I made it home, slamming the door behind me. When I looked around, the house was complete. All the walls were done, and there was furniture in the rooms and glass in the windows. I went to the front door and looked out, and realized I wasn't afraid anymore.

COURTNEY WAS RELEASED from Hillcrest in the winter of 1980, after she turned sixteen. She begged to be emancipated, and I knew her behavior was way too out of control for me to handle. She ran away from any treatment center that could have helped her. I reluctantly agreed that emancipation was the best option.

I thought I could handle this transition rationally. But the grief was so powerful I could only cope by detaching. As a child, I had learned to act as though my birth mother did not exist, though I still fantasized about her. I began to do the same with Courtney. More than once, she described me as cold and clinical. She was right: a wall of self-protection had grown between us, though my dreams always carried me back to when I could hold her close and protect her.

In talking to Clare about Courtney over several years, I had come to realize that my instability with men and difficulty setting firm boundaries had contributed to her struggles in life. Because of my guilt about what I lacked as a mother, I gave in far too easily to her demands, teaching her at a young age that with the right sort of manipulation, she could always have her way. And living with me, as my other children frequently reminded me, could be chaotic. But Courtney had come into the world with a biology that created internal torment. Violent mood swings, troubles with attachment, terrible dreams, and a sense of persecution had plagued her all her life, the flip side of her creativity, generosity, and intelligence. Working with Clare, I accepted that I had not created that temperament.

But accepting that fact did not make her self-destructiveness any easier to bear. I lived in constant terror about what would happen to her. So I shut off, trying to disengage, although I could never tear her out of my heart.

She called frequently, from San Francisco, Ireland, Portland, and Japan, ingeniously finding ways to track me down: in my office with a client, at the home of a friend, even on vacation. She would launch into an explanation of her latest crisis, usually an emergency that required money. If I said I was busy or that I would call her back, she would erupt into an angry outburst.

"You hate me!" she would scream. It was never what she said that got to me—it was the despair in her voice. Desperate though they were, her phone calls did bring a flicker of relief. Her tenacity in finding me demonstrated that she needed our connection, as I did. Along with her anguish, I detected a real, if bizarre, kind of love in her words. And for the moments we were on the phone I could relax, knowing she was still out there somewhere, still alive.

ONE YEAR SHE came home for Christmas. She wore thick, smeared makeup, and her sweaters had holes in them. I tried to remind myself that it was a style, not so different from when I'd dressed in the hippie costume of the sixties. She had just returned from Taiwan, where she had made a lot of money as a dancer, and she arrived with gifts: stuffed animals for her brothers, silk nightgowns for her sisters. For me, she brought a bottle of Joy perfume. I had always said it was my favorite: French luxury made with real roses. She handed me the bottle with satisfaction.

"It's Joy, and don't say it—I knew it was your favorite."

I barely registered the gift. My eyes were fixed on her. She looked pale and worn out, though she was more theatrical than ever. She talked excitedly about her trip and laughed as she told us outlandish stories of her narrow escape from a slave ring. Her sisters looked on, wide eyed with fascination.

Then she paused and turned her attention to me. She was waiting, I realized, for me to react. Her gift was heavy in my hands, and I wanted nothing more than to drop it on the floor.

"Don't give me Joy!" I wanted to shout. What about the sorrow it cost? What about the steady stream of anguished phone calls in the middle of the night that left me shaking for hours?

"It's lovely. Thank you—I'm very surprised," I said, setting the bottle down.

After she left, the bottle sat on a shelf, growing dusty.

CHAPTER 27

As my life in Corvallis deepened, I stayed close with my New Zealand friends. I often sent letters and tapes of music I liked to Mary, Rebecca, Cal, and Tim. Like Judy, Tim was my "truth-buddy"; I felt most comfortable talking with him about my deepest fears and biggest questions. I sent him various books, including one called *The Seasons of a Man's Life* by Daniel Levinson, which introduced a new idea—male midlife crisis. He sent me back a wry note of thanks: "Midlife crisis? No thanks, I think I'll skip that season."

When I was thirty-six, two years after leaving Nelson, Danny and I made a trip back to New Zealand. I stayed with Rebecca and Cal, who threw a dinner party for me the first night. All my friends came, and we delighted in seeing each other. They seemed the same—a little older, all with children and some graying hair, but as full of life as ever.

Later I took a walk with Rebecca. Together we looked down on the lights of Nelson, cradled in dark foothills.

"This place is so magical," I said with a contented sigh. "The years go by and you all continue to live your perfect lives."

"Don't romanticize us," Rebecca retorted. "You see only the outer picture, sitting round a dinner table. People have a lot more troubles than you know."

When we flew home at the end of the week, I realized with surprise that I was excited to return to Oregon. My life was full of good friends, especially Hazel. My private practice was absorbing, and on many days inspiring. And I'd come to an important realization: I was not made for marriage. I loved my life as a single woman.

THE YEAR I turned forty, 1984, I brought Tobias with me on another New Zealand holiday. I spent a week with Cal and Rebecca, and showed Toby the beautiful valley where he and I had hiked together in the moonlight nine years earlier. He stayed on with Cal and Rebecca while I went to visit Tim and Mary for a few days. On arriving at their house, I walked down their path and was greeted by Tim. Something powerful surged in me, as if I was seeing him for the first time. We hugged, and electric energy ran through my body. The intensity was overwhelming, and I pulled away in giddy confusion. Mary arrived, and I shook off the trance and greeted her.

That night we gathered with old friends at a local restaurant. I recounted a story to them. A few weeks earlier, my car had stalled midway on a bridge on a rainy night. There was barely any room to walk off the bridge, and cars whizzed by me as I inched my way back to the road to call for help. I was scared, and looking down at the black waters, I felt, for the first time, a sense of my own mortality, I told my friends.

As I spoke, I noticed Tim push back from the table, set down his knife and fork, and listen attentively to my story. When we returned to his home, he asked that I take a walk with him.

Together, we headed out into the crisp night air. Reaching the top of a hill which looked down on Nelson and the sea, he turned toward me and spoke.

"I want to tell you what I was feeling tonight. I don't think about death much or losing people, but when you told that story, I felt overwhelmed," he said. "It made me see how much you mean to me. I don't think I knew that before."

I was silent for a while, looking at him. "I was thinking about the long talks we had when you brought me along on your vetting trips," I said. "Judy was the only other person in my life I could talk to the way I talked to you."

Tentatively, we held hands and resumed our night walk. Our friendship of ten years was rapidly changing into something different, more powerful. We were falling in love, and we both knew it. Yet nothing could come of it: he was married to my close friend, I was happily single, and we lived half a world apart.

The next evening, the three of us sat around the kitchen table. The sun was setting behind the western mountains, filling the house with golden light.

"Mary, we need to talk," Tim announced. "You know me: I'm not good at pretending. Things are really changing between Linda and me."

Adrenaline coursed through me. I felt like we were about to plunge over a cliff.

" 'Really changing,' " Mary repeated with a mocking smile. "You mean you're falling in love."

"That's right, we're falling in love," responded Tim, a little angrily.

My stomach turned over. I looked anxiously at Mary. She was sitting upright at the table and seemed to be taking this in stride. "It happens at our age," she said. "It happens all the time and people deal with it."

"What do you mean, deal with it?" Tim responded hotly. "Like a flood in the basement? Like a leak in the roof? I don't know how to *deal* with it. I don't think you know what I'm talking about."

Things seemed to be sliding out of control. I shifted nervously in my chair.

"Oh, I know exactly what you're talking about," responded Mary quickly, goaded by Tim's words. "The same thing happened to me, and I *have* dealt with it. I have put it behind me now."

"What are you talking about? What do you mean it's happened to you?"

I suddenly felt this was a conversation I shouldn't be part of, and quietly excused myself. The golden light was fading as I left the room.

The rest of my trip was filled with long, difficult discussions with Tim and Mary. It was clear that their marriage had problems deeper than they had ever acknowledged. They had a lot of work ahead of them. But they also had a deep love for each other and their family. We all promised to stay close, and remain honest with each other. As for Tim and I, we decided we could not pursue our feelings any further.

OVER THE NEXT two years, the three of us kept our promise. Mary and I wrote all the time. And Tim and I never stopped talking, about his feelings about his marriage, his work with animals, our shared spiritual interests. I often talked with him about Courtney, who had been working as a stripper, and had appeared in some cult films, *Sid and Nancy* and *Straight to Hell*. She was heavily into punk music, and was developing a reputation as a musician.

Her desperate phone calls continued, but every so often she would call to tell me she was doing well. During these calls she would report on her newfound interests, like Buddhist chanting and Western philosophy. I sent her books on meditation, creative visualization, addiction and spirituality, Carl Jung. I never understood my firstborn daughter very well, but one thing I knew was true: in her own way, she was deeply committed to spiritual discovery. It was one of the few things we shared.

A few times, she did as I asked, sought therapy or medical help, but it never lasted. Then, as quickly as she asked for help, she would disappear again. I would be left holding the bag of my worries for Courtney, who seemed as driven by the impulse to destroy herself as she was to be a star.

OVER TIME, the difficulties in Tim's relationship with Mary grew intractable. Then, one day in June, Tim called to tell me it was over. "We've really tried," he said, sounding drained. "I just can't do this anymore. Mary is going to visit Scotland with her new partner, Alistair. I want to come and spend a month with you."

We decided to take it slowly, but we both knew where it was going.

Acknowledging that I wanted to share my life with Tim was one of the hardest things I'd ever done. I had made so many mistakes in my past marriages. I was terrified that we would mess it up, and that I would lose one of the best friends I'd ever had. On top of all that, we both had intensely strong personalities, and, at forty-three, were set in our ways.

But I also knew it would be the most meaningful relationship of my life. Though we had very different temperaments, he was the first man I'd met who had the qualities of my best friends. Most important, we shared a deep desire for spiritual understanding and the belief that there was nothing more important than searching for it.

Yet before Tim came to live with me, I had one person I needed to find.

ON A SUMMER afternoon in 1987, I made a phone call that I'd been thinking about making for twenty-five years.

"Lulabelle," Mickey purred into the receiver. "The phone's been getting dusty waiting for your call."

Hearing his voice again, with its touch of an Irish brogue, unnerved me, and I forgot what I had planned to say. Then I laughed, and he did too.

"I'm coming down to the city in a few weeks," I told him. "I'd like to see you."

"It can't happen soon enough," he said.

Two weeks later, we met in the lobby of the Casa Madrone hotel in Sausalito. We had reservations to eat at the restaurant on the top floor.

He stood back to study me as I stepped into the elevator. "You look fantastic!" he said.

I was glad I had chosen a simple black linen dress that accentuated my recent Hawaiian tan.

"I can't believe my eyes," he said. "It's really you."

"Yes, it is," I said. My heart pounded the way it had only for him. No longer a skinny kid, he carried the paunch of middle age, but he made up for it in elegance. He wore a black cashmere sports jacket and Gucci loafers. His hair curled just a little on the right side of his forehead.

We stepped out of the elevator and into Poggio's, an Italian trattoria. The maître d' greeted Mickey with familiarity and led us to a choice spot with a view of Richardson's Bay. Taking it in, I relaxed a little. I turned from the window and met Mickey's gaze. The waiter brought water. I reached for mine and knocked it over. Everything—ice, water, glass—crashed to the floor. I was twelve again. I looked anxiously at the exit, but Mickey's warm laugh reassured me.

"Just like old times," he said. "How could so many years go by? Tell me everything."

"No," I said, still unsettled by my clumsiness. "You go first."

The waiter came to the table and Mickey ordered a bottle of 1975 Brunello di Montalcino.

"Don't you need to see a wine list?" I asked.

"Wine is a passion of mine. I've been collecting it since 1964—the year I dropped out of college and sold my first house."

The waiter brought the bottle and filled our glasses, and Mickey began to talk. He told me about the businesses he had owned, the power he'd acquired, the money he'd made. He had a wife and three sons. "I can afford the best of everything, not just wine," he bragged. Private schools for his children. Summers in the French Riviera. Lately, he had been toying with the idea of going into politics.

I described my years of seeking and stumbling and searching more. "I've had so much therapy, I just went ahead and became a therapist," I said.

"I've always tried to solve my problems myself," he said, and then laughed. "But most of the people I know are in therapy. I imagine business is good."

A quarter century had passed; our differences remained. He had fulfilled his dream to become rich and get out of the Marina. I had kept to my path of self-inquiry. Still, the same features attracted me to him: his wit, intelligence, his way of looking at me as though there was no one else on earth. Mickey poured the last of the wine into our glasses.

"Do you know," he said, "that the willow trees growing in this town were called *saucitos* by the Spaniards? That's how Sausalito got its name."

I nodded and felt a rush of nostalgia. I'd always loved the way he would unexpectedly offer a curious fact like a gift.

We finished our meal, and the waiter brought coffee. Mickey suggested brandy, but I declined. He ordered one for himself.

"Linda," he said. "I've thought of looking for you for years, but you got to me first. Why did you decide to call?"

"For the first time," I said, "I'm with a man who I know is right for me, who I respect and love deeply. I've had such crazy and impulsive relationships I can't tell you how good this feels; maybe the right word is 'solid.' We've decided to get married next year, but I knew I had to look for you before that happened."

I took a deep breath and continued. "I crossed a line with you, Mickey. We were so young. Our time together was unlike anything I'd ever known. Then one day you stopped talking to me, and I never knew why."

He sat silent, looking out across the bay.

"Look, Mickey, it's taken me all these years to sort out the craziness of my childhood. I have a life that works now. But a part of me has never moved past the day you cut me off. I deserve to know what happened."

"You're right," he said, looking tired. "I just don't like to talk about that time in my life." He leaned toward me. "The last time you called me was to tell me about the break-in at your house. Do you remember?"

"Of course." I understood immediately. "You did it."

"Yes, it was me. I knew you were going to be out that night. I'd told some of my friends about Jack's booze collection. It was all done on a dare. We got smashing drunk on Chivas Regal, grabbed a few cartons of cigarettes, and split."

"Just like that," I said, feeling stung.

"Just like that."

"How'd you get in?"

"That was easy. I knew where you kept the spare key."

I looked at him hard, and beneath his mildly contrite expression I saw smugness.

"Jack called," he continued. "He told me he had a friend, a superior court judge, who was just waiting to get the call to put out a warrant for my arrest."

"How did Jack even know it was you?"

"A neighbor spotted us on the way out. She told Jack she hadn't called the police because she recognized me.

Jack said that, with my background, I'd be booked and sent to jail. I had to swear I wouldn't so much as speak to you again, ever. If I said hello to you on the street, he'd make the call to that judge."

"So that was it," I said. "Just like that: a done deal? It wasn't bad enough that you broke into our house, you disappeared without saying good-bye? Do you know what that cost me?"

"Lulu, you have no idea what a scared kid I was. Scared of ending up like the rest of my family, scared of staying poor, scared of being so scared." He drained his glass and signaled the waiter for another. "I'm sorry about what happened between us and how it ended. But, to be honest, the worst part was that your father had such power over me."

"Well, he's been dead for quite a while now," I said quietly. "But I don't think I'll ever get over how sick his relationship was with me and—"

He interrupted. "Don't talk to me about twisted families." He shook his head. "What went on in mine is too perverse to even describe."

"But it's important to remember," I said.

He reached over and gently stroked my fingers. "I have another way of managing."

"I have to leave now to make my flight," I said, pulling my hand away. "I need to get a taxi."

"I'll drive you to the airport," he said.

"No," I said, gathering my things.

Mickey leaned across the table and took my hand again. As he spoke, his eyes never left my face. "Listen to me," he said. "I want you to know I crossed the same line as you. I've been married to one woman for fifteen years. I've slept with countless others, and I've loved many of them. But what happened between us was as intense for me as it was for you. I've never stopped thinking about it."

I leaned back, struck by how comforting his words felt. Though my old image of Mickey had fallen away, I was relieved to hear I hadn't imagined what had happened between us.

"You'll miss your plane. Let me drive you."

I looked at my watch. He was right: my plane was leaving soon.

In silence we rode the elevator down to the garage, where he opened the passenger door of his black Lexus sedan. I brushed by him, and he reached for me.

"Let's finish what we started," he whispered, appearing quite sober despite all the drinking he had done.

Yes, we could do that, I thought. *Let everything else dissolve.* For almost thirty years I'd fantasized about just this moment. All I had to do was follow my body and plunge. Nothing else would matter, at least not for a while.

He stroked my face and said, "Stay for the weekend. We owe this to ourselves."

Gently, I removed his hands from my face.

"I can't, Mickey," I whispered as I sidestepped him and got into the car.

He stared down at me for a moment. "Are you sure? This won't come again."

"I'm sure," I answered.

Without another word, he walked to the driver's side of the car and got in. We were silent as he drove me to the airport. From time to time, he glanced at me and smiled his sweet, sad smile, which had once brought me to my knees. In a strange way, I was relieved that it still could.

At the airport, we looked at each other one last time. I kissed his cheek, got out of the car, and went to catch a plane home.

IN JANUARY 1989, Tim arrived in America. It had taken three month-long visits and had been four long years since our night walk in Nelson to make this decision, for him to sell his veterinary practice and leave his family and the community he had loved for twenty years. He brought with him only one trunk, filled with clothes, books, his father's paintings, and two silver candlesticks that had belonged to his grandmother. He left everything else behind. "I'm here to start over with you," he said when I picked him up.

Tim and I were married in Hawaii on our favorite beach. Hazel helped us write the service, which included most of our closest friends and family, and we were married by our friend, the anthropologist and writer Angeles Arrien. Almost everyone we loved was there, except Jaimee, who was living on a kibbutz in Israel, and Courtney.

Courtney had recently formed a band, which she named Hole. During phone calls she would mention the shows the new band had put on, listing the "important people" who had seen them play. And, she told me after the fact, she had gotten married and, within a few days, divorced. "He's nobody," she snapped when I asked her about the man, a punk-rock musician named Falling James Moreland.

The night before the wedding, Tim and I were sleeping in a little tent near the beach. In the middle of the night, Courtney called, and a friend came and found me. When I picked up the phone, Courtney was screaming and crying inconsolably.

"Courtney, what is wrong?" I asked. In spite of all the time that had passed, and all the late-night frantic phone calls, the sound of her crying always made me feel protective.

"I'm in a hospital and I'm supposed to get another nose job," she wailed. "I don't think I should. I'm scared. What should I do?"

"Courtney, it's the night before my wedding. I know that doesn't mean much to you, but it means something to me. I don't want to talk about plastic surgery."

"You don't give a shit about me—you never did. Enjoy your damn wedding."

She wasn't finished, but I did something I'd never done before. I hung up on her.

CHAPTER   28

In the first years of my marriage to Tim, Courtney shot to fame as a rock star. Songs from her band's album, *Pretty on the Inside*, were all over the radio. I would turn on the television and catch a video of Courtney on MTV. She was a whirlwind of rage and venom and passion in peroxide hair and lacy, torn dresses. She had always wanted to be a star, and she had made it happen. In some ways, I loved seeing her larger than life. Yet it disturbed me that her celebrity image revolved around parts of her—pain, emptiness, anger—that had worried me all her life.

When she started seeing Kurt Cobain, stories about her began appearing in the tabloids. I bought them from checkout stands and read them in private.

Nicole and Jaimee reported seeing the same stories. They were particularly upset by the ones that mentioned me—that I hated her, that I had her arrested for stealing a T-shirt, that I made her sleep in a chicken coop. Reading that last story, I remembered with a sting Mark's thoughtful construction of the *whare*. But the most painful story I read recounted Kurt's mother, Wendy, showing Courtney

Kurt's baby book. Courtney commented that her own mother had never made one for her.

My clients began asking me if the stories were true. I felt violated and angry, at Courtney, at the media, at myself. I called her and said that I wanted the two of us to go to therapy. Her response was to scream obscenities at me. I replied, "Courtney, if you don't stop making up stories about me, I will give an interview and tell every bit of the truth as I remember it."

She hung up on me, but I did notice a change in her stories about me. They were slightly less accusatory, even humorous, such as when an interview would quote her as saying I had owned an organic yogurt factory or lived in a commune.

When I would read the stories her name, Courtney *Love*, seemed to jump right off the page. Of all possible names, why, I wondered, had she chosen this one? It always reminded me of that little girl staring up with delight at the clouds, seeing angels in their shapes.

When Tim and I had been married for three years, Courtney called to tell me I was going to be a grandmother. I wondered what Louella would have thought if she had seen the path of Courtney's life, and it shocked me to realize she had been dead for twenty years.

I remembered when Kate asked me if I would look for my birth mother, and I said "never." Now, with Courtney's pregnancy, I could think about little else.

So I read about reunions. One adoptee discovered he was the product of incest; others learned that their mothers and fathers were long dead. My worst nightmare was that I would find my mother living on the streets. Flat broke and toothless, she would ask to move in with me.

"Oh, my baby," she would cry. "At last I've found the meaning in my life. You've come back."

I read Tim a story about a woman who had found her mother living in a mental institution, smelling of urine.

"The mother didn't even recognize she had a visitor," I said. "What if I found someone like that?" *Someone like Ging,* I thought.

"Nobody who produced a daughter like you could be so horrible," he said.

"You didn't answer my question. What if she's the worst? Will you still love me?"

"It wouldn't take anything away from who you are," he said.

I didn't believe him.

And so I put off the search for her once more.

BUT EVERYTHING CHANGED when I saw my first grandchild, a beautiful baby girl.

Two days earlier, Courtney had called me, hysterical.

"They're going to take my baby away," she sobbed into the phone.

"Who is?" I asked her.

"Children's Services. They read the *Vanity Fair* article and now they're after us," she cried. Courtney had recently been featured on the cover of *Vanity Fair,* pregnant in a wedding dress, two fingers held up to her lips where a cigarette had been air-brushed out. In the accompanying article, Courtney was quoted as admitting that she and Kurt had binged on heroin, not knowing she was pregnant.

"No one in this family will let that happen, Courtney," I assured her. I called my other daughters, and Jaimee offered to take time off from her studies to care for the baby, if necessary.

Tim and I decided to fly down to Los Angeles to meet my son-in-law and newborn grandchild. They were at Cedars-Sinai Hospital in Beverly Hills, where Kurt had checked in for a sixty-day detox program to kick his heroin habit while Courtney gave birth to their daughter.

Nevermind had become a platinum album by this time and the papers were full of stories about Kurt binging on drugs, smashing his guitars on stage. I had read everything I could about him, though I didn't trust much of what I read. I had quit believing the celebrity gossip mills when I read in one that Courtney had spent five years in a Buddhist monastery in China. But I still braced myself to encounter an angry, cynical, aggressive, scowling young man: the kind of person who could exaggerate Courtney's self-destructiveness, even push her over the edge.

We arrived at the hospital in the late afternoon, and Kurt walked down a sunlit corridor toward us. Kurt, his body crouched forward, was slight and boyish, with pixie features and shoulder-length flaxen hair. He seemed out of place in the hospital, as if he had sneaked in the back door and was nervous about being caught. As we made eye contact and introduced ourselves, I saw no animosity or arrogance. A shy smile flickered briefly over Kurt's face, and then he grimaced, bent forward, and placed his hand on his stomach.

"Are you okay?" Tim asked.

"My stomach hurts," Kurt said, his bright blue eyes darting toward us again.

"Do you know what the matter is?"

"Nobody knows what the matter is. I've been to all the doctors and none of them can tell me anything. It just comes on like this and I'm so tense I can hardly walk." Both arms cupped his stomach now as we walked into the hospital suite.

"I'm sorry not to meet you at a better time," he continued a little wistfully, and with disarming politeness.

We sat with Kurt for a while in the suite. Then I decided to go look for my granddaughter. At the newborn room, the nurse told me to come back in half an hour. I went and got myself a cup of coffee and returned to find the suite in semidarkness. Tim sat reading in a chair by the window, and Kurt was lying on the bed, his eyes closed. There was a peaceful feeling in the room. I found a seat and sat, waiting for my daughter.

Then the door swung open, and Courtney came into the room and climbed onto the bed. She was in street clothes, and scarcely looked like she had just given birth. Though I hadn't seen her in two years, she barely acknowledged me. She nodded coldly and lit a cigarette. Parcels of food lay unopened on the bed, and one by one she pulled off their wrapping paper, dumping out the contents. Finding a boiled lobster, she started to pull it apart, making loud cracking sounds. The smell of seafood filled the room. Appearing oblivious of the quiet, she began to chomp and flick ashes on her bed. Soon she was talking to Kurt in a loud voice. Tim and I left the room and went to see my grandchild.

I found myself staring through glass at a room full of newborns. I knew her immediately. Frances. She was sleeping peacefully on her back. As I gazed at her tiny face, I noticed both how much she looked like her parents, and how utterly unique she was.

Standing there, I thought of the strange curse that seemed to surround the firstborn daughters in my family history. I was the firstborn daughter of a woman who had put me up for adoption. Louella was the firstborn daughter of Ging, who deserted her at fifteen. Louella lost her first child in an abortion she didn't want, and could never bear more children. Courtney was my firstborn girl, and over the years, I had managed to lose her as well. My relationships with my other children were solid, but it seemed like some greater force always kept Courtney and me apart.

I wanted to protect my granddaughter—a firstborn daughter of a firstborn daughter—from this curse. I wanted her to feel connected to her family, not orphaned or isolated, as both Courtney and I had felt. One way I could do that, I thought with new determination, might be by uncovering the secrets of my own past.

———

WHEN I RETURNED to Corvallis, I found the name of an adoptee search group in Portland and phoned its organizer, a woman named Betty.

"You're not alone," she said. "Now tell me everything you know."

"I don't know anything except her name," I answered. "Paula."

"That's not much to go on," she said. "Begin by going through every legal channel you can think of. Call the agency you were adopted through. Ask for whatever records can be sent legally and petition the courts for your original birth certificate."

"What if that doesn't work?" I asked.

"Then we dive underground. How deep we dig depends on how far you're prepared to go."

"I can't turn back now," I said. "I'll do whatever I have to."

As I began my search, I found that my mother had been completely hidden, wiped from public records, buried away under phrases like "closed adoption" and "against the law." The clerks, social workers, and lawyers I spoke with told me that finding her would be impossible, illegal, and wrong. Though a few were sympathetic, many were outraged that I wanted to delve into the past.

One woman said, "Honey, trust me, you're best off not looking."

Another told me, "I hope you know what you're doing, because you could ruin your mother's life."

I received a one-page document of "non-identifying information," which informed me that my mother had wanted to be a writer. The letter mentioned that she had been distressed about giving me up, and that she was from the South. This information was intended to satisfy my desire to know about my parents.

I burrowed deeper. I registered with every agency I could find. I located hundreds of other searching adoptees, but found nothing useful. Finally, I called Betty.

"You said to call you if nothing worked."

"Well, it's time, then, to take the next step. You must be frustrated."

"I'm more than frustrated," I said. "I'm sick of being told I don't have a right to know about my own past."

She suggested I call a "search specialist" who had helped many people find their birth parents.

He tried but found nothing. My mother had vanished without a trace.

Her first name, Paula, was all I would ever know.

ON A RAINY morning in March 1993, seven months after I had begun my search, an envelope arrived in the mail from the circuit court in San Francisco.

Anxiously, I slit it open and pulled out a thin slip of paper. And there it was, my original birth certificate from forty-nine years earlier.

I read the name typed on the line above the word "mother."

Paula Fox.

I began to cry.

I didn't know if the tears were from relief or excitement or dread. I didn't know anything except—

She was real. And so was I.

I knew the phone number of a private detective in Reno who promised to find anyone in America for three hundred dollars. I called, speaking to him with a calm that belied my trembling hands and racing heart, and he said I needed to send him a facsimile of all my information. I raced downtown to a store with a fax machine, which was in use. The man at the counter told me to return in fifteen minutes. I went across the street to the public library to wait. Suddenly I remembered that my mother had wanted to be a writer.

I hurried to the reference desk.

"I am trying," I told the librarian breathlessly, "to see if someone might have written something once. I don't know if she was ever published. How can I find out?"

The librarian barely looked at me. "What's her name?"

"Paula Fox," I said.

Her chilly face lit up, and she leaned forward eagerly. "Paula Fox—she's one of the best writers in America. Here, look at this list of novels and children's books."

She typed a few words into a computer, and the printer rumbled to life. Pages of book titles appeared.

"Where can I find out more about her?" I asked.

The librarian pointed to the children's section and showed me the large volume of *The Who's Who of Children's Writers*. I found a listing there and read the speech she had given accepting the Newbery Medal for *The Slave Dancer*. I recognized her words, her manner of thinking, her enthusiasm. She felt as familiar to me as my own skin. I read this passage:

> This effort to recognize is an effort to connect ourselves with the reality of our own lives. It is painful; but if we are to become human, we cannot abandon it. Once set on that path of recognition, we cannot forswear our integral connections with other people. We must make our way towards them as best we can, try to find what is similar, try to understand what is dissimilar, try to particularize what is universal.

"Are you all right, dear?" a woman asked, touching my arm.

I thought I might throw up.

"Paula Fox is my mother," I managed to stammer.

"Oh, aren't you lucky," she replied. "She's one of my favorite authors."

I stared at her. I wanted to stand on a chair and shout. Then the nausea left me, replaced by a sudden calm.

I went home, dialed information, and the operator gave me her number and address. I dialed the number. A woman answered. She only said one word, "Hello," but her voice was articulate, soft and yet firm, more like a statement—hello—than a question.

I felt my stomach clench again. I knew it was her; I hated her; I loved her; I didn't want to know her. I hung up the phone.

I decided to write her a letter. I was angry and tender all at once. I told her a little about my life and asked about my biology and the identity of my birth father. I said I did not need to meet her. I wanted only to know my history. As I began to seal the envelope, I felt a pang of concern for her. I tucked in a card on top that read, "Go Slow."

Three days later, the Fed Ex truck dropped off an envelope at my door. It looked just like the one I'd sent earlier that week.

With horror, I thought that she had refused my letter, *refused me,* and sent the letter back unopened. My stomach somersaulted. I glanced at the envelope. I put it down. I picked it up. Finally, I opened it.

I pulled out a seven-page letter typed on yellow paper and a hand-ful of photographs. There was a photo of her as a child—which re-minded me of one I had of Jaimee at the same age—and another of my great-grandfather's plantation house in Cuba. There were pic-tures of my great-grandmother, Candelaria, who left Spain at sixteen to marry a man in Cuba she'd never met. Also included were pictures of Elsie, Paula's mother; Martin, Paula's husband of nearly thirty years; and Paula's two sons, my brothers. I saw a photo of her father, Paul, and was stunned by his likeness to my sons. Then I found her photo. The woman who looked out at me was no drunken lady, no fallen woman, no Iva Kroger. She was elegant, and the words in her letter were openhearted and generous. She said she was scared, that she knew this would change her life, that she was grateful.

For three months, we wrote daily. We told one another about our past, our daily lives, what it had been like for each of us without the other. There were no phone calls, no meetings—just letters, sometimes two in a day. My husband said it was as though I had taken a lover.

Her younger life had been full of abandonment and loss. Like me, her early marriages had been to men who were wrong for her. In her early forties, she found the right man to spend her life with, as I had. They had been married for over three decades. Through it all, she kept writing.

I read everything I could find about her, but most of all I read her books. I admired the absolute clarity, the unadorned style of her writing, and its brilliant, sharp insights into human interaction. Like me, she had spent her life observing how people worked.

I wondered how different I would have been if Paula had raised me. And who would I be now, with a "real mother" standing beside me?

We agreed to meet in San Francisco, the city where we had parted. Four of my children came to the airport to see me off. I felt panic-stricken.

"Mom, remember how old she is," Jaimee said. "She'll probably have blue hair and use a walker."

As I walked to catch the flight, Daniel whispered in my ear, "It doesn't matter who she is. You just need to know."

Two hours later, in the San Francisco airport, I met Paula as she came off a flight from New York City.

For the first minute, we stared at each other. Then we laughed.

"You're so pretty!" she said.

"You're the one who's beautiful," I said. She was taller than I had imagined, slender and elegant, with cropped gray hair. "Where's your blue hair? Where's your walker? I can't believe you're seventy years old."

We laughed again, then Paula took my arm, and we walked toward the baggage claim.

We spent three days together, holed up in a hotel in downtown San

Francisco, each returning to a separate room at night. She told me about my father, a Jew with Russian immigrant parents, but not a psychiatrist, as the first paper had said. As soon as she got my first letter, she had called to tell him about me. His wife told Paula he had died three months before.

I told her that Jack had said, "All she asked was that you be raised a Catholic."

She shook her head. "Honey, that's not true. I said I wanted you with Jews, because they were the best people I knew. They said they had found you a wonderful Jewish family. They lied to us both." She sighed, then continued. "You can't imagine what it was like then. I was eighteen, and I had no family, no money. I went to an agency called Native Sons of California. The moment they saw me, they told me I had to give you up. I had no idea that I could make choices about my life."

What she was saying was so familiar to me. I nodded intently, waiting for her to continue.

"One night shortly after you were born, I decided I would keep you no matter what. But when I told the doctor my decision ten days later, he said it was too late."

Knowing nothing of her rights, she believed him. She had never returned to San Francisco once she left, she told me. It was too painful. She always wanted to find me, but when she remembered that "wonderful Jewish family" I was with, she felt she had no right to look.

As we talked, I replayed all the stories I had made up and heard about my mother over the years. They were all fabrications, down to the non-identifying information, which had said Paula was from the South, when she was a northeasterner. Even the most incredible stories I could have invented would not have captured her grace and dignity, or the pride I felt walking next to her on the San Francisco streets.

One afternoon, we wandered into the poetry section of City Lights bookstore. I picked up *The Collected Works of Edna St. Vincent Millay*.

"Do you know this?" I asked. " 'What lips my lips have kissed, and where, And why, I have forgotten, and what arms / Have lain under my head till morning.' "

Without missing a beat, she finished the stanza. " 'But the rain is full of ghosts that tap and sigh / Upon the glass and listen for reply.' "

We stood staring at one another for a moment.

"Who are you?" I asked her. "Did I make you up?"

WE SAT IN a café and pointed out the men we thought were handsome. We saw pictures of Courtney and Kurt on magazine covers, and I told her of her granddaughter's rise to fame. Her music and style—baby-doll dresses and heavy, smudged makeup—were influencing a whole generation of young women. Paula told me stories of her parents living in Hollywood in the twenties, writing movie scripts. Douglas Fairbanks Jr. was my father's cousin, she said, and I wondered if there was an invisible genetic inscription that had pulled Courtney so strongly toward the same kind of life.

She brought me into a department store in Union Square, the same one Louella had always taken me to. I remembered our terrible fights over stiff hats and gloves, and how uncomfortable I always felt, standing next to petite Louella. At five-feet-eight, Paula and I had the same stride.

We went to the beauty counter and she asked the woman, "Do you carry Christian Dior nail cream with apricot kernels? I want some for my daughter." Then she said to me, "You have the same cuticles as I do, and this is the best way to manage them."

I called Kate the day after I met Paula. "Can you meet me at a restaurant in an hour?"

"No, I'm in the middle of a dinner party."

"What if I said I was bringing my mother?"

There was a pause of stunned silence. "Oh my God," she shrieked. "I'll be there."

At the restaurant, I listened to Kate and Paula discuss writers they both loved and their favorite restaurants in New York.

When my mother went to the restroom, Kate said, "My God, Linda, she's perfect. Why did you wait so long?"

Paula took me to meet the friend she had lived with when she was pregnant with me.

"She's back," she announced, introducing me to her friend, and we celebrated with champagne.

After our meeting in San Francisco, she told everyone in her life about me. She changed her biography in all of her books and her *Who's Who* entry to include me. I flew out to New York to visit her and meet her husband, Martin.

The taxi dropped me outside their brownstone, and Martin opened the door. I felt intensely nervous, but his warm smile disarmed me. He opened his arms and said, "I'm so happy to have a daughter."

At dinner that night, I was surprised at how quickly our conversation turned to things outside ourselves: politics, history, literature. They were so worldly, so intentional in the words they chose, so deliberate in their movements. Martin radiated confidence in his own thoughts, and the adoration he had for Paula, even after so many years, was evident. He often complimented her, and they laughed easily together. More than anything, I felt, it was their constant reading and writing, each of them in their own offices on the top floor of the house, working mornings and sometimes afternoons, that kept them connected to one another.

After my visit with Paula and Martin, I met my youngest brother, Gabe, at his apartment in Philadelphia. When he opened the door, I was surprised by how handsome he was. We were shy around each other at first, but we soon discovered that we loved animals—he worked with gorillas—and then we couldn't stop talking. We spent the whole afternoon wandering around the zoo where he worked, learning everything we could about each other.

I met my other brother, Adam, at the Newark airport. He was supposed to pick me up at my gate and take me to Paula's. My plane got in early, and I was roaming around the terminal, killing time, when I saw a man walking toward me. From a distance, I could tell it was him, and we both pointed at each other—"you," I said, smiling.

Paula developed relationships with my family. Within two months of our first meeting, Nicole went to Brooklyn and spent a weekend with her. Jaimee went to law school at NYU, and she visited Paula and Martin almost every week. My mother's conversations with Tobias and Daniel about literature deepened their interest in literary criticism and writing. Tim met Paula and was enthralled by her quick intelligence and wit, and they developed a strong and affectionate friendship. In the next few years, both Jaimee and Nicole got married in Oregon, and Paula came to their weddings. As for Courtney, she and my mother met for an hour or so in New York City. But although they both had some interest in each other, nothing further developed between them.

WHEN PAULA AND I told each other our stories, what moved me the most was how similar our circumstances had been when we were pregnant with our first child. We both came to decisions that we thought would free our child of the difficulties we had experienced as daughters.

Paula's parents had left her in a foundling home when she was born. She was rescued by a delightful, kind minister, Uncle Elwood, whom she adored. She lived with him through her early years, and longed to be adopted by him, but her parents returned and took her away. Her father, Paul, was an alcoholic, and her mother, Elsie, was unfathomably cruel, once telling her husband, "Either she goes or I go." Paula spent her youth shuttling from one makeshift home to another, as her parents veered in and out of her life.

She told me, "I thought that you were me, and I was my own mother. I thought that by releasing you at birth, I would ensure you would not have to go through the pain and bewilderment that I went through."

When I became pregnant with Courtney, I had thought: *Now I am my mother, young and pregnant by the wrong man, and this baby is me, but I will do it differently. I will keep her and love her. She will never feel that she doesn't belong.*

CHAPTER 29

S oon after I met Paula, Courtney invited me and her brothers for Christmas Eve at a palatial rented house in Seattle. This was the first Christmas we would be together since the time she had given me Joy perfume. Although anxious, I was optimistic too. I hoped that somehow my reunion with Paula would alter my relationship with my eldest daughter.

The long driveway was iced over as we approached, and the car seemed on the verge of skidding out. A guard buzzed us through the gate.

"Maybe somebody is going to come out to open our doors," Daniel said.

"Not a chance," I said, shutting off the ignition. "Get your jacket on."

We walked carefully up the slick steps and rang the bell. Nobody answered, but I heard voices from inside. A flicker of light came through the door. I pushed it open. We walked through a small foyer into a large, high-ceilinged room where a few people sat on chairs around a tall, thin Christmas tree. Frank and his wife were there, and they gestured for us to join them.

After about twenty minutes, the room fell into a hush and Courtney, dressed in a baby blue Dior suit, crowned in a tiara, and holding a cigarette, descended the long staircase. "Presents, presents," she sang out, exhaling a long plume of smoke. A few of her assistants came and set them down: a TV for Tobias, two shirts from Barneys for Daniel, a camel-haired coat from Italy for me. I dumbly nodded thanks and slipped the coat on. Its gorgeous thick texture against my skin reminded me of the mink coat Jack had given Louella so many Christmases ago. When I had tried on that fur, it felt heavy on my shoulders, laden with the feelings the three of us never expressed. This coat was even heavier. I shrugged it off and folded it back in its box.

Courtney, her eyes wide and piercing, stared at me with a strange grin. I realized later it was an expression of victory.

She refused to open the gifts we'd brought her. She said she hated to open presents. Everyone in the room fawned over her every word, as if she was giving royal pronouncements. After a few more minutes, she stood up. "Ta-ta," she said, and left the room, not deigning to glance our way.

EVEN AFTER THAT Christmas visit, we had been in touch. She had called me from Rome when Kurt overdosed, and also the following month, when he escaped from a treatment center, shortly before killing himself.

That April afternoon, Courtney left a message on my machine. She was wailing, "Mommy, my prince is dead, he's dead, he's dead." At the end, she said, in a broken voice, "Please, come and be here with me now." I heard the message with Nicole standing next to me. We looked at each other, horror-struck. Then the phone rang, and it was a radio station asking me to comment on Kurt Cobain's death. I hung up on them, and turned to Nicole. "Kurt's gone," I said. We stood silent in the kitchen for what seemed like hours, too stunned even to speak.

I remembered a car ride one afternoon when I was visiting Frances in Seattle. Kurt and Courtney sat in front, firing names, albums, groups, singers, songs, and labels back and forth at each other, making the air crackle with their passionate exchange.

Watching them banter in their private shorthand, I had felt the same feeling of hope that I had when Courtney called to tell me of her pregnancy. Though some parts of Kurt and Courtney's life together scared me, their love for each other was obvious to me. Kurt brought out a side of Courtney I hadn't seen since she was a child. She had a tenderness, a softness in her eyes as she looked at him, even as she replied to one of his comments by shouting, "Oh come off it, Kurt, you shit." His gentle intensity was a perfect foil for her warp-speed wit and brazenness. I left that day thinking that Courtney had met her match.

And now he was lost to her. "What will she do?" I whispered. Nicole shook her head, tears streaming down her cheeks.

A FEW HOURS LATER, I got on a plane to Seattle. When my taxi pulled up to Courtney's Lake Washington house, I was astonished at how many people were milling around. It was a surreal mix: businessmen in suits, kids with ripped shirts and bleached hair, paparazzi wielding cameras. Helicopters hovered overhead. Inside the house, fan mail was strewn all over the floor, and there was a heap of broken doll parts—heads, legs, clumps of hair—in one corner.

I found Courtney in her room, lying on her bed. She looked hollowed out by grief. She saw me, and crawled across the bed. We embraced. As I held her I wished, more than anything, that I could gather all her pain and take it into my body instead.

For one brief moment she and I connected again, as if the past had been erased. And then, as we moved apart, the familiar curtain came down between us. She turned away, and eventually, tired of standing there ignored, I left the room.

A few hours later, Nicole, Jaimee, Tobias, and Daniel showed up, and together we went to Kurt's memorial service. Riding back from the service in a limo, a song from Hole's new album, *Live Through This*, came on the radio. It was full of fury and torment and despair. I was staggered by the raw force of her voice, and the beautiful melody that suddenly flipped into angry, driving chords. Somehow, Courtney had harnessed her anguish to make music that resonated with people's most private grief, their deepest rage. The song made me cry with pride at my daughter's amazing creativity, and with sorrow for all that she had lived through.

CHAPTER 30

In May of 1996, my mother and stepfather left for a holiday to Israel. They were each offered residencies at Mishkenot Sha'ananim, a cultural center near the Old City of Jerusalem. The last time we spoke, she was enthusiastic about her trip, describing the relatives of Martin's they would visit, and the places they wanted to see.

The day after they left, my brother Gabe called before dawn. "I'm sorry to have to make this call," he began, and my heart started to pound. I knew the news was bad from the tone of his voice. "Our mother is in bad shape," he said. "She's had a head injury and is in a coma."

She and Martin had been returning from dinner with a friend in Jerusalem on their first night. As they climbed some stone steps, a man walked toward her, head on. He grabbed her purse and ran with it, pulling her along with the purse, then pushing her down roughly. She fell on the cobblestone stairs, her head bouncing on the stones. By the time the ambulance got there, she was unconscious, and now, twenty-four hours later, she was showing strokelike symptoms and moving in and out of consciousness. I booked a flight to Israel right away.

I arrived at the Ben-Gurion International Airport and took a taxi fifty miles to where my stepfather and brothers were staying. When I got there, I spied Adam sitting in the lobby. I sat down and let my head fall against his shoulder.

"It's horrible," he said to me, looking exhausted. "You better prepare yourself. I've never seen her like this." He took me to the room where my stepfather and other brother were. We all embraced, and I was stunned by the change on my stepfather's face. He seemed to have aged years in the few months since I saw him. They told me everything they knew about Paula's condition.

The next morning, we took a taxi to the Hadassah Ein Karem Hospital. Taking a deep breath, I walked with my family through the double doors to the room where my mother lay in bed, her head nodding to the side, her eyes barely open. Seeing her like this, so vulnerable and helpless, was virtually unbearable. Her head was bandaged, and she seemed tiny and alone in the hospital bed. I didn't know what to do or say. I handed her some chocolates and perfume I had purchased for her during my layover in Paris, and she looked woozily at them.

The doctor came in and spoke to us about her head injury. Nobody knew much about it or what would happen, he said. We would just have to wait and see. But we should prepare ourselves, he added, for the possibility that she might never be the same again.

As the doctor continued to talk, I was overcome with anger. I had just found her, and now she might be lost to me forever. How could this happen? Looking at my brothers, I was irrationally furious with them for getting to spend an entire lifetime with Paula, when I had had only three short years. My face flushed, and I clenched my fists tightly, trying to hold back tears. Now was the time to think of her, not me, I told myself sternly. But my anger at the injustice of the situation bubbled under the surface all day.

The next morning I woke up early to golden light and the sound of chattering birds outside my window. For an instant I lay in bed peacefully. Then I recalled why I was there, and the anger surged up again, making a tense knot in my stomach. I got dressed and left the hotel, walking quickly through Jerusalem's streets, trying to calm myself. As I walked, I thought about the last three years of my life with Paula.

At the beginning, all I could see was how she and I were alike. She was the perfect mother, more wonderful than any fantasy I'd created. Then, slowly, we had entered a new phase, where I began to discover all the ways we were different. She didn't like hot climates; I loved them. I tried to read E. M. Forster, whom she loved, but I hated his writing. She didn't like my favorite authors. We argued about the sixties. For me, it was a period of liberation and possibility; for her, it was a time of heartbreak, watching her friends' children lose their way with drugs.

During one trip to New York, I had brought Daniel along, who was then in high school. As we were sitting around the table one night, having dinner, I was telling a story about a former teacher of mine, and used the word "powerful" to describe her. Paula asked me what I meant by "powerful." I began trying to define it, but somehow the words got jumbled, and I couldn't explain myself. I felt Paula and Martin's attentive eyes on me, and felt intimidated and inarticulate. Then I was furious—*I* knew what I meant, and I didn't need to be judged by them.

"You don't understand me!" I shouted, then burst into tears. They looked shocked. I pushed back from the table, tears running down my face, and stalked into the house.

Daniel followed me in after a moment. "What's going on, Mom?" he asked, standing next to me in the kitchen. "You're acting like I did in sixth grade."

I smiled and nodded, wiping my eyes. "That's exactly where I am right now," I said. "Trying to be my own person, separating from my mother. It's like I'm twelve."

After that, my relationship with Paula changed. I saw that it wouldn't have been perfect if I had grown up with her. We would have had struggles like every other mother and daughter. We began to see each other for who we were, with all our flaws and quirks. With this recognition, we moved into a more ordinary family life.

AND NOW THIS accident had happened. My anger burned off, replaced by pure fear. I kept thinking of Paula in her hospital bed, and how frail she looked. I had barely noticed where I was walking, but I soon found that I had reached the Old City.

Towering above everything was the dazzling Golden Dome, Qubbat As-Sakhrah, with its lustrous blue walls. I wondered why it was so familiar, and then I was reminded of a postcard Sister Caroline had sent me from her trip to Israel. She told me the Muslim shrine was built on the Temple Mount, also a holy site for Jews, and that Jewish mystics believe that each prayer from the world finds its way to the Temple Mount, and is released to God. I could hear the Muslim prayers in the distance. The air smelled like fresh bread. People milled around me, hawking food and postcards, talking to each other, going to religious services. Everything buzzed with life, but I felt detached, weighed down with emotion.

I came to an opening, and saw I was standing in front of the Wailing Wall. I was surrounded by Hassidic Jews, Muslims, Catholic nuns, businessmen, mothers with children, travelers with backpacks. Each was facing the wall, writing the names of loved ones on pieces of paper and sticking them into tiny slots. Some were crying; others took photos. I stood watching the scene, entranced, until a friendly looking nun passed me a sheet of paper. I took it, pulled a pen from my purse, and began to write.

Names flowed from me, so many people now dead: my darling baby boy Elki; Jack; Louella; Nellie; Tim's father, John; Hazel; Mickey Malloy, who had died the previous year from an alcoholism-related illness; and Kurt. As I tucked each paper into the wall, I wondered if I would soon be writing Paula's name.

I stood there for a moment, thinking about all the lives that had been a part of my own. And, as always when my mind turned to death, I remembered my friend Judy, and being carried with her into that brief instant when her spirit left her body. When I returned, I didn't come back alone. Something holds me now and bears me forward, something I cannot see or name. In the darkest moments, I forget this, but I always remember once again. I wrote Judy's name on a slip of paper, folded it into the Wailing Wall, and turned away.

I wandered through the catacomb-like city, stopping at stalls to admire herbs and spices, copper, crafts, vegetables. I came upon a little store full of jewels. In the sunlight, a rack of amber prayer beads glinted. I thought of Hannah Steinberg's amber necklace and her words rang in my ears: "Nothing ever dies; it's just transformed." *What an old soul she was,* I thought, picking out three strands of beads, one for each daughter. One day I would tell them about Hannah, and about the peacefulness I felt at the Wailing Wall.

I was about to pay for the beads when something else caught my eye: a row of Russian nesting dolls, neatly lined up in a corner. I picked one up and opened it; inside was another doll, and inside that one was another, and another. The smallest one was tiny, a little scrap of a thing with bright blue eyes. It was perfect for my granddaughter, I thought, holding the smallest one in my palm.

As I put the dolls back together, I thought, *each doll is a mother and a daughter.* Each doll was held by generations of mothers before her, and carried generations inside her. I thought of the women who came before me—Candelaria, Elsie, Paula, Louella—and those who came after me, my daughters and granddaughters. Somehow, we all fit together, in ways I couldn't even begin to understand.

When I was young, I believed that finding Paula would fix everything. I had been raised without a history, I thought. As I grew, I came to see that I made my own history, with Judy, in my slow-dawning love for Louella, with my children and Tim. Still, at forty-eight, I had the idea that uncovering my roots would give me the answers I needed, especially with Courtney. But when I met Paula, though I took immense comfort and pleasure in our relationship, there was still so much about myself, an essential mystery, that I couldn't explain.

It was the same mystery I saw, looking at my children. Each of them possessed some singular quality that I couldn't reduce to genetics or childhood environment—something foundational and inexplicable. Judy and I would have called it our "soul."

Knowing this, I thought, doesn't change what is past. As Paula put it once, "nothing makes up for anything." Nothing could make up for the years of our separation, or heal my fractured relationship with Courtney.

As the day faded, I thought of the curse of the firstborn daughter, carried down through generations of women in my family. Perhaps the curse had something to do with a refusal to accept things as they are, a habit of always looking for something more. Breaking the curse, I realized, might come through acknowledging that there isn't a magic formula to erase life's losses. For just that moment, standing there, I felt the mysterious grace and fullness of the life I'd been given.

I put the last doll together and paid for my purchases. Then I turned and walked back toward the hospital.

AFTERWORD

Paula has largely recovered. In her early eighties, she continues to write and gain critical acclaim. Nicole, Jaimee, Tobias, and Daniel have rich, fulfilling lives and careers in psychotherapy, law, academic scholarship, and writing. After he finished high school in New Zealand, Joshua returned to Oregon and has reunited with our family. He is studying to be a CPA. They, along with their partners, my stepchildren, and grandchildren, are a constant source of challenge and delight.

Courtney follows the path of the phoenix, falling and rising again from the ashes. Her daughter has grown into a beautiful, generous, brave person I am lucky to know.

Tim and I have been married for seventeen years. Our life together continues to enrich and humble me.

I have liver spots on my hands, just as Nellie said I would.

—*June 2005*

Linda Carroll was adopted at birth and only later discovered that her biological mother is the writer Paula Fox. Married at eighteen, and twice more before she was thirty, Carroll lived a classic hippie youth and had five children before finally finishing college, getting a master's degree, and beginning a career as a therapist. Her children, now grown, include two writers, a therapist, a lawyer, and the singer/songwriter Courtney Love. Carroll lives in Corvallis, Oregon, with her husband of seventeen years. For more information about Linda Carroll go to her Web site, www.hermothersdaughter.net.

Printed in the United States
by Baker & Taylor Publisher Services